MW01106096

In the Red

In the Red explains why several prosperous developed countries accumulated so much public debt between the 1970s and the 2000s that they became vulnerable to sudden changes in financial markets and exposed themselves to the risk of default. It compares and contrasts the politics of debt accumulation in Belgium, Canada, Denmark, Greece, Ireland, Italy, and Japan since the 1970s to identify factors that differentiate countries that accumulated dangerous amounts of debt from those that kept their debt under control. It challenges the received wisdom that persistent borrowing reflects the recklessness of governments who indebt their countries in order to please their voters in the short term. The book documents that policy makers invariably initiate painful adjustment measures to correct budgetary imbalances when debt grows at an alarming rate for several years in a row, but the success of adjustment attempts depends on the degree of social support for the spending cuts and/or tax increases proposed. In countries where existing fiscal policies generate intense conflicts of vested interests, mustering the necessary social consensus behind any adjustment package is exceedingly difficult, especially if large parts of society remain unaffected by the negative economic side effects of fiscal imbalances. In countries where existing fiscal policies are less polarizing and fiscal problems negatively affect economic performance, fiscal correction is swift.

Zsófia Barta is Assistant Professor of Political Science at the University at Albany SUNY.

IN THE RED

The Politics of Public Debt Accumulation in Developed Countries

Zsófia Barta

University of Michigan Press
Ann Arbor

Copyright © 2018 by Zsófia Barta
All rights reserved

This book may not be reproduced, in whole or in part, including illustrations, in any form
(beyond that copying permitted by Sections 107 and 108 of the U.S. Copyright Law and
except by reviewers for the public press), without written permission from the publisher.

Published in the United States of America by the
University of Michigan Press
Manufactured in the United States of America
♾ Printed on acid-free paper

2021   2020   2019   2018   4   3   2   1

A CIP catalog record for this book is available from the British Library.

Library of Congress Cataloging-in-Publication Data

Names: Barta, Zsofia, author.
Title: In the red : the politics of public debt accumulation in developed countries /
    Zsofia Barta.
Description: Ann Arbor : University of Michigan Press, [2018] | Includes bibliographical
    references and index. | Identifiers: LCCN 2017053880 (print) | LCCN 2017056805
    (ebook) | ISBN 9780472123469 (e-book) | ISBN 9780472130641 (hardcover : alk. paper)
Subjects: LCSH: Debts, Public—Developed countries. | Developed countries—Foreign
    economic relations.
Classification: LCC HJ235 (ebook) | LCC HJ235 .B37 2018 (print) | DDC
    336.3/4091722—dc23
LC record available at https://lccn.loc.gov/2017053880

To my mother and the memory of my father

Contents

Illustrations

Abbreviations

AMECO	Annual Macro-economic Database of the European Commision's Directorate General for Economic and Financial Affairs
DC	Democrazia Cristiana (Christian Democracy in Italy)
EMS	European Monetary System
IMF	International Monetary Fund
IMF WEO	International Monetary Fund World Economic Outlook
LDP	Liberal Democratic Party (of Japan)
OECD	Organization for Economic Co-operation and Development
PASOK	Panhellenic Socialist Movement (of Greece)
SMEs	Small- and medium-sized enterprises

Acknowledgments

Of the many lessons I learned while writing this book, the one that will stay with me longest is how generous people are around me with their time, support, encouragement and love. I cannot thank mentors, colleagues, friends, and family enough for all they did to make this book possible.

First and foremost, I would like to express my gratitude to my "academic parents," Waltraud Schelkle, at the London School of Economics and Political Science, and Erik Jones, at the Paul H. Nitze School of Advanced International Studies, who have tirelessly advised and encouraged me ever since I embarked on my research on public debt ten years ago. I could always count on them, no matter what obstacle I encountered on the long road from starting a doctoral dissertation to writing a book as an independent scholar. I can only hope to be able to pass on the insight, kindness, and support I received from them to new generations of students, as I can surely never repay them for it. I am also truly grateful to Pepper Culpepper and Sven Steinmo for discussing my work with me during my time as a Max Weber Fellow at the European University Institute in Florence. I learned a great amount from both of them. I would also like to thank my mentors at my new academic home in the Department of Political Science at the University at Albany. Patty Strach and Julie Novkov were instrumental in helping me to get the manuscript finished. Patty not only read and commented on several drafts but she was also immensely helpful with advice on the practical aspects of finishing and publishing the manuscript. Julie organized a workshop for the manuscript that generated crucial suggestions for final improvements.

Many people helped this book with their comments and questions. I am truly grateful to Bruce Carruthers from Northwestern University and Jeffry Frieden from Harvard University for taking the time to come to Albany to discuss the manuscript and for providing invaluable suggestions. I also thank my colleagues in the Department of Political Science at the University at Albany—Peter Breiner, Cheng Chen, Johannes Karreth, Greg Nowell, and Stephan Stohler—for reading and commenting on various chapters. I am also indebted to Dermot Hodson and Daniel Wincott, who both provided feedback on my project at a very early stage, and to two anonymous reviewers whose generous comments were crucial in finalizing the manuscript. I thank Meredith Norwich, Danielle Coty and Mary Hasham at the University of Michigan Press for managing the publication process.

I am also grateful to friends for the support they provided throughout this project. From the first day of research at the London School of Economics, Alison Johnston, Bryon Fong, Andreas Kornelakis, and Léna Pellandini-Simányi have been there for me with both scholarly and personal advice. Since I arrived in Albany, I have often relied on the kind help of Torrey Shanks, Ambarish Chandra, Kat Carlton, and Lewis Davis.

My deepest debt of gratitude I owe to my family. My son, Andor, is too young to read this book yet, but his patience at crucial turning points of the writing process was remarkable. I truly appreciate that. Finishing the manuscript would have simply been impossible if it was not for the dedicated support of my mother, Éva Orbán, who helped me reconcile scholarly ambition and parental responsibilities. I cannot thank her enough for all she has done. It is to her that this book is dedicated and to the memory of my father, György Barta. I will never stop missing him.

ONE

The Puzzle of Relentlessly and Alarmingly Growing Debt

Why do some countries flirt with fiscal disaster? Why do prosperous, advanced industrial states with democratic governments and reasonably well-organized bureaucracies keep borrowing in times of peace and prosperity until they become excessively vulnerable to changing conditions in financial markets and expose themselves to the risk of debt crises and default? The practical relevance of heavy indebtedness hardly needs to be emphasized today in the wake of the wave of sovereign debt crises that engulfed Europe in the recent years and in view of the challenges that many European and non-European developed democracies face in regaining control over their debt. Remarkably, many countries that are currently burdened with the largest debt stocks got into this predicament in the absence of major wars or economic cataclysms, as a result of sustained fiscal imbalances over the course of many uneventful decades. While in countries like Ireland, Spain, or the United Kingdom public debt skyrocketed overnight as a result of the global financial and economic crisis, Japan, Greece, Italy, Belgium, or Canada got dangerously indebted by persistently borrowing heavily for several decades.

Sustained large-scale debt accumulation that puts a country on a collision course with fiscal disaster is a puzzle not (only) because it is bad policy, but because sustained and substantial debt growth is likely to be politically inconvenient for governments. Persistently and significantly growing debt causes economic problems. It constrains policy makers' ability to invest, deliver services, and address welfare needs as they arise. It exposes a country to unpredictable and uncontrollable developments on the financial markets, raising the specter of a destabilizing debt crisis or even default. Finally, it foreshadows increasingly painful austerity measures in the future. As the debt stock swells, risks grow, and economic problems intensify, policy makers with reasonable chances to stay in the political race for future government positions should feel under great and increasing pressure to stop the escalation of debt. So why do policy makers fiddle while Rome burns? Why do successive governments fail to put an end to borrowing once the scope of the problem becomes obvious? Why do they get away with it? And why do some later choose to undertake painful austerity measures when the sacrifices needed to restore the balance of the budget are much larger?

Although persistent debt accumulation is often portrayed as the consequence of a series of irresponsible policy choices, this book argues that sustained and substantial debt accumulation has much more to do with the inability to change an existing fiscal course than with a string of reckless decisions. Analyzing the experiences of Belgium, Greece, Italy, and Japan, this book shows that (although the severe fiscal troubles of these countries had different roots) the unsustainability of fiscal trends was recognized fairly early on in all of the cases and the politics of fiscal policy making revolved around reasserting control over debt growth from that moment on. However, policy makers' attempts to raise taxes or cut spending were repeatedly frustrated by societal resistance. While this latter observation is not very surprising, it is important to note that other countries, for example Denmark or Ireland, had very different experiences when confronted with a debt surge: they managed to put into place drastic tax increases and spending cuts to restore the balance of public finances with fairly strong social support. Furthermore, Italy's and Belgium's experiences demonstrate that policy paralysis is not a fixed feature: in both countries, policy reforms that seemed inconceivable at one point in time were successfully put into place at another. Two questions arise from this cross-national variation in countries' ability to deal with debt accumulation. Why do some countries delay fiscal adjustment dangerously long if others act upon fiscal challenges fairly swiftly? And when and how does inaction give way to action?

This book argues that a country stays on a dangerous debt trajectory when policy makers are unable to enlist broad societal support for painful measures to restore the balance of public finances due to unresolved societal conflicts about what spending should be cut and what taxes should be raised. It identifies two factors that govern how easily the interests of various sections of society can be reconciled behind a specific fiscal stabiliza-

tion package: fiscal polarization and international exposure. It also emphasizes that these two factors interact in a dynamic fashion, implying that the
political conditions evolve as time passes and debt accumulates so that even
if adjustment initially fails, it might later succeed as the problem escalates.

Fiscal polarization refers to the intensity of political conflict about how the
necessary fiscal sacrifices are to be allocated across society, and it depends
on the fiscal policies in place. Fiscal policies are polarizing when different
taxes and spending items affect different sectors, regions, and classes very
unequally. In such a setting, different combinations of tax increases and
spending cuts distribute fiscal sacrifices very differently across society, generating strong incentives for groups with vested interests in existing spending or tax arrangements to resist adjustment to those arrangements and
insist that savings and/or revenue increases be generated through adjustments to other parts of the budget. In countries where major taxes and
spending items are encompassing—i.e., they affect large swathes of society
in relatively undifferentiated fashion—there is little impetus for political
conflict about what parts of the budget should be adjusted, because any
combination of tax increases or spending cuts large enough to close the
gap in the budget affect the majority of society fairly similarly. Under these
circumstances, the majority of society supports the fastest possible adjustment because the size of the necessary adjustment only grows with delay as
debt grows and generates increasing interest pressure on the budget.

International exposure, on the other hand, influences the strength of the
incentives for various sections of society to compromise their fiscal interests
for the sake of speedy stabilization. When a country's economy is strongly
exposed to international economic competition, the economic side effects
of large fiscal imbalances—like inflation or high interest rates—are likely
to impinge on the welfare of a large part of society through reducing competitiveness and negatively affecting sales, profits, wages, and employment.
The same side effects can be more easily accommodated in relatively closed
economies. The more intensely society suffers from the side effects of debt
accumulation, the more urgent it is for groups with different vested fiscal
interests to resolve fiscal problems. Therefore, the greater the economic
openness of a country, the more likely different groups in society are to
reach a compromise about how to share the sacrifices of fiscal adjustment.

Fiscal polarization and international exposure determine the chances
of successful fiscal adjustment in conjunction, but their relative importance changes as adjustment is delayed and fiscal problems escalate. In the
absence of decisive measures to eliminate the deficit, debt keeps growing and generates an increasingly heavy interest burden, compounding

the borrowing problem and giving rise to ever-larger side effects. Therefore, even if fiscal polarization initially prevents a country from adjusting swiftly, the growing negative side effects of the escalating debt problem might later prompt warring groups of differing fiscal interests to find a compromise, giving rise to a strong social coalition supportive of an adjustment package. This allows policy makers to embark on adjustment at a later point in time, despite the fact that the necessary fiscal sacrifices have grown much larger.

In other words, countries are prone to getting stuck dangerously long on an alarming debt trajectory if their existing fiscal policies are polarizing and their economies are relatively closed because the stakes involved in the conflict about how adjustment is to be carried out are very high, while limited exposure of the economy to international competition allows large sections of society to remain insulated from the negative economic side effects of debt accumulation, minimizing immediate incentives to compromise. Fiscal adjustment is prompt in countries where existing tax and spending policies affect the majority of society relatively uniformly and the economy is very open. In countries where targeted spending and tax policies fuel controversy about how adjustment is to be carried out but economic openness generates pressures for stabilization, fiscal adjustment is put into place with delay. Initially, the desire to avoid fiscal pain motivates groups with vested interests in specific fiscal policies to defend those policies even at the price of impeding adjustment in the hope that fiscal stabilization will be carried out at the expense of other vested interest groups. However, as the costs of delay manifest themselves in increasingly painful economic side effects of incessant debt growth, vested interest groups come around to a compromise.

This book explores the diverse experiences of Belgium, Greece, Ireland, Italy, and Japan with debt accumulation and fiscal consolidation since the late 1970s. It shows that countries where entrenched fiscal policies affect different sectors, regions, and classes very unequally, like in Greece, Italy, or Japan and, to a smaller extent, Belgium—policy makers' hands are tied in the face of a growing problem by the intense resistance to painful adjustment from socioeconomic groups who would be hurt by the specific spending cuts or tax increases proposed. Furthermore, the experiences of Belgium and Italy show that exposure to the pressures of international competition can generate the necessary incentives for political compromise that enables policy makers to adjust policies even where existing fiscal patterns are unfavorable to the emergence of societal support for fiscal

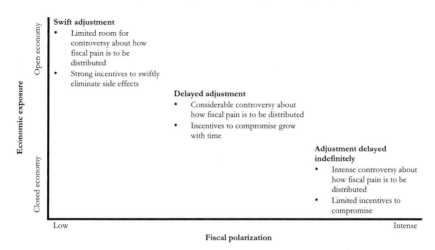

Fig. 1.1. Summary of the polarization-exposure argument

pain. Greece's and Japan's example, on the other hand, indicates that in the absence of such pressures, conflict delays policy adjustment dangerously long. These cases stand in sharp contrast with the experiences of Ireland, a country with a very open economy and encompassing fiscal policies, which has repeatedly demonstrated its capacity to regain control over intense bursts of debt growth in the past.

This introductory chapter lays the groundwork for the investigation of the politics of debt accumulation in those countries. It first surveys the experiences of developed countries with debt growth to get a better general sense of the phenomenon that the book explores and identifies the most perplexing cases of relentless and substantial debt accumulation. It then briefly digresses to reflect on theoretical controversies concerning admissible levels of debt and the best ways to tackle temporary debt surges to clarify that the phenomenon explored in this book—sustained and significant debt accumulation—falls outside of the scope of the recent debate between "austeriterians" and Keynesians, primarily due to its persistent, long-term nature. It then explains why sustained debt accumulation is so puzzling for a political scientist, reviews past approaches to the question of persistent borrowing, lays out the argument put forward in this book in more detail, and summarizes the country cases discussed in later chapters. It concludes by spelling out the contributions of the book.

Recent Experiences with Sustained and Substantial Debt Growth in Prosperous Developed Countries

Every country experiences periods of debt growth. At times of war, economic and financial crisis, heavy public investment, or political upheaval, countries borrow extensively. What is so intriguing about the borrowing patterns of some of the most heavily indebted developed sovereigns of today is that they borrowed persistently over the course of many years and decades, in times of peace and relative prosperity, gradually accumulating a debt stock that poses a significant risk not only to their fiscal health but also to the stability of their economies, financial systems, and, ultimately, their political regimes and societies.

The prime example of this borrowing pattern and a sad reminder of the potential consequences is, of course, Greece. From the late 1970s, Greece's debt-to-GDP ratio increased relentlessly from around 20 percent to over 100 percent by the early 1990s. Never having fully regained control over its large debt ever since, Greece was an obvious target for market panic when economic and financial troubles made investors nervous. The rest of the story, with debt crisis, economic collapse, social turmoil, and human suffering, is well-known to anyone who follows the news. But Greece is far from being the only example. Although no other developed sovereign has been forced to default and suffer the full range of consequences, many are in comparably precarious situations. Italy, with a debt-to-GDP ratio well over 100 percent needed external support to stave off investor panic. Persistent and heavy borrowing throughout the 1970s and 1980s and renewed fiscal laxity in the 2000s burdened the country with an intractably and dangerously large debt stock and substantial interest expenses. Belgium and Canada have remained mostly under the radar in the recent crisis due to their earlier heroic efforts to reduce their debt. However, in the 1990s, they looked at least as bad as Italy or Greece, with debt-to-GDP ratios above 100 percent as a result of their heavy borrowing in the latter half of the 1970s and throughout the 1980s. Much of that debt still continues to burden their public finances. Finally, Japan is an obvious recorder of sustained and substantial debt accumulation with gross debt in excess of 230 percent of the GDP accumulated over the course of four decades.[1]

What is remarkable about these countries' debt accumulation is the combination of its scope and persistence. Many developed countries have experienced debt problems in the past decades. Some saw shorter or longer bursts of intense debt growth, others accumulated debt for many decades at lower rates. Table 1.1 demonstrates the large variation in the intensity, persistence, and scope of the debt issues several developed countries

TABLE 1.1. Periods of debt growth in prosperous developed countries 1970–2007

	Period of debt accumulation	Length of debt accumulation (years)	Speed of debt growth (average, percentage point of GDP per year)	Debt growth total (percentage point of GDP)	Maximum debt within growth period (percent of GDP)
Most sustained and substantial debt accumulation					
Japan	1970–	38	4.5	172	183
Italy	1970–95	26	3.1	81	117
Greece	1981–	26	3.1	82	103
Belgium	1975–93	19	4.2	80	135
Canada	1977–96	20	2.8	57	100
Somewhat less sustained and substantial debt accumulation					
Ireland	1974–87	14	5.0	69	110
United States 1	1981–93	13	2.5	32	73
Netherlands	1978–93	16	2.3	37	78
Portugal 1	1975–86	12	3.6	43	56
Sustained debt accumulation at a moderate pace					
Germany	1975–	31	1.5	46	64
Spain	1977–96	20	2.7	54	66
France	1981–	27	1.6	43	64
Austria	1975–2005	31	1.7	52	68
Shorter bursts of very intense debt accumulation					
Denmark 1	1976–84	9	7.9	71	78
Sweden 1	1977–84	8	7.0	56	58
Sweden 2	1991–96	6	5.2	31	70
Finland 2	1991–96	6	6.9	42	55
Short period of moderate debt accumulation					
Denmark 2	1992–93	4	4.3	17	81
Portugal 3	2001–	7	2.1	15	68
United Kingdom 1	1992–95	4	4.1	16	48
United States 2	2002–	6	1.8	11	64
Portugal 2	1993–96	4	2.6	10	60
United Kingdom 2	2003–	4	1.9	8	44
Finland 1	1977–87	11	0.9	10	16

Source of data: AMECO

encountered in the decades before the onset of the global financial and economic crisis. (The years since the start of the crisis are intentionally left out in an effort to eliminate the confounding effects of the relatively recent economic and financial shocks to many countries' public finances and to focus on the debt that was accumulated over the long run in decades of relative prosperity.) Japan, Greece, Italy, Belgium, and Canada have seen the longest periods of debt accumulation and reached the highest levels of indebtedness.

At the same time, Table 1.1 also demonstrates the impossibility of unambiguously categorizing different countries' experience with debt and drawing a clear line between cases where debt accumulation is dangerously prolonged and excessive and instances where debt accumulation is moderate in scope and length. Japan, Greece, Italy, Belgium, and Canada clearly have the worst track records, but several other countries come close in terms of how long their debt grew and/or in terms of the size of the debt stock they piled up, and the remaining cases are fairly evenly scattered along the whole continuum of both dimensions. It remains a judgment call to decide where the line between harmful and reasonable debt accumulation lies. This book sidesteps this problem by focusing on countries whose debt trajectories are widely considered to be problematic. Nevertheless, it is useful to briefly discuss the theoretical controversies about admissible levels of debt and the tolerable duration of significant fiscal imbalances to explain why it is impossible to authoritatively delineate the universe of truly troubling cases of sustained and excessive debt accumulation from more moderate ones, and to establish that this book does not need to take sides in the academically and politically fraught debate between "austeritarians" and Keynesians.

A Brief Digression on Normative and Empirical Issues Surrounding Debt Accumulation

It is impossible to study the politics of sustained and substantial sovereign debt accumulation without touching on politically sensitive questions concerning admissible debt levels, normative debates about borrowing, and controversies regarding the best ways to deal with debt. Scholarly disputes about these issues have become especially heated—not to say acrimonious—in the wake of the global financial and economic crisis, which left behind considerable stocks of sovereign debt in many prosperous developed countries and lent these debates acute and immediate political relevance. The so-called "austeriterians" clashed violently with scholars of more Keynesian leaning over questions about whether current debt levels represent real risks for countries like the United States, the United Kingdom, or France; whether dealing with those debts is best done through fiscal tightening or growth-inducing stimulus; and whether fiscal sustainability is best served by fiscal rigor or expansion. This book does not take sides in that intense debate because the phenomenon it is concerned with lies outside the area of contention. In looking at *long-term, sustained* increases in the debt-to-GDP ratio to levels that make countries excessively vulnerable to changes in financial market sentiments and threaten with the sudden arrest in financing, the book deals with a policy trajectory that most observers—and, in fact, policy makers and the public of the affected countries themselves—agree constitute an anomaly. This section briefly reviews the debate to explain why that is the case.

The fundamental controversy surrounding debt accumulation is whether borrowing is always unambiguously bad. Scholars of Keynesian leaning have argued that as long as taking on debt allows countries to grow at a faster rate than the interest rate they pay on the debt (through stimulating the economy and enabling higher levels of productive investment), borrowing improves the welfare of a country (Domar 1944). This is because borrowing strengthens the country's ability to service the debt more than it increases the debt service burden, and so income can be boosted without making indebtedness more onerous. By the 1980s, however, a consensus emerged that the conditions for such beneficial borrowing do not hold in the long term because growth rates do not indefinitely exceed interest rates (Sargent and Wallace 1981), which implies that the fiscal pressures created by persistent heavy borrowing cannot be counterbalanced by disproportionately higher growth of income in the long run. Sustained debt accumulation was thus deemed welfare-reducing in the longer term because of the costs of higher taxation needed to service debt in the future (Barro 1979).

As the debt-to-GDP ratio grew to new heights in several countries in the more recent decades, attention turned to the risks and corollary negative economic effects generated by persistent borrowing and large debt stocks. Default—with its potentially catastrophic economic, political, and social ramifications—no longer seemed impossible even for prosperous developed countries, which motivated scholars to look for ways to better gauge the solvency and fiscal sustainability of countries (Buiter 1985; Blanchard 1990; Ostry et al. 2010). Others focused on the economic side effects of debt accumulation and found that as debt grows in proportion to aggregate income, it creates increasing deadweight burden on the economy, reducing investment potential and growth prospects, increasing inflationary pressures and undermining international economic competitiveness (Grilli et al. 1991; Reinhart and Rogoff 2010; Kumar and Woo 2010; but cf. Herndon et al. 2014). Yet others pointed out that growing debt progressively reduces the "fiscal space" available to governments for fulfilling their policy objectives, managing economic cycles, and facing unforeseen challenges (Ostry et al. 2010). These findings cemented the consensus that sustained heavy borrowing does much more harm than good.

However, despite the general consensus that it is better to keep debt at a moderate level, it remains entirely unclear where the distinction between moderate and excessive debt lies. It is impossible to say when a country is too close to default, and indicators of solvency provide little guidance. First, this is because solvency depends on long-term future interest and growth rates that are impossible to predict (Buiter 1985). Debts that seem serviceable under certain economic and financial market conditions might bankrupt a country when those conditions change, as Greece's example demonstrates. Higher debt levels create greater exposure to interest and growth rate shocks, but the relationship between indebtedness and default is not deterministic. Second, solvency also depends on a number of country-specific characteristics that determine the ability to produce large enough surpluses in the future to service the debt, which suggests that the safety limit is different for every country (Ostry et al. 2010). Third, markets might deny further financing to countries that are theoretically solvent but have short-term difficulties in servicing their current debt. Scholars who sought to pin down a debt benchmark based on historical experience have found that some countries default at very low levels of debt, which are obviously unproblematic for others (Reinhart et al. 2003). The same uncertainties prevail when it comes to the negative economic effects of debt: there is no unambiguous limit at which the deadweight burden of debt starts to have tangible slowing effects on the economy.[2]

These ambiguities became important for the controversy that flared up in the wake of the global financial and economic crisis about how to deal with the debt created by the crisis in the short term. With no sure way of determining how close most countries are to default or how likely their debt stocks are to fatally weigh down their economies, even the short-term benefits of borrowing—in terms of providing a stimulus to lift countries out of recession—are considered suspect. Defying Keynesian arguments that large deficits should be temporarily encouraged (or at least tolerated) to avoid deepening the recession (Eggertsson and Krugman 2012), "austeritarians" called for the immediate elimination of the deficits. They contended that growing indebtedness damages market confidence, which leads to higher interest rates and lower growth, both of which jeopardize the fiscal stability of countries (e.g., Alesina and Ardagna 2013; Alesina et al. 2015). In a slightly more tempered version of this argument, a group of IMF economists suggested that only the countries that are more immediately at risk of default need to take action to reduce their indebtedness, while countries that are not in danger of being shut out of financial markets wait for normal economic conditions to return and allow "the debt ratio to decline organically through growth and 'opportunistic' revenues, living with the debt otherwise" (Ostry et al. 2015, 1). While seemingly more pragmatic than calling for austerity across the board, this recommendation sides with the "austeritarian" view that immediate reductions in the deficit are the only way to save the more indebted countries from default because favorable changes in market confidence more than counterbalance the negative effects of austerity on national income, and, thus, on the ability of a country to service its debt.

As Mark Blyth (2013) points out, this debate is highly ideological. Ambiguities about how severe the debt problem is and different views on how public debt and economic growth are related leave room for different interpretations of the current situation, which yield diametrically opposed policy recommendations. Conflicting policy prescriptions, in turn, have very different distributive implications. This is, on the one hand, because fiscal expansion and contraction affect different groups across society very differently. On the other hand, "austeritarians" tend to advocate spending-based contractions—dismissing tax-led consolidations as ineffective in achieving lasting fiscal stability—and spending cuts are bound to affect the poor most severely, as they depend on government services and transfers the most. The political stakes of the debate have understandably impacted the intensity and tone of the controversy and have made it difficult to address issues of debt and adjustment without appearing to take sides in this irresolvable, politically loaded argument.

However, the irresolvability of this debate or the ambiguities about the boundary between moderate and truly troubling amounts of debt do not relativize the political puzzle entailed in sustained and heavy debt accumulation. One does not need to take sides in the debate between "austeritarians" and Keynesians or arbitrarily choose an upper limit for "safe" debt to consider it a policy failure when the debt-to-GDP ratio unremittingly and substantially grows over the course of several decades, and to wonder how this policy anomaly occurs in established democracies. When the debt stock persistently grows at a faster rate than GDP for decades, Domar's conditions for welfare-enhancing borrowing obviously do not hold, because the country fails to "grow out" of its debt even over the course of multiple business cycles. At the same time, economic problems and risks of destabilizing crises escalate. Under these circumstances, it is reasonable to assume that restraining borrowing—through increasing taxation and/or by cutting spending—would be favorable to continuing along the same trajectory of growing debt and to wonder why the trajectory remains uncorrected.

While it is impossible to distill clear criteria for what constitutes excessive debt growth in terms of either length or scope, some cases are clearly problematic. In cases like Japan, Greece, Italy, Belgium, or Canada, there can be little doubt that something was amiss with public finances, not only because these countries borrowed more and for a longer time than any other country but also, and more importantly, because the political and policy discourse in these countries reflected a considerably strong consensus that the debt trajectory was alarming. Debt grew *despite* a professed wish of politicians and policy makers to put an end to borrowing. Why, then, did they fail to do so for decades on end?

The Political Puzzle of Sustained Large-Scale Debt Accumulation

Why does a country borrow heavily and persistently for decades, jeopardizing its economic health, exposing itself to the risk of default and saddling itself with immense interest burdens and large policy challenges for the long term? Beyond its practical relevance for several prosperous developed countries, the phenomenon of sustained and substantial debt accumulation is profoundly puzzling from a theoretical perspective, too. Policy makers should have strong and growing incentives to adjust fiscal policy and stop borrowing as soon as possible once debt accumulation starts to reel out of control. First, they face immense political risks as the danger of disruptive debt crises loom larger. The costs of a default are massive in political terms if the blame for it is attributed to a given political force; and even if explicit default can be avoided, a debt crisis triggers enormously difficult policy problems that the government in power will need to deal with. Second, growing debt undermines policy makers' ability to perform well on a number of issues that have electoral importance. Besides generating potentially large negative economic side effects, the progressive growth of the interest burden constrains policy makers' ability to manage the economy, deliver services, address new welfare needs as they arise, and invest productively. The fiscal problem itself might gain electoral salience and become an important issue on which policy makers' performance is evaluated. Third, the growing pressure on the budget from the ever-higher interest burden foreshadows increasingly harsh fiscal adjustment in the future. Therefore, policy makers with reasonable chances to stay in the political race for future government positions should feel under great and increasing pressure to stop the escalation of debt. Why, then, do some countries keep borrowing for decades?

Against the conventional wisdom, against extensive scholarly consensus and against the approach of European technocrats who tried to bring borrowing in European countries under control via a set of fiscal rules, surveillance, and penalties, this book argues that the main problem underlying sustained and substantial debt accumulation in many developed countries today is not "fiscal indiscipline". It is not the lack of concern for budgetary constraints from policy makers as they try to please voters. Rather, sustained debt accumulation reflects a fundamental adjustment deficiency: the inability of governments to change existing policies once a risky debt trajectory is recognized, in time to stave off the escalation of the problem. Consequently, the book analyzes the conditions under which such incapacity persists and adjustment is delayed dangerously long.

The notion of "fiscal indiscipline" is rooted in a robust literature that emerged from the 1970s around the idea that governments are intrinsically given to irresponsible borrowing due to their short time-horizons. This literature focuses on the dynamics of yearly budgetary decision making. On the one hand, it emphasizes the ways in which spending beyond the available tax revenues enhances policy makers' electoral chances.[3] On the other hand, it highlights the collective action problems that undermine spending control in divided governments.[4] As a result, it argues that governments will be unwilling or unable to respect budgetary constraints unless they are subjected to institutionalized control mechanisms. While this rationalist fiscal governance literature has discovered important factors and mechanisms that induce governments to borrow in any one year, it (somewhat counter-intuitively) cannot explain the puzzle of sustained and heavy debt accumulation. Actually, it is entirely blind to the political puzzle entailed in persistent and heavy borrowing because it looks at fiscal policy making as isolated instances of yearly budgetary decisions and, thus, remains oblivious of the increasing political costs of sustained deficits that emerge as the debt stock swells and starts to generate various economic problems, policy constraints, and risks. A core assumption of the rationalist fiscal governance literature is that the costs of borrowing always arise beyond governments' short time horizons, but that assumption is only tenable if borrowing is sufficiently moderate in scope and persistence. Consequently, this approach provides little help in understanding why policy makers in some countries fail to stop borrowing once it becomes politically inconvenient.

Whereas the rationalist fiscal governance literature seeks to explain why governments are predisposed to borrow, the adjustment approach adopted in this book explores why they might be unable to stop borrowing once debt accumulation starts to give rise to corollary economic or policy problems and financial risks. This approach emphasizes the inertial nature of public finances: the fact that, once in place, spending and taxation patterns are difficult to change, which can become a problem if expenditures substantially exceed revenues. Budgetary imbalances can be caused by deliberate government action—as posited by the rationalist fiscal governance literature—but spending and revenues can also become mismatched due to severe economic crises, adverse changes in long-term economic growth and unemployment, demographic shifts, or increases in the interest rates charged on outstanding government debt. Irrespective of the original impetus, though, a large gap in the budget is unlikely to disappear unless taxes are raised or expenditure is cut (at least in the absence of positive changes in the economic and demographic environment). Worst still, the gap is likely to progressively widen as continued borrowing fuels a growing debt stock, which in turn generates increasing pressure on the spending side through mounting interest costs. However, making large changes to taxes and spending is likely to be fraught with political complications that go beyond the scope of regular year-to-year budgetary negotiations. Since the most important items on both the spending and the revenue sides of the budget are legacies of past redistributive settlements, major adjustments are likely to be subject to considerable social contestation. The adjustment approach adopted in this book focuses on how redistributive conflicts influence governments' abilities to regain control over fiscal imbalances and rein in borrowing, despite the growing pressures generated by debt.

While it is a self-evident truth in political science that redistributive conflicts play a central role in determining the form and success of fiscal adjustment, the exact nature and intensity of these conflicts remain remarkably unexplored. Redistributive conflicts are (implicitly or explicitly) assumed to be sufficiently similar across countries to not warrant specific attention to their nature and intensity as possible explanatory variables for variation in the way different countries adjust their policies in the face of growing debt. This has led some scholars to portray growing public indebtedness as an inherent feature of the latest phase of capitalist development and a general manifestation of class and sectoral conflicts across the prosperous developed world (O'Connor 1973; Streeck 2014). This interpretation highlights important common challenges that place mounting fiscal pressure on all prosperous developed countries—such as globalization, slowing growth, the maturation of welfare systems, and demographic changes (Pierson 2001)—but it inherently underplays the variation in the track records of different countries in adjusting to these pressures and, therefore, cannot provide an explanation for the difference between countries with the most anomalous cases of debt accumulation and ones that asserted control over debt growth.

But the implicit assumption that redistributive conflicts can be reduced to the same class and sectoral conflicts across countries is also omnipresent in comparative studies of adjustment. Since the 1970s, policy adjustment has been at the forefront of research in comparative political economy. Although this literature never looked at fiscal adjustment from a fully budgetary perspective and debt accumulation was never its main focus, studies on welfare state reform, public sector reform, or macroeconomic stabilizations have important implications for fiscal performance, debt accumulation, and budgetary adjustment. These studies overwhelmingly focus on institutional and ideational differences in different national contexts of adjustment, betraying an unstated assumption that variation in adjustment capacity can only come from the different ways in which the same conflicts feed through various political and policy-making institutions and are modulated by different ideologies and policy paradigms (Pontusson 1995). This approach has led to important insights about how institutional circumstances determine the chances of successful reform and how institutional and ideational innovations can lead to policy breakthroughs,[5] but it provides few clues as to *how fast* reform happens. From the perspective of debt accumulation, the speed of adjustment is crucial because of the cumulative nature of the problem. A key issue is not only whether but also how promptly spending and taxation are adjusted to stem further debt growth. Therefore, institutional and ideational analyses of discreet instances of reform failure or success only provide partial understanding of the problem, which plays out across time as a continuous process.

This book proposes a novel approach to debt accumulation and fiscal adjustment that differs from previous approaches in two key respects. First, it pays close attention to the variation in the intensity of redistributive conflicts across different countries, which is likely to be significant due to large differences in existing policies in place. We know from the rich literatures on welfare states, tax systems, and pork-barrel politics that different countries allocate spending, provide transfers, and raise taxes in very different ways, generating very different redistributive consequences across class, sectoral, regional, or generational divisions. These redistributive differences give rise to different conflicts of interests when it comes to radically adjusting existing policies. The more clearly defined the winners and losers of existing policies are, the stronger are the conflicts about what taxes to raise and what expenditure to cut for the sake of restoring fiscal balance; and the more difficult adjustment is. Second, the new approach is also highly attentive to the diachronic dimension of debt accumulation. In the absence of adjustment, the debt problem grows simply by virtue of the passage of time, generating ever-increasing pressures for policy reform. The model proposed in this book investigates how fast the balance changes between the forces impeding and fostering adjustment in different countries to explain why some countries stay dangerously long on a trajectory of persistently and heavily accumulating debt, whereas others successfully adjust their policy when debt starts to grow at an alarming rate.

Why Fiscal Polarization and International Exposure Matter: The Outline of the Argument

The main reason why the puzzle of sustained and substantial debt accumulation has remained unresolved until the present day, despite its pressing practical relevance, is that scholars have never really looked at the issue as a process that unfolds across time. The rationalist fiscal governance literature asks why countries borrow in any one year without acknowledging the cumulative, emerging effects of borrowing, even though debt is arguably a much more consequential policy outcome than yearly deficits are. In contrast, scholars who interpret high public-debt stocks as an inherent feature of the latest phase of capitalism focus only on common pressures without investigating the specificities of the political and policy process that modulate the effect of such pressures across prosperous developed countries. The comparative political economic literature on adjustment concentrates on explaining specific instances of reform without exploring political processes that lead up to a policy breakthrough. In this approach, adjustment is either happening or not. In reality, however, we see that even countries that amass dangerous amounts of debt can make significant, painful, and successful adjustments, albeit after harmful delay. Therefore, in this book, I propose an explanatory model of debt accumulation and fiscal adjustment that traces the road to successful fiscal adjustment across time. In doing so, the model accounts both for policy stasis in the face of ballooning debt and for successful policy change. It also explains why stasis lasts longer in some countries than others.

The argument goes as follows. A combination of significant spending cuts and tax increases can only have the necessary political and societal support to be successfully put into place if sufficiently large sections of society have an immediate stake in fiscal adjustment and cannot reasonably hope for less onerous fiscal sacrifices. These two conditions generally hold in countries where large exposure to international economic competition ensures that the problems associated with debt accumulation directly impinge on the welfare of large sections of society and where there is no room for starkly different distributions of the fiscal sacrifices. In such countries, low levels of fiscal polarization and the urgency of fiscal adjustment for the majority of society lead to swift adjustment. In countries where the existing fiscal architecture lends itself to different avenues of adjustment with significantly different incidence of fiscal pain, conflicts about burden sharing are likely to slow the emergence of societal support for any one package, especially if large sections of society are isolated from the negative side effects of mounting debt in a relatively closed economy. Adjustment in these countries will be delayed and debt will continue to grow even after a consensus emerges that adjustment is necessary. At the same time, adjustment can eventually happen even in these cases as the passing of time—and the ballooning of debt—increases the pressure on the economy and on society above a critical level, forcing a resolution of the conflict about the distribution of fiscal sacrifices. In sum, it depends on international exposure and fiscal polarization how long debt is allowed to grow. The more limited the exposure and the stronger the polarization, the longer a country stays on a dangerous debt trajectory.

This argument is constructed of three building blocks.

1. Its foundation is the premise that if fiscal stabilization is to succeed, spending cuts and/or tax increases need a critical mass of societal support.
2. Its central component consists in identifying the two key factors that influence the availability of social support for such painful measures: fiscal polarization and economic openness.
3. Its third element is the emphasis on the crucial role that the passage of time plays in generating the necessary social support.

The *first* and foundational building block of the argument is its focus on societal support as a precondition for the successful enactment and implementation of painful fiscal stabilization. Before it goes fully into effect, a fiscal stabilization package has to clear obstacles in a number of areas of political contestation. It needs to pass in parliament. It needs to be endorsed by social partners or be able to withstand strikes and threats of capital flight. It needs to endure in the face of political mobilization on the streets. Since Peter Gourevitch's Politics in Hard Times (1986), we think of the source of the societal support that enables a specific policy adjustment package to survive in all these spheres of political contestation in terms of *social coalitions*. Social coalitions are constellations of different socioeconomic groups whose interests can be sufficiently reconciled in a given policy reform to secure their backing. The notion of social coalitions allows for incorporating both of the two important mechanisms that pave the way for policy breakthroughs: compromise and power. Diverse groups need to reach a compromise, a mutually satisfactory reconciliation of their diverging interests within the coalition, in order to have the power to override any opposition to the coalition's preferred policy choice from outside the coalition. Therefore, explaining when fiscal stabilization becomes possible requires understanding how compromises emerge and how conflicts are overpowered. This, in turn, involves analyzing the structure of the conflicts and commonalities of interests between sections of society in a given polity.

The *second* building block of the argument is identifying the factors that generate commonalities and conflicts of interests regarding fiscal stabilization. Economic problems associated with debt accumulation give rise to a shared interest in swift stabilization among groups whose welfare is affected and, thereby, foster compromise and the emergence of a strong supportive coalition behind a given fiscal stabilization package. Acute conflicts about the distribution of fiscal sacrifices, on the other hand, retard the coalescence of a coalition because they make it difficult to find a specific stabilization package—with a specific incidence of fiscal pain—that a large enough section of society is willing to accept and endorse. The speed of stabilization depends on the relative strength of these two countervailing forces in the given country.

Economic problems that arise in tandem with debt accumulation create immediate incentives for biting the bullet and accepting the necessity of fiscal sacrifices for the sake of tackling the debt problem. Large budgetary imbalances are often accompanied by high inflation and high interest rates. These problems are likelier to negatively affect large parts of society when the livelihood of a large proportion of workers and businesses depends on competitiveness in the international economy. Competitiveness, sales, profits, employment, and wages suffer when a country's inflation and interest rates persistently exceed those of their competitors. High inflation and high interest rates can, of course, also affect groups sheltered from international competition, but governments usually have greater latitude in compensating for these negative side effects in relatively closed economies. For example, indexation policies can provide protection to people on fixed incomes against inflation, whereas subsidies can help borrowers in a high-interest environment. In an open economy, however, such compensatory policies engender their own serious problems. Indexation fuels ever-higher inflation, further weakening competitiveness; production subsidies, unemployment benefits, or expanded public employment exacerbate fiscal imbalances; devaluations increase the value of foreign denominated debt; and so on. Therefore, in more open economies, the pressures for swift stabilization are stronger, and they are weaker in relatively closed economies. In the extreme case, if the exposure of the economy to international competition is very limited, compensatory policies might completely insulate the large majority of society from the negative side effects of continued borrowing, implying that the majority of the population first becomes affected by debt when a debt crisis threatens the country's overall fiscal, financial, and economic viability. In such cases, the incentives to make sacrifices for the sake of fiscal stabilization are low all the way until a debt crisis erupts.

While economic problems foster compromise, acute conflicts surrounding the distribution of the fiscal sacrifices necessary for stabilization are the main force working against the emergence of a supportive social coalition. A given budgetary hole can be plugged through many different combinations of tax increases and spending cuts, each of which spread fiscal pain across different sections of society in different ways. Therefore, even when the whole society supports stabilization in principle, there might not exist a specific stabilization package that a large enough majority can agree on and support, as different groups have an incentive to limit the sacrifices they have to bear.[6] The intensity of conflicts of interests about the specific mix of spending cuts and tax increases depends on the existing fiscal architecture. Although the ways in which revenues can be increased and savings can be made are infinite in principle, spending cuts and tax increases are likely to be anchored by the structure of existing spending programs and tax arrangements in practice. This means that conflicts about the distribution of sacrifices arise between groups within society that have vested interests in different spending programs and tax arrangements. In countries where the largest spending programs are inclusive and taxes are broad-based, conflicts about changes to the system are less intense because adjustments that are large enough to close the fiscal gap anyway cannot spare significant sections of society. In contrast, where the bulk of extant expenditures and taxes (and tax relief) serve the interests of specific sections of society delineable along class, sectoral, geographic, or demographic dimensions, there is considerable incentive for the beneficiaries of targeted policies to insist that fiscal stabilization be carried out without affecting the policies they have vested interests in, burdening the rest of society with proportionally greater sacrifices. The polarizing effect of existing taxes and spending policies is strongest when they divide society into a few large blocks with disparate sets of vested interests. In such cases, negotiating a stabilization package that musters enough support to survive is exceedingly difficult.

The *third* and final building block of the argument is that this political economic framework is not static but dynamically evolving even in the absence of exogenous impacts. Even if adjustment is initially impossible in the face of intense societal conflict about the distribution of fiscal sacrifices, the passage of time can endogenously resolve the situation. The constellation of the conflicts and commonalities of interests evolve as time passes, opening the way for the reconfiguration of societal coalitions and, thus, for successful adjustment that brings debt accumulation under control. This is not only because the objective circumstances worsen as time passes—debt accumulates and the economic side effects get more severe—but also because the passage of time conveys important information to different sections of society about the likelihood that successful stabilization could happen without their sacrifices.

According to the famous war of attrition model of fiscal stabilization developed by Alesina and Drazen (1991), any social group has to balance three factors when deciding whether to resist or give in to fiscal pain: the cost of waiting for a pain-free solution, the risks of having to share in the costs of stabilization later when the problem has grown much bigger, and the possible gain from a pain-free stabilization. Resistance to fiscal pain is rational only as long as there is a realistic chance that a stabilization package will be put into place in the foreseeable future that spares the group from fiscal pain. This chance compensates a group for enduring the (growing) negative side effects while adjustment is delayed and for the risk that the group would eventually have to make sacrifices later, when stabilization is more painful, if it cannot wait for other groups to pick up the tab of fiscal reforms.[7] The passage of time increases both of these costs and eventually proves the strategy of resistance to fiscal pain a losing one for groups that suffer from the economic side effects of fiscal problems.

As the passage of time proves to certain sections of society that relentless defense of their vested interests in the fiscal *status quo* will only harm their welfare, they become amenable to adjustment packages they would have unambiguously rejected before. If those groups for whom further delay is most damaging are jointly strong enough to foist their preferred adjustment on others, they form a coalition behind a stabilization package that limits their concessions to the minimum necessary to make stabilization viable and force as much of the fiscal pain as possible onto those sections of society that are not represented in their coalition. If the groups for whom further delay is most damaging are not strong enough to override the resistance of groups for whom stabilization is less urgent, they have to assume as much of the burden as they can to minimize the fiscal pain affecting groups that have less of a stake in swift stabilization in order to make reforms palatable for them.

In summary, this book argues that sustained and substantial debt accumulation is at heart an adjustment failure rooted in fiscal polarization. Fiscal polarization generates strong conflicts over the distribution of fiscal sacrifices necessary to rebalance the budget. Such conflicts are especially difficult to resolve if the economy is relatively closed and a large section of society is mostly insulated from the negative economic side effects of fiscal problems. In such countries, a dangerously long time has to pass to induce a large enough part of society to accept fiscal pain. In the extreme case where society is fully insulated from any adverse economic effect, adjustment will remain impossible until a debt crisis makes the costs of the problem tangible for society.

The Empirical Material

The book will demonstrate the validity of the polarization-exposure argument through analyzing and comparing some of the most puzzling cases of sustained and substantial debt accumulation as they unfolded across time. Given that the argument focuses on the endogenous evolution of the balance of forces fostering and impeding adjustment across time and on the factors that determine the speed at which a critical mass of societal support emerges behind a specific stabilization package, the case studies rely on process tracing as well as paired comparisons. Process tracing allows not only for comparing the explanatory capacities of different theoretical approaches at different critical junctures in the stories of sustained and substantial debt accumulation but also for testing how successful the diachronic argument presented here is in accounting for the process by which critical junctures arise. Pairwise country comparisons allow for gauging the effect of differences in fiscal polarization and international exposure, while controlling for institutional and ideational factors.

Italy's fiscal history, well known both for long periods of debt growth and for impressive instances of fiscal stabilization, serves as the base case through which the mechanism of political change underlying fiscal adjustment is explored. The Italian case study first explains how fiscal polarization coupled with the insulation of relatively large sections of society from the negative side effects of debt in an only moderately open economy to cause a long period of policy paralysis in the 1980s. Then, it traces the process through which this paralysis eventually gave way to major political upheaval and policy breakthrough in the early 1990s as social groups suffering from the repercussions of fiscal problems for international competitiveness abandoned their existing alliances and formed a new social coalition in support of policy reform. It also explains why Italy relapsed into borrowing in the 2000s; after joining the euro severed the link between fiscal problems and economic competitiveness. Finally, it analyzes the emergence of a new social coalition that has lent support to efforts to bring debt under control in the wake of the global financial and economic crisis. By being able to account for every twist and turn of the Italian story, the evolving coalitions approach outperforms alternative institutional and ideational hypotheses previously proposed to explain critical junctures in Italy's history of debt accumulation. It also successfully explains the mechanism that drives alternating periods of political and policy equilibrium and change.

In comparison to Italy, Belgium and Ireland both represent cases where large parts of society are exposed to the negative side effects of debt, due to considerable economic openness. This explains why both countries reacted much faster to the problem of debt accumulation than Italy: both introduced large austerity packages as early as 1982, coupled with drastic deflationary policies to restore competitiveness. However, high levels of fiscal polarization in Belgium hamstrung further efforts to definitively resolve fiscal problems. Large cuts to public consumption and investment initiated in 1982 proved obviously insufficient in stemming debt growth, to a large extent due to the deflationary policies which compounded the interest burden. Nevertheless, successive governments were unable to reinforce stabilization efforts in the face of very strong opposition to tax increases or cuts to social security because existing welfare arrangements strongly polarized the interests of business and labor, while the threat to international competitiveness had been neutralized by deflation. Inability to touch large parts of the budget led to an unhappy mix of fiscal pain *and* persistently heavy debt accumulation until a favorable change in interest rates in the early 1990s eventually rescued Belgium from the chokehold of debt. In contrast, the lack of such polarization allowed Ireland to adjust any large fiscal item and to introduce successful further austerity measures in 1987, which put the debt-to-GDP ratio on a firm downward path long before the rise of the Celtic Tiger.

The comparison of Belgium and Ireland approximates a "most similar" case study design and controls for the effects of alternative institutional and ideational explanatory variables. Besides having similarly open economies, the two countries also have important features in common (most importantly, both have non-majoritarian electoral regimes) and display similar ideational developments over the period concerned (a shift from Keynesianism to neoliberal economic ideas in the 1980s). Where they differ, theory would predict that Belgium should have better adjustment capacities (due to its better established corporatist institutions). In light of these similarities and the institutional advantages on Belgium's side, Ireland's superior performance in regaining control over its debt problem can be confidently attributed to differences in fiscal polarization.

The juxtaposition of the Greek and Japanese cases, on the other hand, approximates a "most different" case study design. The two countries differ significantly on a whole range of economic and social factors, on political institutions (electoral and party systems, the organization of corporatist interest intermediation, and state capacities), and have been dominated by very different economic and political ideologies. Nevertheless, both countries witnessed similarly ruinous debt accumulation since the early 1980s due to similarly intense fiscal polarization and the insulation of large sections society from the negative side effects of debt.

Naturally, the profoundly different economic, social, and political circumstances led to very different redistributive conflicts. In Japan, class and regional differences were manifested in intense conflicts over a strongly biased tax system, the system of subsidies, and infrastructural developments directed to the rural areas and the pension entitlements of urban workers. In Greece, a decade of the infamous "bureaucratic clientelism'" had led to the polarization of vested interests among the populous group of public employees and various groups in the private sector, which made it impossible to curb the costs of public employment and pensions and to start collecting taxes from businesses and the self-employed. Differences in the actual content of redistributive conflicts notwithstanding, the *intensity* of polarization was similar due to the strong geographical targeting of policies in Japan and the highly particularistic nature of the clientelism through which benefits were secured in Greece. The stalemate generated by this polarization was all the more stubborn because of the insulation of large sections of society from the negative side effects of debt due to a combination of low level of exposure to foreign competition and monetary and exchange rate policies that prevented the spillover of fiscal problems into competitiveness issues. This allowed debt problems to grow to truly catastrophic levels in both countries.

The Contributions of the Book: What Can We Learn from Analyzing the Politics of Public Debt Accumulation along the Polarization-Exposure Dimensions?

This book tackles the puzzle of sustained large-scale debt accumulation in prosperous developed countries, which has remained unresolved despite the ever-growing relevance of the problem in the past four decades. Instead of exploring the politics of yearly budgetary decision-making as the existing literature on fiscal governance does, it defines the problem of debt accumulation as a longer term adjustment issue and provides an explanation for why some countries are unable to adjust their existing spending and tax policies for decades after they become manifestly unsustainable, whereas other countries adjust practically as soon as fiscal imbalances appear. It explains how fiscal conflict and the urgency of stabilizing an unstable macroeconomic environment interact in different polities to shape the political conditions for adjustment. The novelty of this explanation lies in specifically identifying the factors—fiscal polarization and international exposure—that bear on the strength of these countervailing forces and, therefore, on the speed of adjustment. The rest of the book demonstrates how targeted fiscal policies in place generate debilitating social conflict in some polities about how adjustment is to be carried out, while encompassing policies limit the scope for fiscal conflict in other polities. It also shows how macroeconomic problems force groups with vested interests in different spending and tax policies to compromise on an adjustment package for the sake of macroeconomic stabilization in countries that are strongly exposed to international economic competition, whereas insulation from the negative side effects of growing debt allows warring vested interest groups to dig in their heels indefinitely in closed economies.

Through analyzing the politics of debt accumulation in different countries along the polarization-exposure dimension, the book also provides a template for delineating the relevant socioeconomic groups—at the intersection of vested fiscal interest groups and different sectors of the economy—whose conflicts and commonalities of interests shape the struggles about fiscal adjustment. It identifies the sources of power they wield and explains the way they form social coalitions to protect their multidimensional interests. As a result, in each country case study, the narrative identifies the winners and losers of the struggles about fiscal adjustment and explains not only the length of the delay but also the eventual composition of adjustment.

Although the book focuses on the clearest-cut and most astonishing cases of sustained large-scale debt accumulation, its argument applies by extension more generally to the question what determines how fast and in what ways countries adjust their policies in the face of growing debt. Furthermore, given that welfare spending and revenues linked to social security have such an overwhelming weight in the budget in most developed countries, the book also has implications for our understanding of welfare state reform. It advances the surprising claim that more encompassing spending programs and revenue arrangements make rebalancing the finances of the welfare state easier, not harder, which goes against the received wisdom that the greatest obstacle to welfare reform lies in the extensiveness of vested welfare interests in society and among the electorate (Pierson 2001, 412–14).

Beyond its practical, policy-relevant claims, the book also makes a number of theoretical contributions. By drawing on disparate literatures, it attempts to generate synergies between different approaches to comparative public policy and political economy. In focusing on the pursuit of material interests among different groups in society and on coalition formation between groups, the argument follows a society-centered approach. It infuses this approach with a rational choice logic by borrowing the results of game theoretical modeling to better understand how the strategic preferences of groups and coalitional affinities evolve under pressure from debt growth with the passage of time. At the same time, the argument is highly sensitive to historical contingencies in the constellation of interests as well as to the path dependent effect of policy choices in terms of shaping political conditions. By taking into consideration existing policy arrangements in delineating relevant groups within society whose conflicts and commonalities of interests shape the struggles about fiscal adjustment, the argument takes seriously the historical institutionalist claim that "policy creates politics" (Hacker and Pierson 2014). This eclectic approach generates four main theoretical contributions.

The first theoretical contribution relates to the analysis of coalitional dynamics underlying policy adjustment. The argument made here emphasizes that structurally given socioeconomic features act alongside existing policies in shaping the conflicts and commonalities of interests that underlie coalition formation in redistributive policy areas. In doing so, it combines traditional coalitional analysis with the characteristic emphasis of historical institutionalism on path dependence and vested interests. Coalitional analysis has traditionally focused on commonalities and conflicts of interests defined by countries' socioeconomic structure in drawing conclusions about the constellation of policy preferences (Gourevitch 1986; Rogowski 1990; Frieden 1991a, 1991b; Hiscox 2001; Iversen and Soskice 2001; Mares 2003). Path-dependence and vested-interest arguments, on the other hand, take existing policies as a starting point in determining the relative forces supporting and obstructing policy change (Thelen and Steinmo 1992; Pierson 2000 and 2004).

The polarization-exposure argument gives equal weight to structurally given determinants of policy preferences and vested interests in extant policies. It juxtaposes these two different dimensions to show that economic and fiscal interests can align and clash in more than one way.[8] On the one hand, it emphasizes that the incentives generated by socioeconomic position are modulated by policies both because vested interests in existing fiscal policies can counteract economic interests and because economic interests themselves are affected by policies. On the other hand, it also stresses that the incentives generated by vested interests never operate in isolation from developments in the real economy and, therefore, their impact on policy preferences cannot be taken for granted. The constellation of conflicts and commonalities of interests—and hence the potential for coalition formation—depends on the complex interplay of socioeconomic structure and past policy choices at any one moment in time. Furthermore, this complex interplay leads to the endogenous evolution of the societal bases of politics by generating changes in the pattern of alignment and conflict among different groups' preferences.

This focus on the dynamic evolution of societal preferences leads to the second theoretical contribution, which relates to our understanding of political, institutional, and policy change. This book explains policy stasis and breakthrough within a single theoretical framework, centering on the endogenous shifts in the coalitional basis of policy making. Simultaneously explaining stability and change has been one of the great challenges in comparative political economy (Thelen 1999). Different theories focused on different phenomena. Many accounted for bursts of change "punctuating" long periods of institutional and policy stasis, citing changes in exogenous conditions (for a review, see Mahoney and Thelen 2009). Others emphasized the multitude of ways in which institutions undergo gradual transformative change through endogenous adaptation (Streeck and Thelen 2005; Mahoney and Thelen 2009). Yet others called attention to the subterranean "drift" in policies as existing policy design fails to keep up with changes in the social and economic environment (Hacker 2004).

This book integrates all of these aspects of stability and change. Its central puzzle focuses on policy stasis in the face of a pressing problem and explores the conditions under which inaction gives way to a burst of reforms. In this context, the book also explains instances of momentous political and institutional upheaval that often accompany long-awaited policy breakthroughs. At the same time, instead of looking for exogenous shocks that trigger these bursts of change, it draws attention to the gradual, subterranean, endogenous evolution of the environment in which existing policies and institutions operate. The book's explanation for the eruption of reforms centers on the gradual endogenous deterioration of economic circumstances that alter the effect of existing policies on the welfare of different sections of society. Changes in the welfare consequences of existing policies trigger shifts in the coalitional structure, which in turn lead to profound changes in the political dynamics, in institutions, and in policy. In this interpretation, the source of institutional and policy change is a shift in the constellation of societal coalitions, but this shift is endogenous to the system and is closely connected to the functioning of existing policies and institutions.

In exploring institutional and policy reform, the book also sheds light on the role of political entrepreneurs as agents of change and ideational innovations as instruments of change. Political scientists have called attention to the role of policy entrepreneurs in redefining debates about certain policy issues; generating the necessary support behind new policy initiatives; and transforming politics, policies, and institutions (Legro 2000; Sheingate 2003; Mintrom and Norman 2009). Some have contended that institutional complexity—uncertainty, heterogeneity, and ambiguity—are the best breeding grounds for entrepreneurial political initiative (Sheingate 2003). A disparate, but related, literature emphasized the role of ideational innovations in helping policy entrepreneurs perform those three functions (Jacobsen 1995; Blyth 2002). This book, however, suggests that political entrepreneurs react to, rather than engineer, changes in the political environment. In the cases presented in this book, those political actors were successful in making political advances who were sensitive to latent shifts in the constellation of the preferences of various socioeconomic groups (from insisting on the defense of their vested fiscal interests to acquiescing in fiscal pain for the sake of macroeconomic stabilization) and exploited new opportunities to represent emergent new societal coalitions. They employed ideational innovations likely to appeal to those groups for whom old societal coalitional arrangements were increasingly uncomfortable. In this sense, political entrepreneurs rode the wave of the endogenous transformation of societal coalitions and their ideational innovations were the response to—rather than the trigger for—profound political change.

Attention to the endogenous evolution of political forces also yields the third theoretical contribution of the book, which relates to our understanding of the temporal, diachronic aspects of political phenomena. Instead of comparing political and economic circumstances at different points in time when reforms are or are not possible, the book traces across time the changes in the economic environment under pressure from growing debt, the evolution of policy preferences of different sections of society as economic conditions worsen, and the shifts in the coalitional structure as preferences evolve to show how these processes—all endogenous to the explanatory model—generate the necessary preconditions for policy reform without any change in the exogenous circumstances. In a sense, the book demonstrates that the passage of time itself can be an important driving force behind momentous change because it allows brewing processes to reach a critical intensity to trigger change. Following Paul Pierson's theoretical work on the role of time in politics, this diachronic approach offers an important corrective to the predominance of comparative statics in comparative political economic analysis and calls attention to the latent, "slow moving" processes that snapshots taken at different points in time will not detect (Pierson 2004).

Finally, the book also speaks to questions of state strength and weakness. As Theda Skocpol noted, "a state's means of raising and deploying financial resources tells us more than could any other single factor about its [. . .] capacities" (1985, 16). By exploring the factors that explain policy makers' ability or inability to deal with the problem of persistent fiscal imbalances and growing debt in a variety of national institutional settings, the book examines state autonomy and capacity by implication. Scholars interested in state strength and weakness have looked primarily at how institutions insulate states from societal pressures when making policy choices and empower them to carry out decisive action (Krasner 1978; Skocpol 1985; Fukuyama 2004). In contrast, this book argues that decisive state action is always dependent on sufficient societal support even in polities where the state is otherwise considered to be institutionally strong. It claims that it is precisely the exclusive focus on institutions of the state and not taking sufficiently into consideration the societal constraints that governments face in their policy making that prevents existing theories of fiscal problems from satisfactorily explaining the phenomenon of sustained and substantial public debt accumulation.

The Plan of the Book

The next chapter situates the polarization-exposure argument in a disparate set of literatures and lays it out in detail, contemplating the implications of a theory built on a model of changing societal preferences for questions of agency, institutions, and ideas, as well as spelling out the observable implications of the argument. The third chapter presents the Italian case at length, focusing primarily on capturing the process through which the constellation of conflicts and commonalities of societal interests changes and affects politics and policy making. The fourth chapter compares the Belgian and Irish cases to each other as well as to Italy in an effort to show the impact of openness and fiscal polarization on countries' ability to regain control over debt growth. The fifth chapter contrasts the Greek and Japanese cases to the other three to test the influence of institutional and ideational factors on the ability to deal with debt in countries where the theory presented here predicts insurmountable obstacles to stabilization. The final chapter sums up and highlights the lessons of the empirical case studies and reflects on the broader relevance of the book from a theoretical and policy perspective.

TWO

Fiscal Polarization, International Exposure, and Sustained Debt Accumulation

The main contention of this book is that countries that amass alarming amounts of debt over the course of many years do so because their existing fiscal policies are too difficult to renegotiate and because major societal groups are not economically hard-pressed enough to compromise. When changes in economic, financial, demographic, or social conditions render existing fiscal policies unsustainable, these countries are unable to sufficiently trim their spending or increase their revenues to stop borrowing in time. The polarization-exposure thesis predicts that once public debt starts to significantly grow in a country, it takes much longer to successfully enact and carry out fiscal reform to stabilize public finances if economic openness is moderate and existing fiscal policies polarize preferences due to their targeted structure than if existing policies are encompassing and the economy is very open. The argument behind this prediction is that reforms are thwarted until a large enough social coalition coalesces in support of (or at least in acquiescence to) a specific combination of reforms. The emergence of such a social coalition implies a certain degree of compromise over the distribution of fiscal pain across society, the conditions for which evolve across time as the benefits of resisting fiscal pain are progressively outweighed by the costs of living with economic problems caused by fiscal imbalances. The costs of waiting for stabilization outweigh the benefits of wrangling over different combinations of spending cuts and tax increases much earlier in countries where existing fiscal arrangements do not allow for significantly unequal distributions of fiscal pain and where the pressures from economic problems are more acutely felt by large parts of society. Conversely, the tipping point arrives much later—and a supportive coalition arises with longer delay—where existing policies keep the stakes of choosing between different stabilization measures high and where large parts of society are immune to the economic problems that potentially accompany debt accumulation.

This chapter develops the polarization-exposure theory in detail. The next section explains why sustained large-scale debt accumulation is best conceptualized as an adjustment problem and develops a society-centered model of fiscal adjustment that draws on diverse strands of the literature on the political economy of adjustment and spells out its empirical implications. The third section explains the relationship of the polarization-exposure theory to possible alternative explanations for sustained debt accumulation: primarily to the rationalist fiscal governance literature, but also to institutionalist and ideational branches of the literature on the political economy of adjustment. The last section derives a plan for testing the relative explanatory capacities of each theoretical approach.

The Polarization-Exposure Thesis

When it comes to explaining sustained heavy debt accumulation, it is less important why borrowing originally started than why it is allowed to continue dangerously long. The reasons for why countries *start* to borrow have been thoroughly explored. Often, these reasons arise from outside the realm of politics (Streeck 2013). Large enduring gaps in the budget are often opened by economic shocks, such as the one experienced by many developed economies in the late 1970s when their economies permanently settled on lower growth paths and their unemployment stabilized at much higher levels, boosting expenditure at a time when revenues were flagging. Fiscal imbalances are also often compounded by disturbances in financial markets, such as the large jump in the world interest rates in the early 1980s, which saddled many countries with a substantially increased interest cost on their outstanding debt. Social and demographic shifts have also generated increasing budgetary pressures in developed countries. At other times, the origin of deficits is purely political as policy makers take on new spending commitments and institute tax cuts without making offsetting changes in other parts of the budget out of electoral motivations. Whatever the original reason for borrowing, though, once a major structural gap opens up in the budget, closing it requires active adjustment to the structure of spending and/or taxation. It often necessitates explicit legislative change, as the better part of spending and taxes is locked in by laws, but even in the case of discretionary spending and revenues, the government has to break with expectations based on past budgetary patterns. The question is why some countries delay making the necessary changes so long that they amass alarming amounts of debt, while others adjust relatively fast.

Obviously, major fiscal adjustments are politically exceedingly challenging. Cuts in transfers, scaling back government contracts, shrinking public employment, curtailing public services, and increasing taxes inflict unambiguous tangible losses on large sections of society. Very often, such losses are particularly painful because private actors had made fundamental economic choices based on past policies, which are difficult to change when policies are adjusted. The order of magnitude of losses to be imposed is often also very significant. A few empirical examples help to appreciate the scale of the necessary change. In Belgium, the (cyclically adjusted) deficit stood at 16 percent of the GDP in 1981, the year before the country embarked on a long period of austerity. Plugging such a hole required increasing taxation by a third or cutting non-interest expenditure by a fourth. The deficit was larger than the entire public employment bill, three times larger than public investment, and barely under the total spending on social transfers. It amounted to as much as the entire direct tax revenue and more than all the indirect taxes. Ireland faced a deficit of 11 percent of the GDP in 1986, the year before it adopted its second major adjustment package, amounting to a fourth of its total revenue and its primary expenditure. Italy was in the same shoes when it embraced austerity in the early 1990s. Greece ran deficits well above 10 percent of the GDP throughout the 1980s, but since its tax revenue and primary spending barely exceeded 30 percent of the GDP, closing the gap would have required a one-third increase in taxes or a one-third cut in spending. Japan ran a deficit of only 6 percent on average in the fifteen years before the global financial and economic crisis hit, but correcting this imbalance would have still required adjustments exceeding what it spent on public employment or public investment.

While imposing considerable fiscal pain on the electorate is bound to give policy makers pause before embarking on major adjustments, they should also be wary of hesitating too long. Since fiscal problems endogenously escalate in the absence of budgetary correction, delay only increases the size of the inevitable future adjustment and intensifies the fiscal pain that will have to be imposed at a later point in time. As borrowing continues, the growing debt stock generates an ever-larger interest rate burden, boosting expenses and compounding existing budgetary imbalances, while also progressively limiting the fiscal space available for addressing newly emerging collective needs and demands. Simultaneously, sustained borrowing generates financial and fiscal risks and corollary economic effects—most typically high inflation, high interest rates, and problems with international competitiveness—which might impinge on the welfare of the electorate. Therefore, policy makers with reasonable chances of staying in the political race for government in the medium-term future have an incentive to carry out adjustment as promptly as they can.

The capacity of policy makers to adjust existing policies, however, depends on their ability to secure the support of a large enough social coalition. This is partly because policy makers will be unwilling to commit political suicide by going against the wishes of their constituencies. Just as importantly, though, they need to have the necessary clout to put changes into place. They not only need the electoral mandate that can be translated into the necessary governmental and legislative power to enact legislative changes but also have to have sufficient societal backing to enable them to avoid or withstand possible pressure from strikes, demonstrations, riots, intense lobbying, or threats of capital flight when putting the reforms to work. As Gourevitch (1986, 20) writes:

> Ultimately, policy choices are made by politicians, by individuals who occupy institutional positions; power comes from the formal authority of those institutions. But somehow political leaders have to get into those institutional positions and hold on to them. And whatever they decide, their policies, to take effect, require compliance or even enthusiasm from countless individuals who work or invest or buy. When politicians make choices, therefore, their choices are constrained by the need to mobilize or retain support. Politicians have to construct agreement from among officeholders, civil servants, party and interest group leaders, and economic actors in society.

In other words, fiscal adjustment can only succeed if a substantial share of society supports it. Technically, there are many possible ways to close a budgetary gap, but in practice, there has to be at least one combination of tax increases and/or spending cuts large enough to close the budgetary gap that a substantial part of society is willing to accept. An adjustment package does not have to be backed by all sections of society to be viable, but it does have to command the support of a large enough share of society so that it can succeed even in the face of potential resistance. Exploring the conditions under which the necessary societal support for adjustment emerges is key to understanding why some countries fail to address their fiscal imbalances for extended periods of time whereas others adjust swiftly.

Understanding the (Delayed) Emergence of Societal Support for Fiscal Adjustment

Finding a package of spending cuts and tax increases acceptable to a large enough share of society is much easier in some countries than in others because of differences in the policy *status quo* and in the economic context across different countries. Differences in the way existing fiscal policies raise and allocate government revenue in different countries generate differential levels of conflict within each society about how the necessary fiscal sacrifices should be distributed across various socioeconomic groups. In countries where existing policies lend themselves to reforms with very unequal distributions of fiscal pain across groups in society, finding an adjustment package that musters the support of a large section of society is more difficult than in countries where different tax increases and spending cuts affect large swathes of society fairly evenly. At the same time, differences in the economic structure—specifically, differences in exposure to international economic competition—create differential incentives for various social groups in different polities to seek compromise in the choice of reforms and acquiesce in adjustments that hurt them for the sake of restoring fiscal balance.

Wherever incentives for compromise are weak and the conflict about the distribution of fiscal sacrifices is strong, it is initially impossible to find a combination of spending cuts and tax increases that can muster the support of a large enough coalition of different social groups. Adjustment attempts founder on the resistance of the group(s) that have most to lose from it. However, as time passes, the balance of these countervailing forces of conflict and compromise might change across time as pressures for compromise increase with the escalation of the debt problem—if the worsening of the debt problem inflicts economic losses on parts of society—allowing a critical mass of social support to emerge. Consequently, analyzing a country's economic profile and existing fiscal policy structure allows us to predict whether its policy makers will be able to address fiscal imbalances swiftly, or their hands will be tied in the face of growing debt for lengthy periods of time before the political conditions for successful stabilization arise.

These predictions rest on a seminal game theoretical model by Alesina and Drazen (1991), which investigates the ways in which societal actors weigh the costs and benefits of supporting or opposing any given fiscal adjustment package.[1] According to the war of attrition model of delayed stabilization, any group in society prefers swift stabilization to a delayed one—to avoid the escalation of the problem explained above—but each group also has an interest in minimizing its own share of fiscal sacrifices and, therefore, in resisting adjustment packages that assign a large share of the fiscal pain to them. Resisting fiscal pain is a gamble, because if other groups similarly refuse to pick up the bill of stabilization, the problem grows and future adjustment only becomes more painful, while in the meantime the economic side effects of the fiscal problem worsen. Obviously, the model assumes that no group has definitive information about how resolutely other actors can resist fiscal sacrifices. If it were clear at the start that a specific group has no chance of avoiding fiscal pain, it would make sense to acquiesce in fiscal sacrifices right away to avoid the harm that delay causes. Resistance to fiscal pain is rational as long as a group can reasonably expect that another, more favorable adjustment package will be put into place—one that assigns most of the fiscal sacrifices to other groups—before the negative economic side effects of the escalating fiscal problem become unbearable.

As time goes by and adjustment keeps being blocked by socioeconomic groups that believe they can do better, the fiscal and economic situation endogenously deteriorates as the fiscal imbalance is compounded by the accumulating interest burden. As a consequence, the passage of time might eventually tilt the balance of incentives for some groups: the longer they have to wait for fiscal stabilization and the more the economic side effects worsen, the less confidence a group can have that it will be able to wait for other groups to acquiesce in bearing the larger share of the burden of fiscal stabilization before the economic harm they suffer outweighs the benefit of securing a more favorable stabilization package. In other words, the passage of time changes the calculus, not only because of the objective deterioration of the situation but also because it transmits information about other groups' resolution to resist fiscal pain. As a consequence, some socioeconomic groups might start to prefer paying the price of adjustment to putting up with the fiscal and economic problems any longer in the hope that other groups will give in first.

How fast the tilting of the balance of incentives for conflict and compromise happens depends on two factors. One is the difference between favorable and unfavorable adjustment packages (Alesina and Drazen refer to this factor as "polarization") because when the difference is large, the benefit of waiting for a better package is considerable. The second factor is the "utility loss" suffered by different groups from having to put up with the economic side effects of fiscal problems while reform is delayed. Groups that are less sensitive to the negative side effects of debt can afford to resist fiscal pain longer. At the extreme, groups that are fully immune to the economic effects of fiscal problems never need to relax their intransigence.

Thus, the war of attrition model teaches us that if it is possible to distribute fiscal pain unevenly across different groups in society, it is initially rational for all groups to take a hard line in resisting any package that assigns more than a minimum share of fiscal sacrifices to them. However, for groups that are sensitive to the economic side effects of fiscal problems, the trade-off between the possibility of escaping fiscal pain and suffering the side effects changes as time goes by. Therefore, some groups initially bent on resisting fiscal pain become amenable to acquiescing in it with the passage of time. Translating these abstract conclusions into concrete predictions about how fast the necessary political conditions for fiscal stabilization emerge in different countries requires three steps. The first is clarifying how unevenly the pain of fiscal stabilization can be distributed across society. The second is exploring the sensitivity of different social groups to the economic side effects of fiscal problems. The third is identifying the relevant groups in society, whose interests govern the politics of debt accumulation, and providing predictions about how their coalitions will evolve.

Step 1: Fiscal Polarization

How unevenly the pain of fiscal stabilization can be spread across society depends on the structure of existing spending and taxes. In principle, the budgetary gap can be closed by an array of completely new taxes, but in practice, fiscal reform is likely to be anchored by existing policies: stabilization packages raise existing taxes and cut spending. Although all countries spend on broadly similar programs and assign broadly similar types of taxes, the incidence of spending programs and taxation varies widely across countries. Vast differences have been documented in the way different welfare arrangements, tax systems, subsidies, public employment, and public investment serve the interests of different classes, income categories, generations, insider and outsider groups, sectors, and regions in different countries.[2] In countries where existing expenditures and taxes are closely targeted to serve the interests of specific sections of society, it is possible to successfully close the fiscal gap through spending cuts and tax increases that allocate losses to a few groups and shield others. In these countries, the existing fiscal structure strongly polarizes the preferences of different groups about different stabilization packages. Therefore, conflict about the specific content of stabilizing measures will be strong even when there is general consensus about the need to stop the accumulation of debt. In countries where major spending programs benefit large majorities of society fairly uniformly and taxes are broad based, any spending cuts and tax increases large enough to plug the hole in the budget are likely to affect the majority of society relatively evenly. In these countries, the existing fiscal policies are not polarizing because the scope for conflict over different stabilization packages is limited.

Given the variety of ways in which different spending and tax arrangements are combined in different countries, it is easier to point out differences in the incidence of spending and taxation in concrete cases than to derive general criteria along which the targeted or encompassing nature of fiscal programs can be diagnosed. Take differences in pensions in the United States and Denmark, for example. In the United States, costs and benefits of the pension system accrue very differently to different groups. On the one hand, Social Security creates divisions between entitlement holders and employers whose labor costs are increased by contributions. On the other hand, tax expenditures on private retirement savings generate further conflicts of interests along income lines, since those with higher incomes can save more for retirement and are therefore entitled to higher tax exemptions. Given high levels of income inequality, this generates very unequal access to tax-financed pension benefits. In contrast, universal pensions financed from general tax revenue spread the benefits and costs of pensions relatively evenly across society in Denmark. Entitlements are available to anyone over the age of 65 and relatively low levels of income inequality dampen the redistributive effect of universalism, whereas the combination of progressive income taxes and regressive consumption taxes takes off the edge of redistributive conflict on the financing side. As a result, in Denmark, pensions are unlikely to stir up severe contention at a time when fiscal stabilization is necessary. In the United States, on the other hand, the pension architecture polarizes preferences about savings to be made on public pension expenditures and about revenue increases. Examples of such variation in the (formal and informal) features of spending and revenues can be drawn from all areas of government finances.

While in concrete cases the targeted versus encompassing nature of certain policy arrangements is quite obvious, deriving hard and fast universal criteria for evaluating the extent to which fiscal policies target benefits and costs to specific sections of society is impracticable. Standard categories of spending and taxation do not capture the entirety of ways in which the incidence of similar policies can differ across countries, especially since similar *de jure* features of policies can hide considerable *de facto* differences. Abstract distinctions between collective consumption versus income transfers, between universalism and selectiveness, or between regressive or progressive taxation (etc.) become blurred and of limited use in evaluating the degree to which some programs serve some social groups at the extent of others. The complexity of existing policies further increases—and the usefulness of abstract categories in gauging redistributiveness and targeting decreases—if we take into consideration the way different spending programs are financed and how the redistributive features of spending and taxation interact.

Types of spending that are normally categorized as collective consumption or collective investment expenditure—like public employment or construction projects—can, in some cases, disguise strongly redistributive and targeted forms of spending if in reality such expenditure is mostly aimed at maintaining the livelihood of specific groups in society. Examples of this phenomenon include the long-term dependence of the Japanese countryside on pork-barrel construction projects for income and employment but to some extent also the reliance of the "military-industrial complex" on defense spending in the United States. Classical transfer spending can be explored using the concepts of universalism, means-testing, and selective eligibility to establish the degree to which welfare benefits are available to large sections of society. However, as Moene and Wallerstein (2001) show, the degree to which a welfare system benefits some at the expense of others also depends on the degree to which income is unequally distributed in the polity. As a result, basic flat-rate pensions are more redistributive in the United Kingdom than in Norway. Furthermore, given the different redistributive effect of benefits financed from general tax revenue and labor-cost increasing social contributions, exploring the incidence of the costs and benefits of welfare spending needs to involve as much attention to the funding side of welfare arrangements as to the analysis of benefits.[3] In Denmark, where pensions are funded from general government revenues, the benefits and costs of the system affect roughly the same sections of society, whereas in Belgium, benefits accruing to labor are financed from contributions paid by employers.

On the revenue side, standard categories of regressive, proportional, and progressive taxation are instructive in terms of the *de jure* incidence of taxes. At the same time, it is important to be aware of the extent to which irregularities alter the actual patterns of burden sharing. The pervasiveness of evasion among certain socioeconomic groups in Greece or the extensive use of specifically targeted tax exemptions in the United States narrow the *de facto* tax base and strongly modify the redistributive character of the tax system by offering selectively available tax relief. At the extreme, even the distinction between corporate and personal income taxes fades away when large parts of the labor force register themselves as companies or as self-employed to minimize their tax burden, as has been a widespread practice in Hungary.

In the absence of universally applicable categories, spending and taxation patterns can only be evaluated on a country-by-country basis. They can be classified as more or less polarizing using a few rules of thumb. Strongly progressive or regressive taxes in the presence of large income inequality, specifically targeted tax exemptions, and selectively available opportunities for evasion polarize preferences about paths to increase revenues in response to fiscal imbalances. In contrast, compressed income distributions dampen the polarizing effects of progressivity and regressivity, while broader tax bases and strictly enforced tax collection limit the possibility of conflicts about targeted *de jure* or *de facto* tax relief. In terms of expenditure, universal access to transfers, services, and opportunities for public employment limits the scope for conflict about the specific ways of retrenchment. In contrast, the more limited and targeted the access to those benefits is, the more polarized preferences will be about cuts in spending. Finally, when a specific program is financed from earmarked revenue sources, preferences will be more polarized the more clearly the beneficiaries and the contributors of the program are separated. Conversely, the more the beneficiaries and contributors overlap, the more muted conflict will be about reforming expenses and benefits of the program. With these general features in mind, welfare programs, patterns of discretionary spending, and taxation can be analyzed to gauge how polarizing the existing fiscal architecture is in a given country.

Step 2: International Exposure

Beside fiscal polarization, sensitivity to the negative economic side effects of fiscal problems is the other decisive factor in the war of attrition model that crucially influences the speed with which fiscal imbalances are tackled. How sensitive different groups are to the negative economic side effects of fiscal problems depends on their position in the economy. Fiscal problems spill over into the real economy to cause inflation and high interest rates and undermine international competitiveness. Those on fixed incomes will be averse to inflation; companies with good investment opportunities will resent high interest rates; while firms and workers in sectors exposed to international competition will suffer from weak profits and falling employment.[4] Clearly, these negative side effects of fiscal imbalances are modulated by policies in place. Incomes can be indexed. Investments can be enhanced by subsidies in a high-interest environment. Competitiveness can be shielded through trade restrictions and exchange rate policies. Inflation can to some extent be counteracted by restrictive monetary policy. Importantly, however, all of these countervailing policies generate their own problems. Indexation worsens the inflation problem. Restrictive monetary policies and low exchange rates can make debt service more onerous insofar as they boost interest on sovereign debt or increase the value of foreign denominated debt. Trade restrictions trigger retaliation. Subsidies compound existing fiscal imbalances.

In general, in more open economies, larger sections of society suffer significantly from the negative side effects of debt. This is not only because larger parts of the economy are vulnerable to the competitiveness-reducing effects of inflation and high interest rates but also because the scope for countervailing policies to dampen these effects are more limited the more closely a country's economy is integrated with the global economy, as capital mobility and openness to trade sharply increase their costs and/or reduce their effectiveness. Therefore, in more open economies, the negative side effects of fiscal problems not only affect a greater part of society, but they are also likely more painful. As a consequence, in more open economies, larger sections of society have significant incentives to compromise their fiscal interests for the sake of speedy stabilization. Conversely, in less open economies, different socioeconomic groups can afford to wrangle longer about the distribution of fiscal sacrifices because their sensitivity to the negative economic side effects of fiscal imbalances is more moderate and there is larger room for policies that mitigate the impact of those side effects.

It bears stressing that the degree of economic openness matters for countries' ability to promptly adjust their fiscal policies to eliminate fiscal imbalances because it influences the *proportion* of the population that is sensitive to the possible side effects of fiscal problems—such as inflation and high interest rates—and the *intensity* of the problems they encounter, as more open economies face steeper costs when trying to mitigate those side effects in the absence of fiscal stabilization. This link between openness and ability to adjust is slightly different from the one usually posited in the political economic literature of adjustment. Since Peter Katzenstein's seminal works (1985, 1987), it has been received wisdom that (small) open economies are particularly good at economic adjustment because of the corporatist institutions of cooperation and compromise they develop to better deal with the vagaries of the international economy. While the argument advanced here is consonant with Katzenstein's insight insofar as it predicts better adjustment capacities at high levels of openness due to societal interests in maintaining economic competitiveness, it diverges from it in implying that the exposure of some groups in society to international economic competition has an impact on a country's ability to stabilize its public finances even at lower levels of openness, independently of the long-term development of institutional structures. In other words, the argument proposed here posits a continuous positive relationship between openness and fiscal adjustment, rather than one that only manifests itself at high levels of exposure over the long term. It also suggests that the interest in maintaining international economic competitiveness need not encompass the entirety of society to influence the speed with which fiscal stabilization takes place. Finally, and most importantly, it assumes that exposure affects adjustment capacity by influencing the incentives for different groups to acquiesce in fiscal pain, rather than through its effect on institutional structures.

It is perhaps also useful to discuss the relationship of the predictions put forward here about the effect of openness on the speed of fiscal stabilization to another key insight of the political economy literature: the finding that more open economies maintain larger government spending—and, in the case of developed Western democracies, much larger welfare state commitments—to buffer the effects of the volatility of the international economy on domestic incomes (Cameron 1978; Rodrik 1996). At first sight, the prediction that countries with more open economies adjust faster might seem to be in contradiction with the heavy welfare commitments of open economies, because the received wisdom is that welfare reform is harder the more extensive the vested interests are in existing welfare provisions (Pierson 1996). However, the thesis advanced here emphasizes exactly that it is not the *extensiveness* of vested interests that matters for the speed of stabilization but their *polarization*. As long as interests in existing welfare state arrangements are relatively uniform across large groups in society, fiscal stabilization is politically relatively uncomplicated irrespective of the size of the welfare state. Furthermore, there is no reason to automatically assume that stabilization can only happen through the retrenchment of the welfare state; the argument proposed here is agnostic about the mix between welfare or other spending cuts and revenue increases in stabilization packages. Therefore, the observation that more open economies tend to have larger welfare states is fully compatible with the prediction that open economies adjust faster due to the larger proportion of society having stronger incentives to compromise their fiscal interests for the sale of swift stabilization and the elimination of the negative economic side effects of debt accumulation.

Step 3: Relevant Groups in Society and the Evolution of Social Coalitions

The argument outlined above suggests that the politics of fiscal stabilization plays out in a two-dimensional political force field shaped, on the one hand, by conflicts of interests generated by existing fiscal policies and, on the other hand, by commonalities of economic interests in a more stable macroeconomic environment conducive to international competitiveness. In this two-dimensional field, the relevant clusters of interests are jointly delineated by stakes in existing fiscal policies and concerns about the negative economic side effects of fiscal problems. Therefore, the societal groups whose incentives drive the politics of fiscal adjustment can be identified at the intersection of those two orthogonal sets of interests: as vested fiscal interest groups, possibly divided according to exposure to the international economy. Differences in existing policies and economic structures draw different maps of conflicts and commonalities of interests from one country to another.

Given the wide variation in fiscal policies across countries explained above, vested fiscal interest groups are different in different countries. It is impossible to identify *a priori*, theoretical categories: vested interest groups have to be identified country by country on the basis of the existing policy structure. For example, workers likely constitute a uniform vested interested group in countries with universal welfare systems; whereas they can be deeply divided about welfare in countries where tight eligibility conditions and targeted benefits create insiders and outsiders to the system. Similarly, business interests align more closely on tax issues where corporate taxes are undifferentiated than in systems where the tax system grants preferential treatment to some firms over others based on size, sector, or other criteria. The clustering of interests could even be geographical in countries where the incidence of spending and taxation varies strongly along regional lines or between urban and rural areas.

Sensitivity to the economic side effects of persistent borrowing cross-cuts the vested fiscal interest dimension and might delineate commonalities of interest in swift fiscal stabilization across lines of fiscal conflicts. Again, the divisions along this dimension are country-specific, due to differences in economic structure and economic policies that might be directed at mitigating the economic side effects of debt accumulation. The analysis needs to focus on the extent to which fiscal problems spill over into high inflation and high interest rates and the way different groups are affected by these problems. In general, though, it can be expected that groups exposed to international economic competition are most likely to be negatively impacted by these issues, and the problems they face will be acuter in more open economies.

Whatever the relevant groups are in any given country, the logic of the war of attrition model suggests that they coalesce into social coalitions in resistance to and in support of stabilization attempts subject to the balance of incentives they face for defending their vested interest and for making sacrifices for the sake of stabilization.[5] Social coalitions initially align along the vested interest dimension as different groups jointly oppose reform to policies they share interest in. Insofar as existing policies reflect the balance of power between different groups in society, uniform resistance to reform by a vested interest group is unlikely to be overcome through pressure from the rest of society. However, wherever significant sections of society are sensitive to the economic side effects of debt accumulation, social coalitions based on the defense of vested interests give way to social coalitions based on shared interest in fiscal stabilization with the passage of time, as groups sensitive to the economic side effects of debt start to prefer to compromise their fiscal interests for the sake of defending economic ones. As parts of vested interest groups relax their intransigence to reform, there is a better chance that still-intransigent groups can be overpowered. As a result, if there is a critical mass of groups open to compromise, they can jointly support an adjustment package that assigns a limited share of the fiscal pain to them and foists the rest of the necessary fiscal sacrifices on others. This process is expected to play out much slower in relatively closed economies with polarizing fiscal structures and faster in open economies with encompassing fiscal arrangements.

To sum up the logic of the argument about how the political conditions for dealing with fiscal problems evolve: countries differ in their adjustment capacities because it takes longer in some than in others to resolve conflicts between different sections of society about *how to share* the fiscal pain necessary to close the fiscal gap. Where there is greater room for very unequal distributions of fiscal sacrifices due to the existence of more closely targeted policies, the conflict is stronger. Where the economic side effects are temperate, typically in less open economies, groups are under less pressure to compromise. Therefore, in countries with moderately open economies and closely targeted fiscal policies, it takes longer for a supportive coalition of different groups to coalesce behind a specific adjustment package that policy makers can put into place. In such countries, reform attempts repeatedly fail in the face of resistance of groups that are affected and debt keeps on growing for a long time, before the negative economic effects of persistent borrowing bring about a realignment in coalitions and a politically feasible adjustment plan. Conversely, social support coalesces behind a stabilization package fairly swiftly in countries with encompassing policies and open economies. This theory is able to account both for why borrowing persists in some countries for a long time and how such countries eventually regain control over debt accumulation. It also distils the factors that differentiate countries with severe problems of sustained excessive debt accumulation from those that fare better at adjusting their policies to changing conditions and thus at keeping their debt under control.

Where Does the Polarization-Exposure Theory Fit?
Interests, Institutions, and Ideas in the Politics of Debt Accumulation and Fiscal Adjustment

The polarization-exposure theory is rooted in the analysis of material interests that govern the evolution of social coalitions whose resistance or support fundamentally determine policy choices, following a venerable tradition built by scholars like Gourevitch (1986), Rogowski (1990), Frieden (1991 a and b, 1996, 2002), Hiscox (1999, 2001) or Ansell (2008). Just like earlier theories in this tradition, the hypotheses provided here are founded on abstract economic theory, specifically, the game theoretical modeling of incentives faced by different socioeconomic groups. At the same time, by incorporating the effect of the existing fiscal policy structures on social coalitions, the predictions of this model also take seriously the historical institutionalist lesson on path dependence and the way in which past policy choices shape politics in the present (Pierson 2000, 2004).

In keeping with the interest-focused tradition, the polarization-exposure theory makes no specific predictions about how changes in the balance of incentives for different socioeconomic groups and the evolution of social coalitions feed through political institutions to effect policy choices and outcomes, or what role ideas and ideology play in influencing this process. This obviously does not imply questioning the importance of institutions and ideas in affecting politics and policy choices. While the polarization-exposure theory puts interests center stage, the mechanism of political and policy change it advances plays out in specific institutional and ideational contexts.

Institutionalist scholars point out that social groups are not political actors that strategize, decide, and take action (Thelen 1999). Therefore, interests, strategies, and the use of power cannot be understood independently of the specific institutional contexts. Varied constellations of political actors and rules of the political game shape how societal conflicts play out in different countries.[6] Constructivists add that these factors cannot exercise their effect independently of ideas, as available conceptual models of the economy and society determine what actors consider possible and desirable.[7] From this theoretical perspective, institutional and ideational factors are bound to crucially influence the extent to which a country is able to adjust its fiscal policies in order to deal with an escalating debt accumulation problem. Some institutional traits help to overcome the resistance of particularistic interest groups,[8] others foster adjustment by encouraging compromise.[9] Ideas matter because certain interpretations of a policy problem provide important focal points around which compromise can arise (Blyth 2002; Culpepper 2008). At the same time, the institutional and ideational context of politics and policy-making is not static. Institutions of coercion and compromise emerge and break down, and new ideas can generate the glue for new compromises.[10] Indeed, it has been one of the central questions of more recent institutional scholarship: why and how institutions, which generate such strong and stable incentives and constraints for extended periods of time change and give way to new institutions, incentives and constraints (e.g., Streeck and Thelen 2005).

Consequently, institutions and ideas are indispensable components of a comprehensive narrative analyzing the way different countries deal with their fiscal imbalances. Understanding how societal interests govern political and policy developments requires attention to the landscape of political actors that represent different social groups and further their interests; to the institutional power they employ in doing so; to the institutional structures that tolerate conflict or foster compromise among them; and to the economic and social ideologies that inform their actions. At the same time, there is no reason to assume that these institutional and ideational frameworks are immutable fixtures of the environment. In fact, analyzing the shifting incentives shaping different groups' approach towards different stabilization packages with the passage of time can be useful in understanding the stability and change of those institutional and ideological frameworks. Observing the congruence or tension between shifting policy preferences of various societal groups and the institutions and ideas through which they are pursued can provide the key to explaining institutional and ideational change.

Thus, the polarization-exposure theory calls for a pragmatic approach to institutions and ideas that expects that societal preferences—which can shift with the shifting of incentives as time passes—always eventually feed through institutional and ideational structures to affect policy outcomes, even if this requires adjustments in institutions and ideas. This approach assumes that interest-representing organizations—parties, unions, employers organization, lobbies, etc.—need to keep their strategies in sync with the preferences of their supporter base, both when resistance to fiscal pain is preferable and when fiscal sacrifice becomes more attractive, on pain of losing support to alternative (old or new) interest-representing organizations. The pattern of interest-representing organizations, the constellation of the supporter bases they serve and their strategies for conflict and compromise with each other jointly embody social coalitions formed in support of or in resistance to different ways of fiscal stabilization. When the underlying preferences of societal groups shift from resistance to acquiescence, organizations either adapt their strategies and their alliances to the new constellation of societal preferences or they are sidelined or replaced by new organizations with new strategies and alliances. This transformation might also lead to changes in ideologies and policy paradigms as political entrepreneurs justify new political strategies and/or rationalize new coalitional affinities and conflicts.

The polarization-exposure theory also privileges the structural power of different social groups over their institutional power in the longer term. For example, workers' ability to disrupt production through industrial action or business' ability to withhold investment is assumed to be more significant in the longer term than co-decision rights granted by corporatist systems, whereas the electoral power of populous social groups is expected to have traction even in unbalanced electoral systems. Consequently, the functioning of institutional and ideational frameworks fostering domination or compromise is expected to be subject to the balance of structural power and the alignment or conflicts of interests. Even time-honored traditions of negotiation and compromise are unlikely to prompt political actors to accept major fiscal losses on behalf of their constituencies if their supporters are opposed to fiscal pain and wield significant structural power.

At the same time, when the priorities of major groups are aligned, systems of coordination might arise to facilitate the actual negotiation procedures needed to hammer out a compromise.[11] In a similar vein, state actors' room for autonomous action is expected to be contingent on social support for (or at least acquiescence in) a general direction of reform.

Therefore, the approach applied in this book implies tracing the impact of the evolving policy preferences of powerful societal groups—and the attendant stability and realignment of social coalitions—when narrating and explaining the actions and interactions of political actors within concrete institutional and ideational frameworks in different countries. The strategic choices of institutional actors—e.g., parties, unions, government coalitions, etc.—concerning fiscal reform are explained with reference to the preferences of their constituencies, with special emphasis on how these preferences evolve with the passage of time under pressure from the escalation of the fiscal and economic problems. Those strategic choices are used, in turn, to explain how policy evolves across time.

How Does the Polarization-Exposure Theory Differ? Competing Explanations for the Problem of Debt Accumulation

Beyond satisfying a realist predilection for exploring the unobservable societal foundations of politics and policy making, focusing attention on the evolution of the preferences of social groups toward different fiscal stabilization packages (and on the factors that govern the evolution of those preferences) also fills a significant gap in the literature on fiscal problems and fiscal adjustment. Arguably, the lack of specific modeling of differences in the commonalities and conflicts of societal interests toward fiscal policy has been a key factor in hamstringing efforts to comprehensively explain why some countries get stuck on a trajectory of debt accumulation dangerously long, whereas others keep debt growth under control. Theories of fiscal problems and explanations of fiscal adjustment alike tend to attribute a fixed set of general incentives to political actors (governments, parties, unions, employers' organizations, etc.) across countries and investigate the ways in which those general incentives exert their effect in country-specific institutional (and, in some cases, ideational) circumstances. While this approach has led to important conclusions about how institutional and ideational conditions influence annual budgetary decision-making to lead to borrowing or balanced budgets year-by-year and how they influence the success of fiscal stabilization, these findings do not add up to a comprehensive understanding of why (and how long) borrowing is allowed to persist and when fiscal stabilization becomes possible.

The increasing prevalence of fiscal problems in prosperous developed countries since the 1970s fostered the development of a robust rationalist literature exploring the forces that lead governments to spend beyond their means. The early strand of this literature hypothesized that policy makers run deficits on purpose to enhance their electoral chances by pleasing the electorate with higher spending, lower taxes, and better economic performance in the short term and keeping them in the dark about the long-term costs of overspending.[12] Empirical studies have found some indication of electorally motivated deficits, but overall, the evidence is far from conclusive.[13] In terms of accounting for the phenomenon sustained and excessive debt accumulation, the key weakness of this approach is its exclusive focus on the electoral benefits of borrowing. Once debt accumulation starts to generate problems for the economy, the electoral benefits of borrowing are likely to evaporate. Attention to the possible economic side effects of debt accumulation, and especially to the ways in which they might affect large parts of the electorate, is necessary to understand the full set of incentives policy makers face and to predict whether further borrowing is likely to be electorally profitable or costly. The polarization-exposure theory presented in this book implies that deficits can only be electorally beneficial as long as large parts of the electorate are immune to the negative economic side effects of deficits, which is more likely in relatively closed economies.

Toward the end of the 1980s, the hypothesis of intentional borrowing increasingly gave way to a different reasoning within the rationalist fiscal governance school: one that focuses on the collective action problems involved in joint budgetary decision-making, which cause policy makers to persistently fall back on borrowing despite knowing better. In this approach, unintentional deficits are a "residual source" of financing when decision makers cannot reconcile their spending and tax preferences so that the budget balances. *Common resource pool models* contend that individual decision makers do not fully internalize the social costs of additional spending benefiting their constituencies, so they keep lavishing more on their voters while taxes lag behind,[14] whereas a *veto-actor* version of this approach focuses on governments' inability to limit spending and raise taxes if different governmental actors veto spending cuts and tax increases that hurt their constituencies (Roubini and Sachs 1989).

While the ultimate driver of borrowing in this approach is the interests of different electoral constituencies—and in this sense, the logic of the theory is similar to the polarization-exposure thesis presented here—the constellation of these interests is never substantively explored or used to explain the severity of the collective action problems. Instead, the focus is on the governmental sphere and on the way institutions give representation to or suppress the multitude of interests in the decision-making arena. The collective-action problem is expected to be more severe (and, thus, borrowing to be more persistent) in settings where the decision-making process incorporates a greater number of divergent political preferences, such as in proportional electoral systems with multiparty governments.[15] However, the problems should be mitigated by the adoption of institutional mechanisms that enforce coordination.[16] Although there have been attempts to use intragovernmental ideological differences as a proxy for the substantive divergence of policy preferences among parties within governments, these are few and far between, and they are hampered by the fact that some of the most important conflicts of fiscal interests are sometimes housed within parties rather than between them.[17]

Empirical evidence supports the expectation that appropriate coordination mechanisms significantly improve the chances of balancing the budget.[18] It is therefore unsurprising that fiscal targets, deficit ceilings, penalties, commitment to a specific path of corrective action, surveillance, and transparency became part of the design of the fiscal oversight system that was meant to protect the European Economic and Monetary Union from the excessive borrowing tendencies of some of its members. In practice, however, the European experiment showed that successful coordinating institutions cannot be implanted into political contexts that do not endogenously generate them. Especially in countries with track records of persistent borrowing in the past, fiscal limits were routinely circumvented and transparency was undermined by creative accounting, while commitments to targets were regularly broken. The manifest failure of the European fiscal system to correct the fiscal paths of some of the most delinquent European countries suggests that the lack of a well-functioning coordinating mechanism might be a symptom of a deeper underlying cause of the permanent deficit problem, which imposed institutions cannot resolve.[19] The question then becomes why some countries are unable to adopt the institutional mechanisms that would protect them from persistent borrowing.

The importance of why some countries adopt better coordinating mechanisms than others has not been lost on scholars in the fiscal governance approach.[20] In attempting to account for differences in budgetary institutions across countries, Mark Hallerberg and his colleagues emphasize that institutional constraints on budgetary decision-making are adopted and operate essentially by consent of the very policy makers whose discretion needs to be constrained (Hallerberg et al. 2009). This implies that it is not so much the adoption of the appropriate budgetary coordination mechanism that allows a country to limit borrowing, but the willingness of policy makers to constrain their own ability to pursue the fiscal interests of their voters at the price of perpetuating debt accumulation. Coordinating budgetary institutions become an intervening variable, while the ultimate explanation lies in what policy makers prioritize: fiscal balance or the particular fiscal interest of their constituencies. While Hallerberg et al. seek to account for the presence or absence of consent to constraining institutions within the government-centered framework—citing volatility in ideological polarization within governments and the fiscal conservativism of the electorate—their results do not allow for drawing definitive conclusions on this matter.[21]

The difficulty of the rationalist fiscal governance school with explaining how policy makers prioritize between the fiscal interests of their constituencies and controlling debt accumulation draws attention to the limitations of focusing attention strictly within the confines of the governmental sphere and of treating fiscal policy as the outcome of a yearly budgetary exercise. Better understanding policy makers' priorities requires moving the investigation beyond the governmental arena to explicitly model the constellation of the interests of the different constituencies. This, in turn, involves accounting for the costs of debt accumulation for different constituencies as well as the benefits arising from the protection of a constituency's fiscal interests. While the fiscal governance approach emphasizes the political benefits of defending vested fiscal interests, it is practically blind to the costs[22] because it focuses on discrete yearly budgetary decisions without taking into consideration the cumulative effects of persistent borrowing and, thus, the growing negative economic side effects that accompany the accumulation of debt. The polarization-exposure approach offered in this book implies that policy makers are more likely to prioritize the promotion of the fiscal interests of their constituencies (and, thus, refuse to abide by fiscal institutions that constrain their ability to do so) when extant fiscal policies create intense conflicts of fiscal interests and when moderate international exposure limits the sensitivity of different constituencies to the economic side effects of debt accumulation.

Moving beyond the strict governmental-parliamentary sphere also allows for incorporating political actors that exert their influence outside of the electoral channel into the explanation of fiscal trajectories.[23] The importance of such encompassing analysis of the polity in modeling policy choice is demonstrated by the literature on the political economy of policy adjustment, which calls attention to the role of unions, employers' confederations, or other organized interest groups in the politics of policy reform. This literature has provided invaluable insights into the ways prosperous developed economies adapted their policies to challenges from globalization, deindustrialization, technological shifts, population aging, and the like since the late 1970s.[24] Since these challenges significantly contributed to the fiscal problems of developed countries (Pierson 2001; Streeck 2014), the adjustment literature is highly relevant when it comes to exploring the differential experiences of different countries in dealing with debt.

However, the adjustment literature does not provide a ready-made explanation for why some countries accumulate debt dangerously long, while others assert control over their fiscal imbalances relatively swiftly. Scholars in this tradition have never focused directly on the issues of persistent borrowing and debt accumulation. Although they investigate instances of fiscal stabilization as components of broader macroeconomic reform, they are more interested in the *conditions* under which adjustment becomes possible and the *substantive content* of reform than in the *speed* with which countries take control over their fiscal imbalances, which—given the cumulative nature of the fiscal problem—crucially influences the severity of the resulting debt situation. Studies of macroeconomic reform highlight how institutions facilitate compromise among various political actors about spending and taxes, and emphasize the role that ideas play in providing shared understandings of the origins of the macroeconomic problems among those actors.[25] At the same time, they also demonstrate that neither institutional structures, nor ideas are fixed features of the political environment by documenting how *ad hoc* social pacts can form around new ideas to enable reform even in countries that lack time-honored corporatist and consociational institutions.[26] The question then becomes how the institutional and ideational preconditions for compromise *arise* and *how long this takes* in different countries, but these issues remain outside of the purview of studies of macroeconomic adjustment. The polarization-exposure thesis implies that it takes longer for the institutional and ideational preconditions of compromise to arise in countries where the obstacles to fiscal compromise—rooted in conflicts generated by the extant policy structure—are more severe and where resolving macroeconomic problems are less urgent due to the limited exposure of large parts of society to international economic competition.

In summary, the polarization-exposure thesis helps to fill in the gaps in our understanding of long-term heavy debt accumulation and answers questions about persistent borrowing and fiscal adjustment that existing theories—in the rationalist fiscal governance school of thought or in the adjustment literature—cannot. It does so by approaching debt accumulation from a novel angle. It expands the analysis beyond the strict governmental sphere of yearly budgetary decisions to explicitly explore the evolution of societal preferences toward adjustment under the changing pressures of aversion to fiscal pain and the economic pressures created by debt accumulation. In doing so, it also looks beyond the institutional and ideational circumstances to better explain how the conditions for compromise arise in time and to explain how long it takes in different countries.

Methodological Considerations

The rest of this book gauges the empirical relevance of the polarization-exposure thesis through a set of qualitative case studies that explore the history of debt accumulation in Belgium, Greece, Ireland, Italy, and Japan. It employs process tracing as well as within-case and cross-case comparisons. A qualitative approach is arguably more suited to investigating the fit of the polarization-exposure explanation than a quantitative one for two reasons. The lesser of those two reasons is the difficulty involved in standardizing fiscal polarization, one of the two key explanatory variables of the model. (This issue has been explained in depth above.) The more significant reason is that quantitative measures taken at specific points in time are unable to capture the diachronic dimension of the mechanism that is hypothesized to drive the politics of debt accumulation. Process tracing allows for exploring how well the diachronic mechanism of realigning social coalitions posited here explains the twists and turns of the politics of debt accumulation in the real world, and for comparing the explanatory capacity of the model to alternative hypotheses at each important critical juncture (Pierson 2004). At the same time, cross-case comparisons allow for probing the capacity of the two explanatory variables (fiscal polarization and international exposure) to explain the length of time it takes from diagnosing debt accumulation as a serious problem to putting successful reform packages into place. Because the two independent variables interact, several pairwise comparisons are necessary to sample different combinations of fiscal polarization and international exposure.

The universe of cases from which the sample was drawn consists of distinct instances of debt accumulation in OECD member countries between 1970 and 2007.[27] Instances of debt growth prior to 1970 are not considered here, due to problems with the availability of consistent cross-country debt data from before 1970. However, the years between 1970 and 2007 provide a fairly exhaustive collection of all the periods of debt accumulation between the Second World War and the global financial and economic crisis, because in the decades of high economic growth prior to 1970, most countries were dramatically decreasing the debt-to-GDP ratios they inherited from the war. The only exception is Ireland, which accumulated debt between the mid-1940s and the late-1950s, but by the 1970s, debt was on the decline in that country, too (Reinhart and Rogoff 2010). The debt spurts since 2007 are not included in the universe of cases because there is insufficient perspective at the time of writing to definitively evaluate how successful countries are in handling the debt issues triggered by the global financial and economic crisis.[28] Table 1.2 in chapter 1 provides an overview of the cases of debt accumulation between 1970 and 2007, including details on the duration and severity of debt growth.

In an effort to sidestep theoretical controversies about admissible levels of debt and acceptable delays in tackling growing indebtedness—explored in detail in chapter 1—the book samples as its case studies instances of debt accumulation from cases where there can be little doubt that the problem warranted policy response. Belgium, Canada, Greece, Ireland, Italy, and Japan—with the largest scope and longest duration of debt accumulation—constitute such cases. Other countries had significantly more benign experiences with debt prior to 2007, and therefore, there is much greater ambiguity about whether and when debt accumulation should have been stopped.[29] Of these six countries, the rest of the book explores five—Belgium, Greece, Ireland, Italy, and Japan—in detail in a series of within-case and cross-country comparisons, selected and matched along criteria described below. (Canada is briefly discussed in the conclusion to evaluate the degree to which this sixth case of large-scale debt accumulation is consistent with the predictions of the thesis advanced here.)

Despite similarities in the severity of their debt problems, the five chosen countries display significantly different track records in dealing with their fiscal issues. Japan and Greece have never been able to effectively address their fiscal problems. Greece accumulated debt at a very fast rate throughout the 1980s, and although the debt-to-GDP ratio roughly stabilized around 100 percent by the mid-1990s due to a number of favorable exogenous factors, high levels of debt and the failure to deal with fiscal imbalances made Greece vulnerable to adverse changes in the global economy and financial markets, which led to a debt crisis and default in the 2010s. Japan's debt accumulation started at a slow rate in the 1970s, but it has intensified considerably since the early 1990s and remained practically unaddressed in the past four decades, apart from a brief interlude of tightening around the turn of the millennium. Although Japan has avoided major debt crises, it is the most indebted country in the world with gross debt amounting to two-and-a-half times its GDP in 2015. Italy exemplifies a case where fiscal stabilization was long delayed but eventually succeeded. Italy accumulated debt between the mid-1970s and the mid-1990s without adopting any significant stabilizing measures, but it was eventually able to reverse debt accumulation and reduce the debt-to-GDP ratio through resolute consolidation by the second half of the 1990s, although it relapsed in the 2000s. At its peak, the debt amounted to 117 percent of the GDP. Belgium and Ireland addressed their fiscal issues relatively early on. Both launched drastic austerity programs in 1982 to arrest the debt spurt that started in the late 1970s. When these programs fell short of fully bringing borrowing under control, the two countries' paths diverged. Ireland reinforced its earlier measures with a new stabilization package in 1987, setting debt on a steep downward path. Belgium, on the other hand, failed to redouble its efforts and saw its debt snowball further until favorable changes in financial market conditions allowed it to reduce its debt-to-GDP ratio from the mid-1990s.

In terms of fiscal polarization, the five countries are distributed along a continuum.[30] Ireland represents the least polarized fiscal structure, particularly around the time when it was facing fiscal challenges in the 1980s. It had tax and spending policies that distributed benefits and burdens in fairly undifferentiated fashion among the bulk of society. In the other five countries, policies created distinct large clusters of vested fiscal interests. In Belgium, a fully contribution-based social security system polarized interests between business and labor. In Italy, similar conflicts about a conservative welfare state were compounded by the dependence of the population of the South on transfers, public employment, and construction contracts and by the ability of small firms to escape fiscal burden-sharing through evasion. In Greece, vested interests were polarized by bloated public employment, a conservative pension system, and immense tax evasion. In Japan, conflicts about an unsustainable pension system added to the polarization of interests between urban and rural populations due to distortions of the tax system as well as regionally targeted subsidies and construction contracts.

In terms of international exposure, the five countries range from extremely open to mostly closed (see figure 2.1). Ireland and Belgium represent the most open economies. In both countries, the sensitivity of large sections of society to the negative side effects of debt accumulation was particularly high at the time of acute fiscal challenges, as both countries

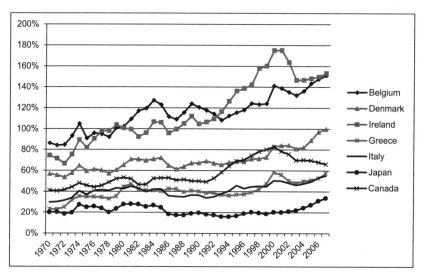

Fig. 2.1. Exports plus imports as a percentage of GDP in Belgium, Canada, Denmark, Ireland, Greece, Italy, and Japan from 1970 to 2007. Source: Ameco.

were members of the fixed exchange rate system of the European Monetary System (EMS), which implied that inflationary problems accompanying fiscal imbalances inflicted particularly significant harm on firms and workers in the exporting or import-competing sectors. While Italy and Greece have had roughly similar proportions of trade within their national incomes, exporting and import-competing sectors were arguably more sensitive to the negative economic side effects of debt in Italy due to the country's membership in the EMS. At the same time, accession to the euro—and the delegation of monetary policy to the supranational level—has significantly weakened the link between fiscal problems and competitiveness for Italian producer groups since 1999. Finally, Japan's economy has been mostly insulated from international economic competition, with imports and exports amounting to less than a quarter of the GDP.

Given this pattern of variation and similarities, the rest of the book evaluates the explanatory power of fiscal polarization and international exposure through a series of within-country analyses and pairwise comparisons that help to control for alternative explanations. Italy serves as the base case through which the mechanism of political change underlying fiscal adjustment is explored. The country represents a middling case both in terms of fiscal polarization and international exposure. It is a case that lends itself particularly well to within-case comparisons because Italy's fiscal, political, and economic history is characterized by many sharp changes (impressive instances of fiscal stabilization after long periods of debt growth, momentous changes in political institutions, and the transformation of the economic environment after euro accession) that help to explore the explanatory capacity of alternative factors.[31] The comparison of Belgium and Ireland allows for gauging the effects of fiscal polarization. It approximates a "most similar" case study design that controls for international exposure as well as alternative institutional and ideational explanatory variables. Besides having similarly open economies, the two countries also have important institutional features in common and display similar ideational developments over the period concerned. Where they differ, theory would predict that Belgium should have better institutional adjustment capacities. In light of these similarities and the institutional advantages on Belgium's side, Ireland's superior performance in regaining control over its debt problem can be confidently attributed to differences in fiscal polarization.[32] The juxtaposition of the Greek and Japanese cases, on the other hand, approximates a "most different" case study design. The two countries differ significantly on a whole range of economic and social factors and on political institutions and they have been dominated by very different economic and political ideologies.[33] Nevertheless, both countries displayed similarly ruinous inability to address their debt problems. (Table 2.1 summarizes the main parameters of each case study.)

The concluding chapter adds brief sketches of two further cases. As mentioned above, it briefly discusses Canada's experiences with debt to provide the missing case for a full overview of the most serious instances of debt accumulation. Canada displays many similarities with the Belgian and Italian cases. Its track record in dealing with its debt problems parallels Italy's almost exactly: it accumulated large stocks of debt throughout the 1980s and the early 1990s but managed to effectively reverse debt growth in the mid-1990s, after the debt-to-GDP ratio had reached 100 percent. Its fiscal structure was similarly polarized at the time of its greatest fiscal troubles as Belgium's, with conflicts about the welfare system interacting with issues of interregional redistribution in a federal system. Canada is somewhat more open to trade than Italy, and its exposure to international economic competition increased in the 1990s upon the free-trade agreement with the United States and subsequently, the adoption of the North Atlantic Free Trade Agreement (see figure 2.1). The conclusion also briefly explores a more benign case of debt accumulation. The Danish case complements the Irish one, providing further evidence for the role of low fiscal polarization in swift and resolute stabilization—in two instances of intense debt spurts in the early 1980s and 1990s—even when the government's welfare commitments are significantly more extensive and exposure to international competitiveness is less extreme than in the Irish case.

The exploration of fiscal trajectories of different countries in this book does not rely solely on the investigation of fiscal figures but blends numerical analysis with qualitative accounts of policy choice. This is because the variable of interest—the length of time it takes from diagnosing debt accumulation as a serious problem to putting successful reform packages into place—cannot be fully captured through observing the ascents and descents of the debt-to-GDP ratio. On the one hand, it is reasonable to assume that fiscal problems are diagnosed with some lag as the size and persistence of fiscal imbalances become clearer to policy makers. On the other hand, debt accumulation is not a function of fiscal policy alone: it also crucially depends on economic performance. Major revenue and spending items automatically change with changes in national income and unemployment, influencing yearly borrowing in unanticipated directions, while the proportion of outstanding debt to GDP depends on economic growth. Therefore, the evolution of the debt-to-GDP ratio is an imperfect indicator of fiscal policy and the number of years spent on an upward debt trajectory inadequately measures the delay in policy adjustment. For these

TABLE 2.1. The main parameters of the cases and case study design

	Independent variables		Dependent variable		
	International exposure	Fiscal polarization	Speed of response to fiscal problems	Case study design	Location in book
Italy	moderate-low	high	delayed stabilization, then relapse	cross-temporal variations explored	Chapter 3
Ireland	high	low	swift response, problem fully tackled	most-similar institutions and ideas	Chapter 4
Belgium	high	high	swift response, problem only partially tackled		
Greece	low	high	no effective response	most-different institutions and ideas	Chapter 5
Japan	low	high	no effective response		
Denmark	moderate	low	swift stabilization	short comparison with Ireland	Chapter 6
Canada	moderate-low	high	delayed stabilization	short comparison with Belgium and Italy	Chapter 6

reasons, the narratives in this book analyze different countries' fiscal trajectories by jointly investigating fiscal figures; the policy discourse; and the presence or absence, success or failure of concrete policy measures. The policy discourse is explored to gauge the extent to which fiscal imbalances that seem significant in retrospect were interpreted as problematic at the time and to establish when tackling deficits became a professed policy objective. Policy measures—planned and actual reforms—are identified with the help of existing expert analyses of fiscal policy in the given country to determine policy intentions and their level of success.[34] Fiscal figures are used to ascertain the effect of such measures on the evolution of deficits and the debt-to-GDP ratio.

Qualitative analysis is also privileged in exploring the two explanatory variables of the model. This is emphatically true for fiscal polarization. Due to difficulties with standardization noted above, numerical examination of the size and proportion of different spending and revenue items in itself cannot adequately describe the incidence of the benefits and costs of different governmental programs. Therefore, the case studies rely on expert accounts of policy to better understand patterns of redistribution arising from taxes and expenditures than what is immediately obvious from numerical analysis. Exposure to international economic competition lends itself better to numerical assessment: the proportion of exports and imports within GDP provides a good primary indicator. Although this proportion changes somewhat across time—and therefore a single figure cannot precisely describe exposure over several decades—the basic patterns of trade are stable enough to consistently characterize a country as more or less open to international trade. At the same time, complementary qualitative investigation of the monetary environment and trade-related policy choices allows for better understanding the conditions under which different parts of society face international economic competition.

The methodological design of the rest of the book entails the detailed investigation of debt accumulation in five countries over extended periods of time. The analysis involves process tracing in each country as well as comparisons within and across countries. It entails exploring developments on three different levels: policy, politics, and the socioeconomic environment. Such analysis is bound to rely mostly on secondary sources. As Lustick (1996) warned, such an empirical strategy needs to be executed with care because there is a risk that selection bias among sources used might lead to a distorted interpretation of history. Therefore, special care needs to be taken to compare and contrast several sources in discovering each component in this complicated process. At the same time, the multi-level nature of the analysis automatically helps such triangulation, because it necessarily draws on sources from very different fields and integrates various types of data (e.g., economic and fiscal figures; electoral data; sociological studies; political analysis; works in economics, public finance, and public administration; etc.). This provides a possibility for cross-checking whether information drawn from disparate sources about developments in the three disparate spheres of analysis are compatible with each other.

The next three chapters execute this empirical strategy and tell the story of debt in Italy, Belgium, Ireland, Japan, and Greece. The sixth chapter pulls together the lessons from all of these studies to provide a full set of comparisons; to complement them with short sketches of the Danish and Canadian cases; and to return to the theoretical considerations discussed at length in this chapter.

THREE

Evolving Social Coalitions, Intense Polarization, and Moderate Exposure

Italy

Default hung over Italy like Damocles' sword in 2011. With debt at 116 percent of GDP and yields on government bonds rising fast, Italy seemed likely to become the next domino in a series of European debt crises. It took significant intervention from the European Central Bank and the replacement of a democratically elected government with a technocratic one, as well as a series of drastic austerity measures to calm markets and avert immediate crisis. Troubles with sovereign debt did not befall Italy overnight: they had been in the making for the past half-century, over the course of which debt rose from less than 30 percent of the GDP in the mid-1960s to over 130 percent in 2015, making Italy one of the most baffling examples of sustained and heavy debt accumulation. The debt-to-GDP ratio had slowly edged up from the mid-1960s, but it only started growing in earnest when slowing economic growth and increased financing costs compounded existing fiscal imbalances at the beginning of the 1980s. There was no significant attempt to rebalance the budget throughout the 1980s, despite ever-greater alarm in policy circles about growing indebtedness. The breakthrough finally arrived in 1992 when Italy adopted a program of severe spending cuts and tax increases, which it reinforced with additional measures throughout the rest of the decade, setting the

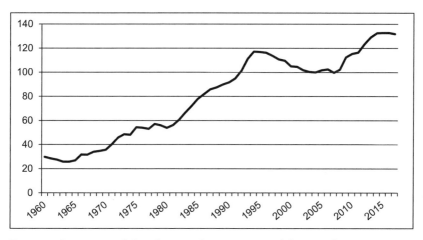

Fig. 3.1. Gross consolidated general government debt in Italy as a percentage of GDP from 1960 to 2015. Source: Ameco

debt-to-GDP ratio on a firm downward path. After 2000, however, the decline of the debt-to-GDP ratio progressively slowed—despite the windfall fiscal benefits of precipitously falling interest rates—as deficits started to widen again. The decline of the debt ratio had completely stopped by the time the global financial and economic crisis struck at the end of the 2000s, leaving Italy in a precarious situation just when markets started to fret about the creditworthiness of highly indebted sovereigns.

This chapter explains this puzzling fiscal trajectory—the baffling inaction in the face of dramatic debt accumulation in the 1980s, the heroic breakthrough of the 1990s, the relapse of the 2000s, and the desperate austerity of the post-crisis years—by tracing how social coalitions evolved across time, governed by the changing balance between the forces of intense fiscal polarization and moderate exposure to international competition. It shows that intense polarization of fiscal interests between four major vested interest groups initially fostered a coalitional pattern centered on the defense of major features of the existing fiscal architecture that the four groups had important stakes in. Large businesses formed a social coalition with small- and medium-sized enterprises (SMEs) and the dependents of the state in the South to keep a five-party conglomerate (the so-called *pentapartito*) in power throughout the 1980s, which guaranteed the continuation of subsidies and targeted tax exemptions to large enterprises, continued to tolerate tax evasion by SMEs, and maintained public employment and the flow of investment funds to the South.

This social coalition and the governments they backed were confronted with the fourth group, organized labor, which was strong enough to veto curtailments of the generous welfare system or increases in the tax pressure on labor. Under these circumstances, any significant fiscal adjustment was impossible.

With the passage of time, however, several of these vested interest groups came under increasing pressure from growing problems with international competitiveness, which eventually induced large businesses and SMEs in the exposed sector to defect from their old coalition and to ally with organized labor in support of the drastic adjustment efforts of the 1990s. United by their shared interest in improving macroeconomic conditions for international competitiveness, this coalition helped to keep in power austerity-minded policy makers and strengthened their hands in raising taxes and cutting spending, while it also enabled a series of compromises between social partners. However, the common ground on which this coalition was built was lost when Italy entered the common currency in 1999, and the link between macroeconomic stability and public finances was broken. The competitiveness-coalition disintegrated. The awkward coalition of large and small businesses averse to taxation and the dependents of the state in the South was reinstated. It supported a series of center-right governments, which restored many of the policies that had been affected by previous reforms. Labor reassumed its role as a veto actor in further welfare reform and was excluded from policy making apart from a brief stint in power by the center-left in the middle of the decade. It was only in the early 2010s that this coalitional structure was broken up again as the specter of sovereign debt crisis loomed over the country and required immediate fiscal correction.

The twists and turns of the Italian fiscal story—the alternation of periods of debt accumulation and determined adjustment—provide a chance to explore how fiscal polarization and economic exposure shape the evolution of social coalitions across time and how the changing coalitional bases of politics affect a country's ability to deal with heavy debt accumulation. Furthermore, they provide a unique opportunity to evaluate the explanatory capacity of the diachronic social coalitions model against a wealth of alternative institutional, and ideational explanations of adjustment, which were proposed in the wake of the historic turnaround of the 1990s to account for the sudden change from policy stasis to a burst of reforms. This chapter demonstrates that none of the competing explanations of the developments of the 1990s is consistent with Italy's subsequent policy trajectory, whereas the model centering on the evolution of social coalitions across time can explain the trajectory in its entirety. Institutional and ideational changes that various accounts of the policy reforms of the 1990s focus on—such as the increased autonomy of the state, electoral reform, the transformation of the party system, evolving patterns of corporatist consultation, and shifts in policy paradigms—are important components of the political sea-change that enabled policy reform, but they are better understood as manifestations of momentous shifts in the societal foundations of politics. When those shifts were reversed—by the early 2000s—fiscal policy relapsed despite the endurance of some of the institutional and ideational features that had helped reform; revealing that without the appropriate societal foundations, those features were insufficient to sustain control over debt accumulation.

The next section describes the Italian fiscal trajectory in some detail. The third section engages with alternative explanations of Italy's fiscal history in depth and evaluates their explanatory capacity against the theory centering on changes in societal coalitions. The fourth section explains how and why societal coalitions realigned from one period to the other under the countervailing pressures of fiscal polarization and international exposure, and it describes the observable manifestations of these realignments in terms of changes in the party system, electoral shifts and corporatist cooperation. The last section summarizes the lessons of the Italian case and briefly relates it to the case studies of the next chapter.

Italian Fiscal Policy by Numbers

The past half-century of Italy's debt history resembles an underwhelming roller-coaster ride with long, steep ascents and short, disappointing descents. Already on a mild upward slope throughout the 1970s, debt was rising steeply and relentlessly throughout the 1980s. The budget was not simply in the red; deficits averaged a whopping 11 percent of the GDP. Through exceptionally large fiscal effort in the 1990s, borrowing was reduced to close to 0 by 2000 and the debt-to-GDP ratio fell. However, the favorable trend in the debt-to-GDP ratio was halted and then reversed as the 2000s ushered in a renewed period of fiscal laxity with quickly widening deficits that lasted throughout the decade, apart from a brief attempt at tightening between 2006 and 2008. By the time the global financial and economic crisis hit, Italy's public finances were in very vulnerable shape again. At the height of the European sovereign debt crisis, renewed austerity efforts were made. This section describes the main characteristics of fiscal policies in these four decades to provide a more nuanced analysis of the trends that shaped fiscal outcomes since the 1970s.

The 1980s were characterized by a puzzling mix of ever-growing alarm about the state of public finances and virtually no serious attempt to close the enormous budgetary gap. By 1980, Italy had looked back on a decade of growing fiscal problems. Debt had grown from under 40 percent of the GDP in 1970 to almost 60 percent as spending soared due to new welfare programs, increased public employment, and growing debt-servicing costs, while tax revenues lagged behind. In the 1980s, pressure on the budget only worsened as growth slowed, unemployment increased, and real interest rates shot up as a result of attempts to restrain inflation after Italy joined the European Monetary System (EMS) in 1978. As the decade progressed, the policy discourse was increasingly dominated by calls for *"risanamento"* (Radaelli 2000) as ministers and central bank officials urged austerity measures to stabilize public finances (Walsh 1999). One budgetary reform followed another,[1] and major adjustment packages were announced (Bosi et al. 2003; European Economy 1993). At the same time, the fiscal effort remained remarkably limited: spending growth was slowed but not reversed, revenues increased only hesitantly. Borrowing stayed firmly above 10 percent of the GDP as the pace of the correction of the primary deficit fell behind the rate of increase of the interest burden.

On the expenditure front, policy makers shied away from taking on any of the major spending items. Social security expenditures continued to increase significantly until 1983 as the result of a large boost in temporary income-replacement benefits[2] and early retirement[3] in the wake of a large industrial restructuring campaign. For the rest of the decade, they slowly edged up with the gradual maturing of pension liabilities. Attempts to restrain the costs were less than half-hearted. Marginal adjustments on pensions[4] were never followed by comprehensive reform despite discussing several proposals. Although stricter rules on disability benefits were introduced, these were not enforced, so the widespread abuse of these entitlements continued (Ferrera and Gualmini 2004, 94). The compensation of public employees also marginally increased. Although the large waves of hiring in the public sector seen in the 1970s had stopped, employee numbers kept drifting up and salaries increased in line with rest of the economy (Morcaldo 1993; Bosi et al. 2003). Public investment was also kept up. Only two fields stood out where the government could achieve savings: health care, where co-payments were introduced (Ferrera and Gualmini 2004, 95), and production subsidies, because state aid was gradually phased out after 1986 in compliance with rules of the

Single Market. In all other areas of spending, inertial forces were stronger than savings efforts.

On the revenue front, the improvement was larger. Between 1980 and 1991, revenues grew by almost 8 percentage points of the GDP. This, however, was not the outcome of government intervention, but the result of the combination of the extreme progressivity of the personal income tax system and high inflation (Giavazzi and Spaventa 1989). Revenues from personal income taxes grew by almost 5 percentage points during the decade, although the momentum of revenue growth considerably slowed after the government readjusted the brackets in 1983, 1986, and 1989 under pressure from trade unions. Other sources of revenue growth included taxes on previously exempt government bonds, increased withholding tax, and increased excise taxes on fuel after 1986 (Guerra 1993). Other revenues stagnated. Although the corporate income tax rate was raised from 25 to 36 percent as early as 1983 and the rate of local taxes on productive entities grew from 15 to 16.2 percent, this had little effect due to the frequent use of tax rebates to help industry and also due to widespread tax evasion (Guerra 1993). A reform on income reporting and tax collection was put forward in 1984 to deal with the latter problem, but it was adjusted in the face of fierce opposition from self-employed groups (Ginsborg 2003, 154). Evasion continued to be a major drain on public revenues. Social security contributions on the income of the self-employed were raised several times, but revenue from contributions remained flat until the end of the decade. At the same time, privatization—a possibly considerable source of extra revenue—was not on the agenda in this decade. The sale of public enterprises remained sporadic and was usually motivated by the companies' financial problems rather than by the urge to raise revenues (Goldstein 2003).

Despite the growing sense of emergency, fiscal policy was lacking decisive action on both the spending and the revenue front throughout the 1980s. Even when apparently drastic action was taken—such as the increasing of the corporate income tax rate by almost a half—results failed to come forth due to lax enforcement and countervailing decisions to soften the blow. At times, policy makers even set fiscal consolidation back by agreeing, for example, to adjusting the income tax brackets. This hesitancy took its toll. By 1990, debt approached 100 percent of the GDP, and the interest burden on the budget had grown to 10 percent of the GDP. With this high interest burden, debt would snowball indefinitely even though the gap between non-interest expenditures and revenues was gradually closing.

In the early 1990s, the long years of deleterious inaction gave way to furious-paced reforms in the context of mounting economic problems and political upheaval. With the economy in a slump, the country went through a major currency crisis in 1992 and had to leave the European Monetary System. The Treasury ran into difficulties in selling bonds, and there were signs that confidence in the banking system might be waning (Ginsborg 2003, 271). To make matters worse, the process of European integration was to move to a higher level, and Italy seemed destined to be left behind due to its macroeconomic problems. In the midst of major political turmoil, technocrats took over the main policy-making positions and embarked on reforms that were to characterize fiscal policy throughout the rest of the decade, even after the return of elected governments.

The fiscal zeal improved the primary balance by nearly 7 percent of the GDP in the next five years and brought borrowing down to almost 0 by 2000. Spending was reduced by around 2 percent of the GDP, mainly as a result of major savings on the compensation of public employees—due to a hiring and salary freeze—and the closing of the *Cassa per il Mezzogiorno*, the agency channeling public investment funds to the underdeveloped South (Bull and Baudner 2004). Cutbacks were also achieved in health expenditure and by the tightening of the eligibility conditions for disability benefits (Ferrera and Gualmini 2004, 23). Although four major pension reform packages were also passed in this decade, these yielded few immediate savings due to the long phase-in times they mandated.[5] The one pension reform attempt that sought to achieve immediate cost reduction in 1994 failed in the face of fierce opposition.

Revenues grew mostly as a result of the increasing fiscal pressure on businesses and a huge wave of privatization. Corporate tax revenue expanded not only because of the increase in tax rates and social security contributions[6] but also because certain tax deductions were ended[7] and evasion-safe new taxes were introduced[8] in an effort to bring into the fold of taxpayers companies that consistently reported no profits. These efforts to increase corporate tax revenues and strengthen the credibility of tax collection suffered a temporary setback in 1994 when a three-year tax credit program eliminated taxes on reinvested profits and an amnesty on previous tax irregularities was announced, but they were back on track again with the 1997 tax reform that pursued the joint aim of shifting some of the fiscal pressure from labor costs to corporate profits and increasing the transparency and enforceability of corporate taxation (Bernasconi et al. 2005). Privatization was a major source of revenue throughout the decade, averaging 1 percent of GDP a year and peaking in 1996 and 1997 (Goldstein 2003).

Drastic and sustained austerity bore fruit as the debt-to-GDP ratio started to decline after peaking at 122 percent in 1994. The interest burden dropped precipitously from almost 13 percent of the GDP in 1993 to a little over 6 percent by the end of the decade as austerity increased Italy's chances of adopting the common currency and thus allowed it to benefit from the downward convergence of interest rates in the prospective euro area. Seemingly set to be sucked into a debt-interest spiral at the beginning of the 1990s, by 2000, Italy was in a virtuous circle of improving fiscal performance, falling interest rates and declining debt-to-GDP ratio.

This happy state of affairs was not to last into the 2000s. After Italy joined the euro and a new government came into power, fiscal discipline seemed to take a back seat again. Despite the continued fall of interest rates in the eurozone and the consequent decrease in the interest burden on the budget, deficits widened again and the descent of the debt-to-GDP was stopped and reversed by the middle of the decade. Fiscal policy in this period seemed to be aimed at undoing the changes of the 1990s. Revenues fell as the 1997 tax reform was repealed, the corporate income tax rate was repeatedly decreased, a new investment tax credit program was launched, and the credibility of tax enforcement was weakened by amnesties (Maurizi and Monacelli 2003; OECD 2005a). Spending was on the rise due to new public investment projects (mostly in the South of the country) and the significant growth in the compensation of public employees as both the number of employees and wages increased at all levels of government (OECD 2005b). Apart from one brief attempt to reverse these developments between 2006 and 2008, this trend persisted until Italy found itself in the eye of the storm of the European sovereign debt crisis.

Faced with the need to calm markets and to earn the support of the European Central Bank, Italy adopted a drastic austerity program at the end of 2011. Similarly to the early 1990s, the first reform measures were put into place under a technocratic government. The composition of the program, however, was quite different. On the revenue side, it strongly relied on regressive tax increases like the raising of VAT and gasoline excise tax rates and the extension of the real estate tax to first residences, although these measures were complemented by the introduction of a luxury tax, while efforts to crack down on tax evasion were also renewed (Culpepper 2014). On the spending side, savings came from immediate pension cuts.[9] The fiscal effort has since been kept up, although growth-enhancing reforms seem to take a clear precedence to budgetary consolidation.

This overview of the past four decades of fiscal history highlights some consistent features beyond the puzzling alternation of long periods of persistent debt accumulation and drastic austerity. One issue that stands out is the prominent place of the revenue-generating capacity of corporate taxation on the fiscal agenda. Reforms attempting to increase or decrease the fiscal pressure on corporate income have been frequent. This is not only manifested in the repeated changes in the corporate rates and social contributions—hikes in the 1980s and 1990s and reductions in the 2000s—but also, and perhaps more importantly, in policy efforts directed at the actual collection of the revenue. Cracking down on evasion and the closing of tax loopholes have been hallmarks of periods of fiscal tightening, whereas tax amnesties and the proliferation of tax breaks and exemptions have characterized periods of fiscal profligacy. In contrast, reforms of personal taxation have been mostly revenue-neutral.

Another central fiscal issue is more notable by its absence. Although pension reform was constantly on the agenda, immediate savings were never achieved before the most recent austerity program, despite the huge weight of this expenditure item for the budget and the deficit.[10] Nor were any of the generous income replacement schemes trimmed. Social security outlays remained on an increasing path throughout the past four decades. Very minor adjustment to these costs only happened through cracking down on the abuse of disability benefits in the 1990s. Appreciable cuts on the spending side only came from reducing the public wage bill and public investment, but these savings were reversed when austerity ended. The next section incorporates this information into the testing of alternative explanations for the long period of excessive debt accumulation in Italy until the early 1990s and for the subsequent dramatic changes in the policy trajectory.

Explaining Italy's Immutable Problems and Heroic Breakthroughs: Social Coalitions versus Political Institutions and Policy Paradigms

After Italy broke the habit of incessant borrowing and brought its debt under control through painful austerity in the 1990s, scholars offered a large number of rival theories to explain what made the 1990s so different from the 1980s. The early 1990s were a time of tremendous upheaval in Italy that ushered in many conspicuous political changes: a succession of technocratic governments, electoral reform, a complete overhaul of the party system, changing relations of social partnership, new economic paradigms, and a new phase in European economic integration. Different theories focused on different institutional, ideational, and interest-based aspects of this momentous transformation.

Many institutionalist scholars emphasized the strengthened capacities of the state in the 1990s to override the divergent preferences of societal groups, whose untrammeled influence on policy making had precluded asserting control over spending and taxation throughout the 1980s (Della Sala 1997). Enhanced state strength in the 1990s was attributed to institutional changes that shifted power from a spendthrift legislature and factious coalition governments to a stability-minded "core executive." One variant of this argument stressed the importance of technocratic governance in the early 1990s. Whereas parties held sway over the budget in the First Republic, a small circle of policy makers most concerned with macroeconomic stability—previously concentrated in the Bank of Italy—controlled the budget in the early 1990s (Sbragia 2001). Another variant underlined the role of changes in the electoral and party system. In the First Republic, members of coalition governments treated the budget as their "fiefdom," whereas increased electoral competition in the Second Republic forced parties in governments to give greater priority to fiscal discipline and to delegate budgetary decision-making authority to the treasury, where fiscal balance took precedence over particularistic interests (Hallerberg 2004; Hallerberg et al. 2009). Furthermore, others pointed out that the new electoral rules also reduced the incentives of members of parliament and party factions within government to keep lavishing fiscal favors on their narrowest constituencies. Under the old system, preferential voting had motivated candidates to differentiate themselves from rivals—even within their own party—by providing selective benefits to their voters (Cox and McCubbins 2001). Removing this element of the electoral rules weakened the centrifugal forces affecting the budget.

Other institutionalist explanations focused less on the newfound autonomy of the state. Instead, they emphasized governments' ability to successfully negotiate policy adjustment with influential interest groups. Whereas hostility between unions and employers had tied the hands of governments in trying to assert control over welfare costs and taxation in the 1980s, the institutional innovation of social pacts allowed for tri-partite compromise between social partners and the government on these fundamental issues throughout the 1990s (Regini and Regalia 1997; Molina and Rhodes 2007; Baccaro 2003). Social pacts generated a common informational basis for enabling different interest groups to successfully coordinate their preferences and to arrive at a compromise about policy adjustment (Culpepper 2002 and 2008).

Ideational explanations focused on the gradual spread of the stability-oriented paradigm of macroeconomic policy making from a narrow group of experts in the Bank of Italy to much broader circles of political, economic, and policy-making elites. While Keynesian ideas still had important influence in the 1980s, they were fully replaced by the new paradigm by the 1990s, especially in the context of the clear European consensus on the primacy of macroeconomic stability, giving rise to the conviction that Italy's problems could only be solved by tight fiscal (and monetary) policies (McNamara 1998; Quaglia 2004).

Finally, a prominent interest-based explanation concentrated on the central role of business in the exposed sector in bringing about stabilization (Walsh 1999). It argued that fiscal stabilization became possible when a window of opportunity opened for export-oriented businesses to exercise influence over policy under technocratic governments. The combination of devaluation and fiscal tightening suited export-oriented groups, but it disadvantaged sheltered sectors. Since the latter had strong leverage over parties in government throughout the 1980s, stabilization only became possible when those parties lost control over government policy in the 1990s.

Most of these explanations also incorporated the theme of European integration. They argued that the "national imperative" that Italy joins the Economic and Monetary Union upon its launch in 1999 strongly reinforced the beneficial effects of the institutional reform, ideational innovations, and shifts in interest group influence they focus on. The impending deadline for fulfilling the Maastricht criteria generated exceptionally strong penalties for fiscal problems, lending exceptional authority to technocrats, inducing parties and members of parliament to delegate budgetary decision-making to guardians of fiscal discipline, fostering compromise between social partners on reforms of welfare and taxation, bolstering the stability-oriented paradigm, and strengthening the determination of businesses in the exposed sectors to pursue fiscal stabilization.

The shared emphasis of these disparate explanations on the role of the "national imperative" of early euro accession in fiscal consolidation is problematic. Notwithstanding its ubiquity, the "national imperative" argument is inconsistent with the sequence of events. Euro accession was made a "national imperative" in the second half of 1996, but the bulk of the most painful fiscal austerity measures had already been passed by then. The debate about early accession was open until the last moment, with businesses, unions, and technocratic and political elites being equally divided on the issue. The final decision to adopt the euro along with the first group of countries was only taken after the Prodi-government realized in September 1996 that Italy would likely be the only country other than Greece to be left out of the first round (Radaelli 2000, Quaglia 2004). Although the fiscal effort was stepped up at that point in a last-ditch attempt to make the grade, real austerity had already happened—and the institutional and ideational changes and shifts in interest group power that the different theories focus on had already taken place—in the previous years, when the euro still represented an issue of contention rather than a "national imperative."

Without the auxiliary argument that the run-up to EMU was a period of exceptional politics and exceptional fiscal policy making, however, the above-described theories are at a loss to explain subsequent turns of fiscal policy. Why did Italy relapse into fiscal profligacy in the 2000s? The new electoral and party system persisted and budgetary decision-making continued to be centralized in the treasury. Why did these institutional changes fail to exercise their beneficial effect beyond 2000? Why did social pacts lose their capacity to foster cross-class support for sustained reform? Why did European consensus on the primacy of macroeconomic stability stop protecting Italy from the temptation of destabilizing fiscal policies? Why did business in the exposed sector lose its ability or willingness to keep lobbying for fiscal stability despite its emphatically good relationship with center-right governments of the time? The brief attempt at tightening between 2006 and 2008 remains equally puzzling. Why was determined fiscal stabilization initiated by a non-technocratic government—that was beholden more to labor than to business—in this instance? Why did it not revive the practice of social pacts? What triggered it in the absence of profound institutional changes[11] or paradigm shifts? Finally, what explains the renewed success of fiscal rigor since 2011 despite the shortness of the spell of technocratic governance, the delay in institutional reforms, and the conspicuous absence of social pacting?

The explanation for the wildly changing patterns of Italian fiscal policy lies at deeper levels of politics than directly observable in institutional and ideational factors: namely, at the level of societal coalitions. Large fiscal imbalances mark the reign of governments that rely on an awkward social coalition of socioeconomic groups averse to taxation and dependent on the state for their livelihood. Both the so-called *pentapartito* governments that held power throughout the 1980s and the center-right governments of the 2000s drew support from various business groups, who prioritize low corporate taxes, and from the population in the economically depressed South that is highly dependent on state spending (public employment, public investment projects, and disability payments) for its income. This is why the *pentapartito* governments of the 1980s were so reluctant to allow corporate tax pressure to grow, to crack down on tax evasion and disability fraud, and to cut public employment and investment. It also explains why center-right governments were so eager to reverse corporate tax increases, grant tax amnesties and restart public projects. The anti-tax-state-dependency coalition puts great strain on the public budget. Therefore, balancing the budget would require very large net contributions from other groups in society. However, in the past four to five decades, this coalition was not strong enough to pressure its main opponent, organized labor, to accept higher taxes or a stunted welfare state. The strike potential of labor prevented adjustment in social security outlays. The stalemate between the two sides led to persistent large imbalances and debt accumulation.

Fiscal stability is only possible under a different coalitional constellation. The coalition that emerged at the beginning of the 1990s united organized labor with businesses exposed to international competition under the banner of restoring competitiveness. This competitiveness coalition supported the policies of the technocratic governments of the first half of the 1990s and the center-left government of the second half of the 1990s. It secured crucial concessions from all members of the coalition: acquiescence in long-term pension reform (albeit not in immediate cuts) from labor and the acceptance of the increase in corporate taxation by business in the exposed sectors. Furthermore, this coalition was also strong enough to dominate policy making and force painful sacrifices upon groups not represented in the coalition. Dependents of the state suffered from cutbacks on public employment and investment while sheltered businesses had to suffer the increase in *de facto* tax pressure. It was this competitiveness coalition that the center-left attempted to revive when it briefly got into power in 2006 and embarked on painful austerity, but the economic circumstances no longer fostered such a coalition; austerity was rejected and the center-left government fell after two years.

The years since 2011 have seen the emergence of a third type of coalitional constellation, whose exact contours are still uncertain as is the direction fiscal policies can be expected to take. This coalition also seems to be centered on business, but it excludes organized labor and is likely to woo the so-called labor market outsiders instead. Accordingly, fiscal stabilization under this coalition is likely more heavily focused on trimming the welfare privileges of organized labor.

The competing explanations presented in this subsection are all summarized in Table 3.1. The table shows that the coalitional pattern corresponds exactly to the different phases on fiscal policy, whereas the evolution of the institutional and ideational frameworks does not follow all the twists and turns. The logical question is, of course, how and why the coalitional patterns that are so consequential for the fiscal health of the country

TABLE 3.1. Overview of alternative explanations for the different phases of fiscal policy in Italy in the past four decades

	1980s	1990s	2000s	2010s
Policy	large deficits and debt accumulation	adjustment and debt reduction	widening deficits, return to debt accumulation	austerity from late 2011
			brief austerity attempt between 2006 and 2008	
Societal coalitions	stalemate	dominance	stalemate	dominance
	labor VS anti-tax-state-dependency coalition	competitiveness coalition over rest of society	labor VS anti-tax-state-dependency coalition	new coalition (exposed businesses and labor market outsiders?) over rest
			brief attempt at resurrecting the competitiveness coalition between 2006 and 2008	
Electoral system	proportional with preference vote	near-majoritarian	near-majoritarian (added bonus for winner after 2005)	near-majoritarian with bonus for winner
Party system	polarized pluralism	two electoral blocs	two electoral blocs	realignment
Technocracy	no	yes: 1992 to 1994, 1995 no: 1994, 1996 to end of decade	no	yes: late 2011 to early 2013 no: 2010 to late 2011 2013–2015
Budgetary institutions	decentralized	increasingly centralized	centralized	centralized
Concertation	no	yes	yes (formally)	no
Dominance of stability paradigm	no	yes	yes	yes
"National imperative"	no	not until 1996 yes (euro-accession) after 1996	no	yes? (crisis)

arise. The next subsection turns to this question. It describes the historical roots of the anti-tax-state-dependency coalition and explains the mechanism through which this coalition disintegrated by the early 1990s to give way to the competitiveness coalition. It also accounts for the surprising reversal of coalitional patterns after 2000 to call attention to an underappreciated side effect of the common European currency on the domestic political dynamics surrounding policy making. Finally, it contemplates the political situation arising in the wake of the global crisis.

Evolving Social Coalitions, Fiscal Polarization, and International Exposure

The coalitional dynamics that so strongly determine Italy's ability to ensure fiscal stability originated in the late 1960s and the first half of the 1970s. Both the political balance of power and the main contours of redistribution changed in this famously turbulent period in a way that would shape the politics of fiscal policies in the coming decades. Organized labor forcefully asserted itself through a wave of strikes and demonstrations. It challenged business's previous hegemony over policy making under successive coalition governments led by Christian Democracy (DC). It achieved a dramatic expansion of welfare policies as well as a tax reform that was to put a large part of the increased tax burden on business and the wealthy (Ginsborg 2003). On the defensive and unable to control the main contours of policy any more, business sought protection from increased taxation in two ways: large businesses lobbied for targeted tax exemptions, whereas small entrepreneurs increasingly relied on the tacit toleration of tax evasion (Guerra 1993). At the same time, if the DC was to retain its dominant governmental position and its ability to protect business interests, the political support of the population of the economically backward South had to be secured. This population had always supported the DC, but during the tumultuous years of the late 1960s and early 1970s, it had signaled its disenchantment with the lack of policies to alleviate the poverty of the region through riots and demonstrations as well as through electoral defection. Therefore, new flows of public funds were directed to the region to boost public employment and investment projects (La Palombara 1987).

Besides blowing a sizeable hole in the budget, these dramatic spending increases—arising from welfare expansion and the intensified flow of funds to the South—and the arrangements to limit the tax exposure of business through tax exemptions and evasion also defined the vested interest groups that were to play a crucial role in the politics of fiscal policy in the next decades. The new policies interacted with socioeconomic cleavages present in the Italian polity to delineate four main vested interest groups: organized labor concentrated in the North of the country, the population of the South, large corporations, and small entrepreneurs. Intense class conflict, dramatic economic disparities between the North and the South, and the dualization of industry between large corporations and small family firms were given features of the socioeconomic structure, but these divisions were magnified by the new policies. The new welfare provisions reinforced disunity between northern and southern labor. The system was heavily biased towards pensions and temporary unemployment relief that accrued to workers with long, stable careers (Ferrera and Gualmini 2004). This suited labor in the economically dynamic North but gave workers in the South little stake in this system because they had little chance to fulfill the eligibility requirements due to the limited access to stable jobs in the region. Instead, southern workers shared a strong interest with local business in the steady flow of state funds as the main source of the region's income. Meanwhile, the fiscal interests of large and small businesses in the North diverged pronouncedly due to the difference in the strategies available to the two types of businesses to shield themselves from tax pressure.

The shifts in the political balance of power that generated these policy changes also ensured that vested interest groups would be able to block unfavorable changes. On the one hand, labor in the North had the power through the lingering threat of devastating industrial action to veto any changes to the welfare system or attempts to increase taxes on labor. On the other hand, the marriage of convenience of large firms, small businesses, and the dependents of the state in the South ensured that all three groups had the necessary leverage over successive DC-led coalitions to protect targeted tax exemptions, block efforts to make tax collection more effective,[12] and to maintain the flow of funds to the South.

The 1980s: Stalemate, Policy Paralysis, Brewing Discontent, and Breakthrough

This stalemated politics and policy making started to have really deleterious consequences when the original gap in the budget was magnified by a series of unfavorable exogenous changes. Debt started growing on an alarmingly steep path after growth slowed, unemployment increased, interests on government debt rose, and it became impossible to fully monetize deficits after Italy joined the fixed-exchange rate regime of the EMS in

1979. Although successive governments continuously spoke of the urgency of *risanamento* (Walsh 1999), nothing could be done as long as each group was bent on defending their vested interests in existing fiscal policies. With no way of adjusting major expenditure or revenue items, efforts to balance the budget were constrained to relatively minor areas like health care and excise taxes but could not take on any of the big-ticket items and major revenue sources. Therefore, they had little chance of slowing down, let alone halting, the fast accumulation of debt.

At the same time, as the growing fiscal problems increasingly impinged on the real economy, they set in motion latent shifts in the policy preferences of certain groups that were to change the political dynamics profoundly. Groups whose livelihood depended on preserving the competitiveness of Italian industry suffered more and more from the real appreciation of the *lira*. The partial monetization of the deficit fueled inflation,[13] which remained consistently and significantly higher in Italy that in its trade partners. In the fixed exchange rate system of the EMS, this translated into a 42 percent real appreciation between 1978 and 1991 despite repeated adjustments of the exchange rate (Fratianni and Spinelli 1997, 236–37). The substantial deterioration of international competitiveness led to losses of market share, profitability, and employment in many industries (Guerrieri and Milana 1990, 147–63). In light of these growing economic problems, the gridlock between DC-led governments and intransigent unions became ever more costly for labor and businesses of all sizes in the exposed sector. For these groups, the balance started to tilt in favor of compromise for the sake of fiscal stabilization.

The political change motivated by these shifts in preferences had subtle signs already in the 1980s, although the real breakthrough only came in the early 1990s. In the second half of the 1980s, groups in the exposed sector displayed increasing disaffection with the political actors that were supposed to protect their interest. Large businesses criticized successive DC-led governments ever more vehemently for their failure to stabilize the economy (Walsh 1999), while small businesses in the export-oriented industrial districts of the North deserted the DC in droves in favor of the emergent political movement of the so-called *lega*-s (Ginsborg 2003), who demanded better policies for businesses. Among workers, dissatisfaction with the unions was evident in the deterioration of the relationship of the leadership with the rank-and-file as well as in declining membership, especially among the younger cohorts that were worst hit by the loss of jobs and were not eligible for the protection accruing to workers with longer employment histories (Regini and Regalia 1997).

Despite these obvious signs of disgruntlement, it was difficult for both the DC and the unions to change tack because important elements of their supporter base were sheltered from the effects of declining competitiveness and remained averse to fiscal compromise. The firmest supporters of unions, older workers protected by stringent redundancy laws, generous income replacement, and early retirement schemes would have been loath to give up that protection or agree to pension reform. The hands of the Christian Democrats were similarly tied by their need to retain backing from small entrepreneurs in the sheltered sectors and from the southern dependents of the state in the face of their losses of support from exposed groups. Policy change was only possible if the entrenched front lines were redrawn.

In the event, redrawing the entrenched frontlines involved a complete regime change. The political shifts finally came to a head in the early 1990s. Disenchantment with the *status quo* had become ever more tangible: support for protest parties like the *Lega Nord* increased, the use of empty and spoiled ballots in elections surged, and a referendum movement calling for constitutional reform was launched (Bull and Newell 1993). In 1992, disaffection culminated in an "electoral earthquake" that saw the DC's vote share plummet (*ibid.*). The fate of the old political elite was sealed when the *Mani Pulite* campaign swept away not just the DC but practically every party of the so-called First Republic (Ginsborg 2003).

Space opened up for the reconfiguration of societal coalitions. After the fall of the DC, the vested interests of large business, small entrepreneurs, and the dependents of the state in the South ceased to be politically linked. At the same time, the unions came under increasing pressure to face up to the plight of their younger members in the wake of a new boost to unemployment in the industrial North and scrambled for a strategic solution to reconcile their responsibilities towards their younger and older cohorts. Amidst the political chaos, the contours of a new societal coalition started to take shape between large businesses, small entrepreneurs, and organized labor under the banner of international competitiveness.

The 1990s: Fiscal Stabilization under the Reign of the Competitiveness Coalition

The competitiveness coalition manifested itself in a variety of forms. The most conspicuous and most intensely studied of these was the series of social pacts between unions and the employers association *Confindustria*, which settled many conflicts that had put organized labor and business so starkly at odds in the previous decade and that were now universally recognized to be obstacles to restoring international competitiveness (Regini 2000; Culpepper 2002 and 2008; Baccaro 2003 and 2007; Molina and Rhodes 2007). But the coalition also worked through partisan-electoral cooperation, which was just as important a forum for collaboration, especially because it helped to tie small entrepreneurs in the industrial districts of the North—who were ill-represented in forums of social partnership—into the alliance via the *Lega Nord*. Technocratic governments of the first half of the decade as well as center-left governments of the second half were openly supported by parties of the center-left electoral bloc—which received the bulk of the labor vote and also had good ties with large businesses—but the tacit toleration and passive support of the *Lega* was just as crucial in ensuring the viability of these austerity-minded administrations.

The central role of the *Lega* in the success of the reforms of the competitiveness coalition is easy to miss because the party is normally associated with the center-right—due to its track record of being part of that bloc throughout the 2000s—whereas the reforms were put into place by technocratic and center-left governments. In the 1990s, however, the party very much retained its independence from the center-right and was crucial in ensuring the survival of technocratic and center-left governments as well as the success of their policies. Although the *Lega* never officially backed these governments—it even often ostensibly protested against their policies—its decision to keep its distance from the opposing center-right electoral bloc was critical in tilting the balance of power. By bringing down the center-right government after eight months in office in 1994, supporting the technocratic government that followed it, and refusing to join the center-right electoral alliance for the 1996 elections, the *Lega* neutralized throughout the decade the political alternative to the political proponents of the reforms and stabilization measures that the competitiveness coalition supported.

The groups left out of the competitiveness coalition were overpowered. The "orphans of the DC," the dependents of the state in the South and those small entrepreneurs who had not wished to change the old DC-dominated system, quickly found new champions to represent their interests in the National Alliance[14] and *Forza Italia* (Diamanti 2007), but these parties were unable to meaningfully influence policy making throughout the 1990s. Without the *Lega*, their center-right electoral coalition was not strong enough to win elections on their own. For the 1994 election, they managed to woo the *Lega*, but the alliance fell apart within months. The anti-tax message of *Forza Italia* fit well with the *Lega*'s low-tax platform, but the *Lega* could not afford to support the center-right's entire policy mix. This mix coupled tax amnesties and tax breaks with the allocation of funds to the South, which was bound to undermine fiscal balance in the absence of savings on welfare spending, which the center-right was unable to deliver in the face of union opposition. It conspicuously resembled the policy-mix of the erstwhile DC that the *Lega* had forcefully campaigned against on behalf of small business in the North. Therefore, the *Lega* had no other choice than to refuse forming coalitions with the center-right throughout the 1990s and instead grudgingly and tacitly support the policies of the competitiveness coalition under the technocratic and center-left governments despite the ratcheting up of the tax pressure.

The reign of the competitiveness coalition saw the introduction of a series of austerity measures, which imposed fiscal pain on groups across society: it affected the three major groups forming the competitiveness coalition but also placed at least as heavy burden on the groups left out of it. Organized labor agreed to pension reform, but the unions successfully negotiated an exemption for older workers. Business acquiesced in raising the corporate tax rates and social security contributions even though tax exemptions were now ruled out under the Single Market. Smaller businesses also had to suffer the tightening of tax collection and the introduction of new, evasion-safe taxes on net worth and real estate. Obviously, this increased tax pressure on all businesses engaged in the practice of evasion, whether they had a stake in restoring international competitiveness or not. The austerity package also dealt a heavy blow to the livelihood of the dependents of the state in the South when the *Cassa per il Mezzogiornio*, a major source of subsidies and project funds for the region, was closed and state enterprises were put up for privatization.

These measures eliminated the enormous budget deficit of the previous decade and put the debt-to-GDP ratio on a firm downward path. They represented a major step toward restoring macroeconomic stability and international competitiveness. At the same time, these achievements required great sacrifices from those who supported them just as much as from those who opposed them. The competitiveness coalition was willing to pay the price, as well as enforce the pain on others in order to avoid the economic costs of fiscal problems, which had become so painfully tangible by the late 1980s.

The Fall of the Competitiveness Coalition and Policy Relapse

However, the calculus of maintaining the competitiveness coalition at the price of painful compromises changed profoundly when Italy joined the common European currency in 1999. This was not because the coalition's purpose had been euro accession. In fact, as discussed above, business and unions had harbored major doubts about early accession until the very last moment. Euro accession removed the raison d'être of the competitiveness coalition because it insulated international competitiveness from the effects of fiscal problems. Once monetary policy was delegated to the European Central Bank, deficits could not be monetized and generate immense inflationary pressures. Furthermore, the crowding-out effect of public debt on private investment would be dispersed in the integrated European financial markets. These factors diminished the motivation for further sustaining the compromises that a strong competitiveness-alliance required and allowed old conflicts of interests to resurface.

The competitiveness coalition unraveled quickly both in the electoral and the corporatist sphere. Demonstrating the fatigue of small businesses with increasing tax pressure, the *Lega* joined the center-right bloc in the first election after accession in 2001 and stayed in the fold afterwards. Large corporations also defected to the center-right and supported confrontation instead of concertation in issues of reforming of the welfare system (Molina and Rhodes 2007). These political shifts reunited exposed sectors of business with their counterparts in the sheltered sectors and with dependents of the state in the South under the center-right umbrella, restoring the awkward anti-tax-state-dependency societal coalition that the DC had represented in the 1980s. After the defection of business from the competitiveness coalition, the center-left was emasculated. Although it managed to field an electoral coalition that won the 2006 elections by a whisker (in part, thanks to a reform of the electoral rules passed in 2005), the austerity program that it sought to put into place had no societal support and its government fell. Deserted by its allies, and thus too weak to be in government, labor could do little else than to return to its strategy of the 1980s and resist encroachments on its fiscal interests.

As the politics of the 1980s were recreated, fiscal outcomes also conformed to old patterns. Tax cuts and toleration for evasion coupled with increased public spending in the South without new savings on welfare expenses. Deficits increased and debt started to grow again, despite the fact that a precipitous fall of interest rates dramatically eased the debt service pressure on the budget. The equilibrium that politics settled back into had detrimental consequences for policy, and since fiscal problems ceased to exercise a negative effect on the welfare of different groups, there was no countervailing force to upset the equilibrium. The political and policy space was paralyzed until the global financial and economic crisis and a series of successive sovereign debt crises in Europe made fiscal disaster a tangible possibility in late 2011.

Question Marks in the Wake of the Crisis

The acute pressure for policy change in the face of impending crisis broke apart the paralyzing anti-tax-state-dependency coalition, but it is not entirely clear yet what is emerging in its place. The partisan-electoral sphere is in flux. The center-right is splintering; it has been hemorrhaging votes in the South as well as in the industrial districts of the North, and it lost the support of large business to the centrist political force that emerged around former technocratic Prime Minister Monti's policy platform (Culpepper 2014). Meanwhile, the center-left is in the process of redefining itself, signaling important shifts in the party's policy preferences away from the staunch defense of policies that organized labor is wedded to. The ambiguity is compounded by the emergence of a large protest party, the Five Star Movement, which captured a whopping 25 percent of the vote in 2013, without ever clarifying what policies it would prefer instead of the ones it so vehemently opposes or what other political forces it would be willing to ally with, if any. Similarly, in the corporatist sphere, it is clearer what is not in the cards than what is. Social pacts seem to be out (Culpepper and Regan 2014), but it still remains to be seen if any alternative form of policy concertation might develop.

The direction of change in Italian politics is difficult to predict, not only because of the lack of perspective on an ongoing process but also because the balance of political power seems to have definitively tilted away from organized labor, making the 2010s very different from previous decades. When organized labor asserted itself in the late 1960s, it changed the balance of power and created the policies that then determined the conflicts of interest within the Italian polity for the next half-century to come. By now, only a fraction of the active labor force supports unions and benefits directly from the welfare policies and protection that they fought for. In the 1980s, organized labor was a formidable force. In the 1990s, it was still a useful partner who managed to square the circle of compromising for the sake of younger labor market outsiders while protecting the vested interests of the older insiders. In the 2000s, it could still cause headaches to center-right governments. By the 2010s, unions can neither offer coordinating capacities, nor threaten with major disruptions (Culpepper and Regan 2014).

With the weakening of organized labor, new coalitional possibilities open up for large business. It does not necessarily have to choose between painful compromises with unions and expensive coexistence with tax-evading small businesses and dependents of the state any more. Instead, it might choose to sideline unions and seek to strike a deal with labor market outsiders to reform the costly welfare system that only benefits the insiders. The shift in the policy preferences of the center-left under its new leadership signals that a suitable redefinition of labor interest might be underway, while the present grand coalition of the center-left with splinters of the center-right and Monti's business-friendly political force suggests that a political alliance capable of delivering a business-labor outsider deal is feasible at least in the short run. However, ambiguities remain. First, it is questionable if drawing conflict lines in the midst of labor along generational dimensions will work in a society where the young are known to rely heavily on the support of their parents. Second, it is not clear where other social groups, small businesses, and the dependents of the state in the South would fit into this coalitional pattern. Finally, it is all the more difficult to answer these questions because a quarter of the electorate that voted for the Five Star Movement in 2013 is still to reveal its policy preferences. In any case, whether Italy is about to leave behind the coalitional pattern that governed the politics of the past half-century will have immense consequences for its ability to break the curse of uncontrollable debt growth.

Conclusion

The twists and turns of the Italian story of debt conform closely to the predictions of the model of evolving societal coalitions. The policy paralysis of the 1980s and the relapse of the 2000s illustrate how stalemate between societal coalitions bent on protecting the vested interests of their constituent groups can render policy makers helpless in the face of an ever-growing problem when militant unions, parties in government, and influential lobbies make every major item of the budget untouchable. The policies at the heart of the conflict (exclusive welfare arrangements, regionally targeted relief, designated tax exemptions, and the toleration of tax evasion by firms small enough to engage in it) exemplify how the polarization of vested interests encourages intransigence when the costs and benefits or existing policies are narrowly targeted at different groups, making it easy to design adjustment packages that only affect some groups and spare the others, thereby encouraging different groups to insist that stabilization be carried out without their sacrifices. The breakthrough of the early 1990s underlines that the only escape route from the stalemate is if some groups find the side effects of fiscal problems on their economic performance increasingly unbearable and defect from their existing coalition; whereas the relapse in the 2000s under the euro shows that if economic performance is insulated from the direct harm of fiscal imbalances, the motivation to form and maintain compromise-based coalitions evaporates. Finally, the tumultuousness of the early 1990s and 2010s demonstrates how the realignment of coalitions leads to policy breakthrough despite any previous institutional and ideational constraints on politics and policy making. In these two periods, a combination of electoral "earthquakes," constitutional changes, profound transformations in the party system, major innovations in social partnership, and ideological adjustments removed the obstacles to the political cooperation of groups that had previously been on opposite sides of the battle over fiscal policy and cleared the way for radical policy reform.

The next chapter investigates the process of debt accumulation and stabilization in Belgium and Ireland and compares them to each other and to Italy in order to show the effects of fiscal polarization and international exposure on the way this process enfolds. Swift reaction to growing debt problems in both Ireland and Belgium—with the first wave of drastic stabilization launched as early as in 1982 in both countries—attests to the importance of exposure to international economic competition. Both Ireland's and Belgium's economy is very open and the competitiveness-reducing effects of inflationary pressures arising from persistent borrowing forced large groups of society to consent to radical fiscal reform early on, a decade ahead of Italy. The divergence of the two countries' adjustment patterns in later years, however, underlines the significance of fiscal polarization. The first wave of stabilization successfully brought inflation under control, but fell short of stemming debt growth in both countries. Low levels of fiscal polarization allowed Ireland to reinforce its stabilization efforts in 1987 with a program that targeted those areas of the budget that had been spared in the previous austerity package; whereas in Belgium, further consolidation was prevented by the polarization of interests concerning the reform of the social security sector, whose enormous deficit undermined efforts to stop the snowballing of debt.

The comparison of Belgium and Ireland is particularly instructive because their adjustment patterns contradict what institutionalist theories would lead us to expect. The two countries show considerable similarities in political institutions and where they differ Belgium seems to have adaptive institutional advantages. Yet, it was Belgium that remained mired

in debt until exogenous changes—a precipitous drop in European interest rates—rescued it from fiscal disaster while Ireland pulled itself up by
its bootstraps long before conditions turned for the better. This pattern
reinforces the finding of this chapter that the constellation of political
institutions is secondary to the evolution of societal coalitions in determining adjustment capacity. Whenever stabilization can muster the necessary
societal support, the institutional framework for compromise will be created. Whenever the necessary societal consensus is missing, however, even
well-established institutions of compromise will fail to secure successful
adjustment.

FOUR

Fiscal Discord and Accord
in Open Economies

Belgium versus Ireland

In the 1980s, Belgium and Ireland accumulated debt with such alarming speed and persistence that Italy's problems paled in comparison. Belgium was the most indebted sovereign of the time and its debt stock was surging faster than that of any other developed nation, while Ireland followed as a close second. Reeling from the economic shocks of the 1970s, neither country could regain control over the alarming growth of its debt. Although both countries adopted sizeable fiscal adjustment packages as early as 1982, the adjustments proved to be vastly insufficient in the face of ballooning interest costs and only succeeded in slowing, but not reversing debt growth in both countries. In the late 1980s, however, the debt trajectories of the two countries diverged. Belgium's debt continued to snowball alarmingly in the absence of radical new adjustment due to ever-more onerous interest payments. It reached 135 percent of the GDP by the time the precipitous fall in European interest rates finally started to ease the interest burden in the mid-1990s. Ireland, on the other hand, adopted a second major adjustment package in 1987, which rapidly reduced the country's indebtedness long before interest and growth rates changed for the better in the mid-1990s. Subsequently, the debt-to-GDP ratio decreased consistently in both countries until the global financial and economic crisis struck in the late 2000s and pushed the debt-to-GDP ratios over 100 percent again in both countries (see Figure 4.1).

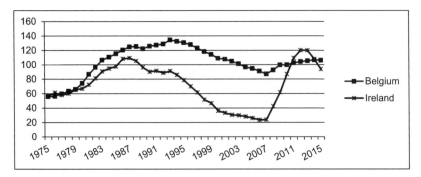

Fig. 4.1. Gross consolidated general government debt in Belgium and Ireland from 1975 to 2015. Source: Belgian Statistics Office and Ameco.

This chapter compares and contrasts the politics of debt accumulation in the two countries in order to explore the effect of fiscal polarization in two similarly open economies. It argues that the relatively fast reaction to fiscal imbalances in both countries was motivated by their intense exposure to international economic competition. It explains how the severe negative effects of high inflation on trade, employment, and profits created the necessary political conditions for stringent deflationary policies, underpinned by radical fiscal tightening in both countries in 1982. At the same time, the chapter emphasizes that Belgian and Irish governments had very different room for maneuver in raising taxes and cutting spending due to different levels of fiscal polarization. In Belgium, the polarizing architecture of social security generated intense conflicts between business and labor. These conflicts were temporarily suppressed at the height of the economic emergency in the early 1980s, but they immediately resurfaced once the first adjustment package had brought inflation under control and they made it impossible to increase taxes or to retrench entitlements. As a result, fiscal effort was constrained to cuts in public investment and collective consumption for the rest of the decade, which proved insufficient to stop the snowballing of debt as the interest-burden grew, despite an astonishing reduction in these expenditures. Thus, Belgium remained on a path of incessant debt growth until the steep fall in interest rates finally freed the country from the chokehold of debt in the mid-1990s. In contrast, policy makers had much greater latitude in adjusting various spending and taxation items in Ireland because the encompassing nature of existing policies ensured that any adjustment affected large parts of society fairly uniformly and, thus, limited the room for contention about who should bear the burden of fiscal stabilization. In the two waves of adjustment, taxes were raised, welfare transfers were retrenched, and public investment and consumption were cut with minimal political resistance.

Focusing on international economic exposure and fiscal polarization helps to account for the two countries' fiscal trajectories more comprehensively than alternative explanations do. The common claim that debt accumulation arises from fiscal indiscipline has little bearing on the Belgian and Irish experiences. In both countries, the vast fiscal imbalances were originally triggered by a series of exogenous economic and financial shocks, to which both Belgium and Ireland responded with resolute fiscal tightening from 1982. Notwithstanding the lack of effective political control mechanisms to ensure spending discipline under divided governments in both countries (Hallerberg 2004), both Belgium and Ireland achieved remarkable and sustained reduction in spending in this period, evidencing the commitment of successive coalition and minority governments to spending control. The trouble was that the improvement in the primary balance could not keep pace with the increase in the interest burden. The divergence in the two countries' fiscal trajectories in the second half of the 1980s had to do with differences in policy makers' ability to extend fiscal effort beyond the realm of discretionary expenditure. Belgium was unable to change course due to its failure to complement spending discipline with adjustments to entitlements and taxes, whereas Ireland's turnaround was made possible by achieving both.

Other explanations shed light on important aspects of the politics of policy adjustment in the two countries but fail to explain all significant similarities and differences. It has been noted that the ability of governments to enlist the support of the social partners was crucial in enabling the stabilization package of 1982 in Belgium (Jones 2008; Kuipers 2005; Hemerijk and Visser 2000) and the reforms of 1987 in Ireland (Baccaro and Lim 2007; Baccaro and Simoni 2008; Culpepper 2008). It remains to be explained, however, why further compromise proved elusive in Belgium since 1982 or how Ireland could already put into place a major adjustment package in 1982 without a social pact. Similarly, the ideational shift from Keynesianism to a neoliberal policy paradigm in the 1980s (McNamara 1998) helps to better understand the ideational background of the decisive deflationary turn in 1982 in both countries, but it does not explain why Belgium failed to step up its fiscal efforts the same way Ireland did when the first stabilization package proved insufficient to stem debt accumulation.

By analyzing the interplay of economic pressures and redistributive conflict in the two countries, this chapter fills in these gaps in our understanding of the politics of debt accumulation and fiscal stabilization in Belgium and Ireland. It explains why divided governments could exercise surprisingly strong spending control in both countries, under what conditions governments could count on the support of social partners, and why the neoliberal policy paradigm was more fully embraced in Ireland than in Belgium. The first half of the chapter discusses how the economic pressures on Belgium's open economy created the preconditions for a rightward shift in the government coalition and for a compromise between employers and part of the labor movement, which made it possible to embrace a new, stability-oriented policy paradigm and to put into place the drastic fiscal adjustment package of 1982. Then, it demonstrates how conflicts between business and labor about the social security system undermined the government coalition that had launched the first wave of stabilization and reignited hostility between social partners once the worst economic side effects of fiscal problems had been neutralized. The second half of the chapter discusses Ireland's success in adjusting its fiscal policies in the face of alarming debt growth. It shows that political conditions were conducive to fiscal adjustment practically irrespective of the composition or strength of the government in power or the presence or absence of corporatist consultation, because intense exposure to international economic forces made stabilization urgent while the encompassing nature of existing fiscal policies implied that no political actor could spare any major social group from fiscal pain. (For an overview of the alternative explanations for the pattern of similarity and divergence between Belgium and Ireland in the 1980s, see Table 4.1.)

TABLE 4.1. Overview of alternative explanations for the pattern of similarity and divergence between Belgium and Ireland in the 1980s

	early 1980s		late 1980s	
	Belgium	Ireland	Belgium	Ireland
adjustment	successful	successful	unsuccessful	successful
fiscal conflict	low	low	high	low
	(high fiscal polarization neutralized by competitiveness emergency)	(low fiscal polarization, plus competitiveness emergency)	(high fiscal polarization, competitiveness insulated from fiscal problems)	(low fiscal polarization)
government structure	divided (coalition)	divided (coalition)	divided (coalition)	divided (minority)
corporatist relations	compromise	adversarial	adversarial	compromise
policy paradigm	stability-oriented	stability-oriented	stability-oriented	stability-oriented

The next section analyzes Belgium's fiscal policies in the 1980s and early 1990s in detail to show that drastic fiscal effort in public investment and consumption was coupled with practically complete inaction in the field of revenues and entitlements. The third section explores the societal bases of this lopsided fiscal effort. It discusses the conflicts between business and labor over the social security system and the shared interests of the two classes in macroeconomic stability in the economically more dynamic and internationally more exposed Flemish region of the country. Then, it discusses the political and policy manifestations of these conflicts and commonalities of societal interests. The fourth section reflects on the longer term implications of the foregoing analysis for Belgian politics. The fifth section turns to the Irish case. It briefly discusses the fiscal policies of the period and goes on to explain why fiscal effort could encompass the entirety of public finances. It analyzes the structure of societal interests and how they were represented in the political sphere. The sixth section argues that Ireland's effectiveness in dealing with its recent fiscal problems is still rooted in the same socio-political structure that allowed the country to overcome its debt problems in the 1980s. The concluding section draws the main lessons of the chapter.

Fiscal Rigor and Recklessness in Belgium since the 1980s[1]

Belgium's serious fiscal troubles began with the oil crises. The country had previously been on a favorable fiscal path. Although it inherited a large debt stock from the time of the war, the debt-to-GDP ratio dwindled swiftly in the postwar decades due to robust economic growth and moderate deficits (Reinhart 2010, 23). In the second half of the 1970s, however, the budget was thrown out of balance by the effects of the major economic downturn triggered by the two oil crises and by a jump in the costs of outstanding debt. Expenditure was set on an explosive trajectory, growing from 45 to 64 percent of the GDP within ten years after the first oil shock. Social expenditure grew by 8 percentage points as the welfare system was flooded with unemployed and early retirees in the wake of the economic downturn (Hemerijk and Visser 2000). Non-social security expenditure also increased by 5 percentage points as successive governments tried to remove excess workforce from the job market by boosting public employment (Hemerijk and Visser 2000). The increase in primary expenditure was compounded by a jump in the interest burden around the turn of the decade—from 4 to 10 percent of the GDP—due partly to increased borrowing but, more importantly, also to a two-thirds increase in the interest rates charged on Belgian sovereign debt (Barro and Sala-i-Martin 1990). Initially, the expenditure explosion was partially counterbalanced by a surge of revenues, because double-digit inflation generated extra tax income via fiscal drag (Blöndal 1986, 117). However, when Belgium joined the fixed exchange rate regime of the European Monetary System in 1979, it became crucial to rein in inflation to maintain parity with low-inflation Germany. As inflation was brought down, revenues leveled and the full scale of the fiscal damage of the economic and financial shocks became visible. By the beginning of the 1980s, it was also clear that the damage would last beyond the immediate crisis years.

By 1982, the debt-to-GDP ratio had grown close to 100 percent, and annual borrowing was above 10 percent of the GDP. Fiscal imbalances had started to cause problems with maintaining a fixed exchange rate within the EMS due to high inflation and balance of payments issues. Belgium was forced to devalue the franc in the wake of several currency crises, but other member states only consented to such realignment on the condition that austerity measures were taken (Hemerijck et al. 2000, 236; McNamara 1998, 142). In view of the direness of the situation, a radical austerity package was adopted.

Spending on public consumption and investment was cut back via the introduction of the rule that expenditure cannot grow in real terms and that additional cuts would be made whenever this was necessary to ensure that the nominal value of the deficit does not increase (European Economy 1993). As a result, such expenses shrunk 11 percentage points to 20 percent of the GDP, a fifth lower than their pre-crisis level in the early 1970s. Investments were cut by two-thirds; subsidies to firms were halved, and the compensation of employees decreased by a fifth. In these years, Belgium moved from spending on public consumption and investment on par with countries of similar levels of development to spending the least on public consumption and by far the least on public investment (IMF 1998, 17).

Adjustments to social security, on the other hand, were much smaller, especially in view of the enormous shock to the sector around the turn of the decade. The austerity package of 1982 included some tightening of the unemployment benefits and increases in contributions paid by employers (Hemerijk and Visser 2000); but beyond that, changes remained minimal, and Belgium continued to spend significantly more on social security than comparable countries (IMF 2004, 6). Outlays in this sector decreased slightly during the decade but only by 2 percentage points, which was a rather small improvement in light of their preceding surge. Importantly, the reduction happened mostly endogenously: family allowances dwindled in the wake of a decrease in the number of births, while unemployment transfers decreased thanks to the relative improvement of the labor market situation in the second half of the 1980s (Festjens 1993, 236).

It was not for the lack of trying that adjustments failed to happen. The 1980s saw four attempts to retrench the social security sector. The 1981 Disaster Plan, which attempted to freeze pension expenses and tighten conditions on several social security benefits failed because coalition partners (Christian Democrats and Socialists) disagreed over how radical the retrenchment should be and the government fell over the issue. A proposal to reform the pensions of civil servants put forward in 1983 was withdrawn in the face of strikes. The St. Anna Plan of 1986—which included heavy cuts in the unemployment insurance and limited future pension entitlements—also stirred up fervent labor demonstrations and was left unexecuted after the government that proposed it had to resign. It was only in 1982 that cuts in social security were actually enacted and pension contributions increased, although they proved ultimately insufficient (Anderson et al. 2007, 321–23; Marier 2008, 88). The deficit of the social security sector shrank somewhat during the decade—from 11 percent of GDP in 1980 to under 8 percent by 1990[2]—but the gap was still sizeable and started to widen again.

In contrast, there was almost no attempt to involve the revenue side in the consolidation effort. On the contrary: after a prolonged period of growth, revenues declined from the mid-1980s onward due to two personal income tax reforms—the Grootjans tax-reform of 1985 and the Maystadt tax-reform of 1988—which led to a significant decline in direct tax revenues (European Economy 1993), while the so-called "Maribel operation" of 1981 granted employers of manual workers exemption from contribution to social security. Indirect taxes were left untouched throughout the decade to avoid detrimental impacts on inflation. The only revenue increases came from the raising of pension contributions and the creation of new levies in 1982, but these were more than offset by the decrease in other sources of revenue. (Anderson et al. 2007, 322).

As a result of the sustained campaign of austerity, the primary balance climbed to a surplus of 5 percent in 1990, 13 percentage points higher than at the beginning of the decade. Nevertheless, net borrowing still amounted to 7 percent of the GDP because the interest burden had kept steadily growing throughout the decade to 12 percent of the GDP by 1990. The steady growth of the debt-to-GDP ratio was only paused for a single year, on the peak of an economic boom in 1989, but it was rising to new heights

again in 1990, and it surpassed 130 percent in 1993. It was in this dis-
heartening situation that the decision about creating a common European
currency arrived and Belgium looked very far from being able to fulfill the
fiscal criteria for accessing the monetary union.

In 1993, the government embarked on a renewed consolidation effort.
First, it announced a "Global Pact on Employment, Competitiveness, and
Social Security," which included plans to reform and significantly retrench
social security, especially in the field of unemployment benefits (Kuipers
2005, chap. 5; Marier 2008, 89). When this pact failed in the face of fierce
opposition from the social partners, the government put forward a new
"Global Plan" to save the day through limited cuts in pensions (a reduction of the highest pensions and a 1 percent solidarity tax on the highest early retirement benefits), a mix of minor tax increases (raising VAT
by a percentage point; increasing excise rates on alcohol, tobacco, and
energy; and introducing a new real estate tax) and one-off measures like
the sale of the central bank's gold reserves and privatization (IMF 2005;
Kuipers 2005, chap. 5; Marier 2008, 89–90). While these measures managed to further improve the primary balance by the late 1990s, they—once
again—achieved little in terms of closing the gaping deficit of the social
security sector. In the following year, plans were discussed to increase the
financial viability of the pension system through an increase of the retirement age, higher taxes on the highest pensions, and a decrease in civil servants' pensions, but when the unions expressed their disapproval, the plan
was dropped (Anderson et al. 2007, 331; Marier 2008, 90–124). This 1994
attempt to rebalance the social security sector proved to be the last one
ever since.[3]

Nevertheless, the headline deficit figures improved significantly in the
second half of the 1990s as the external financial environment dramatically changed for the better. Interest rates sharply dropped across Europe,
and the interest burden on the budget melted away from its peak at 12
percent of the GDP in 1990 to under 7 percent in 2000 and further to
around 3 percent in 2010. The fiscal efforts of the 1980s and 1990s finally
bore fruit: high primary surpluses translated into a balanced budget and
Belgium's debt-to-GDP ratio started to rapidly decrease without further
fiscal adjustments. By the late 2000s, just before the global financial and
economic crisis struck, the debt-to-GDP ratio was back at 87 percent.
Thanks to its steadfastness in controlling its public consumption and
investment expenses and to the fortuitous change in interest rates, Belgium
was saved—and managed to enter the monetary union with the first group

of countries—despite its inability to tackle the enormous problems of its social security sector.

The next section investigates the political background of policy making in this period to explain this curious, lopsided fiscal effort, which combined the greatest rigor with remarkable lack of progress on the issue of consolidating the social security sector either through significant retrenchment or through revenue increases. This policy mix inflicted considerable fiscal pain on the country while it simultaneously jeopardized fiscal stability through relentless debt accumulation. Belgium escaped acute trouble as conditions on global financial markets turned better just in time to avoid crisis and to meet the requirements for euro-accession. However, its travails are intriguing from the perspective of understanding the political bases of the country's ability or inability to deal with the problem of sustained excessive debt accumulation.

The Societal Bases of Rigor and Recklessness

Belgium's prolonged battle with debt provides a glaring example of the limits of governmental power in resolving acute redistributive conflicts and, thus, in solving budgetary problems. This section demonstrates that successive Belgian governments' maneuvering room in making adjustments to the budget were circumscribed by the preferences of business and different labor groups. Heightened conflict between business and labor about social security excluded the possibility of revenue increases and entitlement cuts, except at times when acute economic troubles forced the two sides to compromise. In 1982, labor groups in the economically more dynamic Flanders, which suffered heavily from the rapid decline in foreign competitiveness, defected from the united labor front defending generous entitlements. They showed themselves to be ready to compromise with business, which was itself in great distress due to the macroeconomic problems Belgium's open economy experienced. This made limited retrenchment and increases in employers' contribution possible. This "reform-coalition" between business and Flemish labor also enabled the government to launch the wave of deflationary reforms that included cuts to collective consumption and investment spending as well as measures insulating monetary matters from fiscal problems.

However, this coalition was short-lived. The first wave of reforms averted the most acute danger to foreign competitiveness, and fiscal problems ceased to directly bear on the welfare of labor or business. As a result, the unified labor front was restored in its rejection to retrenchment to social security, while business was more concerned with the size of social contributions than with the deficit of the social security sector. In this situation, all that successive governments could do was to step up their efforts in cutting expenditures that had less direct impact on the interests of well-delineable social groups. The resultant dramatic shrinking of funds available for public consumption and investment contributed greatly to the heightening of regional conflict between Flanders and Wallonia over the distribution of such funds, but it had no bearing on the conflict between labor and business and, thus, on the social security issue, which proved to be impossible to solve ever since.

Conflicts and Commonalities of Interests and Social Coalitions

Social security was the focal point of political wrangling over fiscal stabilization in Belgium not only because the fiscal imbalances of the sector were massive—they amounted to more than a tenth of the GDP in the early 1980s—but because its architecture strongly polarized the interests of contributors and beneficiaries. As in all Bismarckian welfare states, the social security system in Belgium was designed to provide generous, contribution-based entitlements to workers from funds generated by payroll taxes that directly increase the costs of labor (Hemerijk and Visser 2000). Unlike in arrangements where general tax revenues dissipate some of the welfare costs across society and allow for more undifferentiated burden-sharing in consolidation efforts, losses from benefit reductions or revenue increases in this contribution-based setup fall squarely on one group, creating incentives for each side to demand solutions that place the entire burden of consolidation on the other side.

Yet, in 1982, both cuts and revenue-increasing measures were successfully enacted under the Special Powers Act. When sacrifices hurt most—at the peak of unemployment and in the midst of a wave of bankruptcies—they were made. It was later in the decade, when growth and profitability picked up, unemployment somewhat subsided and the opposing sides could have better afforded to thrash out a compromise that front lines hardened and further reform proved elusive. Successive governments put forward proposals that favored business interest by seeking to rebalance the system exclusively through entitlement cuts. These invariably failed in the face of fierce union opposition.

At first sight, this pattern of discord and compromise simply confirms the importance of "crisis" in fostering compromise noted by several experts of Belgian politics (Pochet 2004, Kuipers 2005). The compromises of 1982 were achieved in the context of economic emergency. High inflation had fueled serious problems with international competitiveness from the time Belgium joined the fixed exchange rate system of the EMS in 1979, causing a catastrophic rise in unemployment and a wave of bankruptcies. In 1982, problems culminated in a currency crisis. Taming inflation—to restore international competitiveness and to strengthen the credibility of the fixed exchange rate—required immediate macroeconomic stabilization, especially the consolidation of public finances.

However, the crisis narrative conceals the fact that different sections of Belgian society had different incentives to compromise their fiscal interests in the economic emergency of 1982, depending on how much their welfare depended on the country's international competitiveness. Macroeconomic stabilization was very urgent for businesses and workers in the economically more dynamic Flanders because they could reasonably hope that sales, profits, and employment would rebound if the inflationary pressures subsided. Rapidly declining Wallonia, on the other hand, had such profound long-term problems due to its outdated industrial structure that macroeconomic consolidation in itself was unlikely to improve the Walloon economy enough to compensate for fiscal sacrifices. It was the shared interests of Flemish labor and business in international economic competitiveness that gave rise to a powerful social coalition in support of the stabilization package of 1982. The acquiescence of Flemish workers in moderate welfare cuts was particularly important in enabling the compromise on social security because strikes by Walloon workers only had no chance of successfully blocking reform.

The Flemish competitiveness coalition did not last. After the first wave of stabilization had improved macroeconomic conditions and businesses and employment somewhat recovered in the second half of the 1980s, the incentives for further compromise evaporated. The front lines hardened again as Flemish labor reverted to its alliance with Walloon labor and business started demanding cuts to labor-cost increasing contributions. Despite ever more alarming debt accumulation, significant reform to the social security sector was unfeasible because the debt problem ceased to have direct bearing on economic conditions. Inflation had been brought under control, and it was insulated from fiscal problems through institutional changes that ensured the independence of the central bank. Even the announcement of plans for a monetary union and the adoption of the Maastricht criteria for membership failed to change this situation, despite the importance of accession for business and labor in the more dynamic export-oriented regions. The previous decade had shown that the government could effectively improve the primary balance by cutting collective consumption and investment expenditure whenever reforms to social security failed, weakening the urgency for compromise on this divisive redistributive issue.

In sum, the politics of consolidation were governed by developments along two dimensions. Class conflict over the issue was particularly acute due to the polarizing nature of the social security architecture. However, regional divisions—especially within the ranks of labor—modulated class conflict depending on the extent to which fiscal problems bore on economic performance. Workers in economically healthy Flanders had a strong incentive to compromise for the sake of eliminating the negative economic side effects of debt. These incentives induced them to defect from their alliance with labor in persistently declining Wallonia whenever their employment prospects were endangered by macroeconomic imbalances. A coalition between business and Flemish labor was strong enough to trump opposition not only from Walloon workers, who were especially strongly wedded to the welfare safety net due to the hopeless state of the Walloon economy, but also from any other interest group that might have had a stake in blocking cuts to collective consumption or investment expenditure. However, the reforms launched by this temporary coalition in 1982 eliminated the link between fiscal and macroeconomic problems, making it possible for class conflict to dominate the strategic context of consolidation for the rest of the 1980s and 1990s.

The Observable Manifestations of Evolving Coalitions: The Behavior of Parties, Unions, and Employers' Organizations

This analysis of conflicts and commonalities of interest across groups in society and their effect on the formation of social coalitions is consistent with the behavior of different political actors in this period. Clusters of labor and business interests were represented by an intricate web of institutional actors in the partisan and the corporatist sphere, which allowed the commonalities and conflicts of interests between the different clusters play out in a complicated arrangement within the political scene. Yet, patterns of government coalitions and trade union behavior in the 1980s and early 1990s clearly reflect the détente between business and some labor groups at the height of economic troubles, the role of Flemish labor in making this compromise possible, and the renewed straining of class relations after the most pressing economic problems were addressed and Flemish labor restored the unity of the labor front. Showing this requires a brief intro-duction of the Belgian political system first.

The Belgian party system had been historically structured around three sets of cleavages—religious issues, acute class conflict and regional-linguistic differences—and thus came to be dominated by Christian-Democratic, Liberal, and Socialist parties with a Flemish-speaking and a francophone party in each ideological family[4] (Deschouwer 2009). For most of the 1980s, the Christian Democrats dominated elections due to their overwhelming electoral strength in Flanders, drawing on a mixed constituency of labor, business, and the self-employed in the economically more dynamic areas (De Winter 1996, Claeys 1996). Socialists were not far behind—in fact, they pulled ahead of the Christian Democrats in the 1987 elections—enjoying solid support in the declining heavy industrial areas of Wallonia and pockets of heavy industry in Flanders around Antwerp and Ghent (Delwit 1996). Liberals were firmly in third place throughout the decade, relying on the steady electoral support of relatively younger, better educated, white-collar employees, managers, and self-employed from the economically most dynamic areas of Flanders, Wallonia, and the Brussels area alike (Fitzmaurice 1996).[5]

The trade union movement was also divided along ideological lines, but all three unions—Christian, Socialist, and Liberal—retained their national unity, despite different linguistic proportions within their memberships. The Christian union was the largest of the three, and its membership was biased towards Flemish speakers. The Socialist was a close second, with a balanced membership across the two linguistic communities. Lib-eral unions were rather insignificant (Claeys 1996; Marier 2008). On the employers' side, a single national organization participated in the system of social partnership, representing enterprises on both sides of the linguistic divide, but this organization was in competition with an alternative Flem-ish organization for the support of Flemish business. The social partners wielded policy influence in their institutionalized roles in administering the social security funds and participating in the National Labor Coun-cil or in the Central Economic Council. More importantly, however, they achieved power through cultivating strong ties with the political parties, achieving synergies from the mobilization capacity and the electoral power of their membership.

In this setup, the Christian Democrats (especially the successful Flem-ish party) and the Christian union represented the pivot in the conflict between different labor groups and business over the social security issue.

The standpoints of Liberals and Socialists were clear on each end of the spectrum. Liberal parties and the employers' organization pushed for the retrenchment of social security on behalf of business. Socialist parties and the Socialist trade unions fought tooth and nail for keeping entitlements to protect the interests of pensioners as well as workers in declining areas stricken by long-term unemployment. In contrast, the Flemish Christian Democratic parties and the Christian union faced hard dilemmas. The Flemish Christian Democrats were confronted with contradicting demands from their varied constituencies: businesses clamored for lower social security contributions, whereas labor was wedded to entitlements. To make things more complicated, businesses themselves worried that a too aggressive stand on retrenchment might trigger large-scale labor unrest at a time they were barely coping (Jones 2008, 170). These contradicting demands were directly represented in the party's decision-making as the different Christian Democratic constituencies (usually referred to as *standen*) exerted influence on the party's policy choices not only via electoral channels but also through their representatives within the party.[6] The Christian union was ambivalent between compromising with employers for the sake of better employment opportunities, which would have benefited its Flemish majority, and the defense of social entitlements, which was in the interest of all of its members, but was especially crucial to the Walloon minority. The political balance of power and the fate of social security hinged on the behavior of these pivotal actors not only because they represented something of a middle ground in the conflict but also because they represented such powerful forces in the partisan and corporatist spheres.

The stance of these actors evolved with the changes in the economic environment. At the beginning of the 1980s, Christian Democrats had been governing with the Socialists for a decade. With the deepening of the economic, monetary, and fiscal crisis, the government came under increasing pressure to adjust policies, but intragovernmental disagreements about policy reform caused cabinets to fall in rapid succession. In 1981, the government was about to put into place a "Disaster Plan" to restore macroeconomic stability, but it foundered on Socialist resistance to pension cuts. It was in this situation that Christian unions started to signal their readiness to support painful reforms for the sake of economic recovery. In secret negotiations with the Flemish Christian Democratic leadership, they consented to breaking up the Christian-Democratic-Socialists coalition and to forming a new government with the Liberals. This secret consent given by trade union leaders only became known to the wider public in 1991 (Jones 2008, 188). In an economic recovery plan, the Christian unions also laid out some welfare sacrifices they would be willing to accept to ensure the success of this new coalition in putting forward a stabilization package (Jones 2008, 170–71). The new Christian-Democratic and Liberal coalition passed the Special Powers Act in 1982, which represented a compromise as cuts to social security were balanced by increased social contributions. Socialist parties protested and Socialist unions organized strikes, but the Christian unions kept their promise and refrained from striking, rendering Socialist protest ineffectual. Importantly, the reforms met with the approval of the constituencies of the political actors involved, despite the secrecy surrounding the initial negotiations about political and policy changes. Christian union leaders faced no backlash for not joining the Socialist strikes in opposition to welfare cuts; Christian Democrats got more votes in the next elections, while the Liberals maintained their vote share. The new political alliance between these actors was supported by a social coalition between business and Flemish labor.

This social coalition did not survive for long, though. Although the Christian Democratic and Liberal government coalition lived on after the 1985 elections and continued to push for further consolidation, the tacit alliance with the Christian unions disintegrated and further reforms to social security proved elusive. Christian unions had much weaker incentives to consent to further sacrifices on behalf of their members after the threat to international competitiveness had been successfully averted, growth gradually picked up, and unemployment started to decline in Flanders (Jones 2008, 52). Liberals and business constituencies of the Christian Democrats were also less willing to tolerate high social security contributions. The coalition adopted the so-called St. Anna Plan in 1986, which included heavy cuts in the unemployment insurance, limited the accumulation of benefits, and decreased the level of future pensions, with no corresponding sacrifices from businesses' side. Christian unions strongly objected and this time they did join the Socialist unions in the mobilization for strikes. The government had to resign not long afterwards due to pressure from the Christian workers movement on the leadership of the Christian Democratic Party to break with the Liberals (Marier 2008, 88). The St. Anna Plan remained unexecuted (Anderson et al. 2007, 325).

The new elections in 1987 only reinforced the significance of class conflict in structuring the political scene. The Christian Democrats lost votes to the Socialists in Wallonia, who now wielded the strongest electoral force in the country, and to the Liberals in Flanders, who continued to siphon off Flemish Christian Democratic voters from then on (Fitzmaurice 1996). The Socialists and the Christian Democrats were in government together again. The Socialists made sure that cuts to the social security system were off the agenda for the rest of the decade. In fact, they even achieved some corrections in entitlements that had not been indexed under the previous governments. The Flemish Christian Democrats could not confront them without alienating their labor section. At the same time, they were sorely conscious of losing business support to the Liberals and, thus, (successfully) sought to decrease the fiscal pressure on businesses. The Christian-Democratic and Socialist coalition survived until 1999.

In 1993, while in coalition with the Socialists, the Flemish Christian Democrats seized upon the emergency generated by the combination of monetary integration, a disastrous fiscal situation, and a recession to try to broker a "historic compromise" between labor and business. The Global Pact on Employment, Competitiveness and Social Security[7] was to solve the persistent imbalances of social security, decrease the cost of labor, and help make sure that fiscal problems would be resolved in time for the euro deadline. Unsurprisingly, it also promised to resolve the conflict that was breaking the Flemish Christian Democrats' constituency apart. The odds of a breakthrough seemed better than ever because of the major challenges the country was facing. First, joining the euro with the first group of countries was of immense importance to the Flemish economy, which was so dependent on competitiveness in the European markets. Second, the recession had increased unemployment—although mostly in Wallonia, less significantly in Flanders—and created problems for business. Third, debt reached truly alarming proportions and borrowing was still high.

In the event, the "Global Pact" failed spectacularly, proving the crisis discourse of the government and the reference to the country's problems ineffectual in the absence of direct incentives for labor and business to make painful sacrifices. Euro accession had real urgency, but it was far from clear that better fiscal figures could only come from social security reform, given the decade-long experience with successive governments finding ever-newer savings through cuts in public consumption and investment. In Flanders, the slump in employment and growth was much less serious than the economic troubles of the late 1970s and early 1980s, while Wallonia was much harder hit (Dejemeppe-Saks 2002). Moreover, in the low-inflation environment of the early 1990s, it was much less clear that fiscal consolidation would be a remedy to economic problems than in the early 1980s when the link between exchange rate troubles, inflation, and fiscal policy was much more obvious. Finally, in the absence of any indication of a looming debt crisis, debt was not of immediate concern to either business or labor.

This lack of pressing motivation for compromise is evident both in the design of the "Global Pact" that was put forward by the government and in the response by unions. Presumably as a result of the desperation of the Flemish Christian Democrats to win back the business support they had been losing to the Liberals, the proposal presented to the public was tailored entirely to business' liking and offered little to labor by way of a compromise. The unions had been involved in preliminary bargaining, but their demands were left out of the final draft (Kuipers 2005, chap. 5; Marier 2008, 89). The proposal contained plans to reform the structure and administration of the social security system, to make it more selective, to limit expenditures, and, thus, to restore the system's financial balance. It was especially in the field of unemployment benefits that substantial retrenchment of entitlements was to take place. Simultaneously, the plan proposed to decrease social security contributions on specific types of employment in order to decrease the costs of labor for business. If the Flemish Democrats were hoping that they would be able to strike a similar deal with the Christian unions as in the early 1980s, they seriously miscalculated. Even if Christian union leaders had been inclined to further negotiate about the pact, they had no other choice than to reject this unbalanced pact under immense pressure across the board from the rank and file for strikes (Kuipers 2005 p97). In the face of united labor opposition, the pact could not survive.

The Enduring Problems of a Fiscally Polarized Polity

Remarkably, the "Global Pact" of 1993 has been the last attempt to rebalance social security despite persistent (and, in the recent years, further widening) deficits of the sector. The precipitous fall of interest rates since the 1990s stopped and reversed the snowballing of debt, reducing the urgency of the issue and allowing it to be shelved. Nothing demonstrates better that social security ceased to be a sore point of Belgian politics than the fact that Liberals and Socialists were able to form a coalition in 1999—ejecting the Christian Democrats from government for the first time since the Second World War—and they successfully governed together through 2007.

As class conflict cooled, interregional differences took center stage. Party competition has revolved ever more intensely around the protection of the regional interests, especially in Flanders, where increasing attention has been directed to the unequal contributions to and benefits received from the public purse across regions. The Flemish political discourse first started to focus on the unequal fiscal capacities between regions after a number of studies showed that Flanders was paying the bills of high unemployment and disproportionately high health costs in Wallonia in the second half of the 1980s (Kuipers 2006; Marier 2008; Beland and Lecours 2008). The issue then increasingly gained ethnic overtones as structural unemployment plaguing Wallonia and the inability to control health care costs started to be traced back to factors like "bad life habits" or a "culture of dependency" (Beland and Lecours 2005). As the growing successes of separatist parties like Volksunie and Vlaams Blok/Belang highlighted the electoral appeal of Flemish nationalism, Flemish Liberals rebranded their party as protectors of Flemish interest (Jones 2008, 205). Christian Democrats followed suit and entered into electoral cooperation with the openly separatist New Flemish Alliance (Jones 2008, 218). By 2010, the New Flemish Alliance was winning the elections on its own.

The dramatic shrinking of funds for public consumption and investment in the 1980s surely contributed to the intensifying of this conflict. Tension between the two linguistic communities and, thus, the two regions had been an important factor in Belgian political life in the postwar period,[8] but the divisions had not gained economic-redistributive relevance before the 1980s (Beland and Lecours 2008, 153). The intensification of cross-regional tensions led to a series of constitutional reforms that separated the financing of collective consumption and investment expenditures between the regions and devolved decision-making to the regional level.[9] It also led to increasingly insistent calls from Flemish political actors for the regional splitting of social security. Unsurprisingly, the Walloon side has used its constitutional veto to stop further devolution, as no political actor in Wallonia can agree to reforms that reduce interregional transfers that increase the per capita disposable income of an average Walloon household by more than 8 percent (Caruso et al. 2002).

This had grave consequences for the country's political stability. The question of state reform is threatening to break up the country, and it has dramatically increased political uncertainty, best exemplified by how astonishingly long coalition formation takes after each election (nine months in 2007 and 541 days after the 2010 elections.). At the same time, the shift to regionally motivated politics also has serious implications for the issue of social security reform. Political attention is no longer centered on how the imbalances of the redistributive system can be resolved but whose problem they should be. Flanders could operate a balanced system (without having to ask business to pay more in or labor to take less out). Wallonia would be bankrupt because it is unlikely to be able to borrow the necessary funds to finance the enormous discrepancy between contributions generated and entitlements drawn by its population. In a sense, this would resolve the issue, but at the price of possibly breaking up the country and bankrupting half of it.

The immense political turmoil of the past years—in the midst of years of serious financial and economic crisis—reveals the costs of the persistent failure of Belgian society to renegotiate existing terms of redistribution in the past four decades. Although favorable changes in interest rates freed the country from the chokehold of debt in the 1990s and decreased the price of the conflict in fiscal terms, the political costs remain. Decades of class strife—in which labor and business were able to insulate themselves from the negative side-effects of debt and dig in their heels in protect-ing their polarized interests—are now followed by intense regional con-flict in another negative sum game. In view of the veto that constitutional arrangements guarantee to the two communities, this conflict is unlikely to be resolved as long as the Kingdom of Belgium exists, but its intensity does not seem to subside. It fuels continuous political uncertainty. During the global financial and economic crisis, strong control over collective con-sumption spending and the continuation of low interest rates limited the damage to public finances. The debt-to-GDP ratio grew by only 20 per-centage points in the past eight years to 107 percent. However, unfavorable changes in interest rates could easily plunge the country into similar fiscal troubles as in the early 1980s. With politics paralyzed by the issue of state reform, the country would be ill-prepared to deal with such an emergency or, in fact, with the economic hardships and emerging problems of popula-tion aging that are already on the horizon.

Ireland and the Benefits of TINA

The Irish case provides an interesting contrast—and a useful shadow case—to the Belgian one. Ireland was hit by similar fiscal and economic shocks as Belgium in the late 1970s and early 1980s, but it dealt with them much more effectively. Just like Belgium, it adopted a sizeable deflation-ary and fiscal adjustment package in 1982, which proved to be similarly insufficient in the face of ballooning interest costs and only succeeded in slowing, but not reversing, debt growth. Unlike Belgium, however, Ireland soon responded to this situation by renewed efforts, which affected many of those areas of the budget that the previous consolidation package had not and set the debt-to-GDP ratio on a steep downward path well before the fall of interest rates, and the famous growth spurt of the Celtic Tiger helped further lighten the debt burden.

This section explains that Ireland was better able to adjust its fiscal policies because economic pressures made fiscal stabilization equally urgent, but there was much more limited room for wrangling over the distribution of fiscal sacrifices due to the structure of conflicts and commonalities of interest within society. It shows that successive governments were able to make a wide range of adjustments to spending and taxes that affected households across society because the large majority of society had a crucial economic stake in swift stabilization, but could not hope to be spared of the sacrifices necessary to make it happen. Policy makers could convincingly use the "there is no alternative" argument. This section also briefly reflects on the way Ireland has been dealing with the debt problem that it encountered in recent years as a result of its banking crisis to demonstrate that enduring patterns of societal interests give rise to similar pathways of fiscal stabilization today as in the 1980s.

Just like in Belgium, the fiscal troubles of the 1980s were ushered in by the oil crises in Ireland, too. Having amassed a considerable debt stock in the 1950s and 1960s, Ireland had been successfully decreasing its debt-to-GDP ratio for a decade when things turned sour in the mid-1970s. As growth slowed and unemployment increased, the government experimented with fiscal stimulus in vain (Honohan 1999). As a result, debt surged. By 1980, the debt-to-GDP ratio had grown to 67 percent from a low of 40 percent in 1973. When interest rates shot up in the early 1980s, the debt started to snowball at alarming speed. Within two years, the debt-to-GDP ratio was over 80 percent.

In 1982, Ireland embarked on stabilization. It broke with Keynesian stimulus and embraced austerity. VAT and personal income taxes were increased, while public investments and food subsidies were radically reduced (Alesina and Perotti 1996; Honohan 1992 and 1999). This achieved a 6-percentage point improvement in the structurally adjusted primary balance. However, this was not enough to counterbalance the growth of the interest burden and, therefore, only succeeded in significantly slowing, but not reversing, the accumulation of debt (Honohan 1992; IMF 1998). By 1987, the debt-to-GDP ratio was at 109 percent. Consequently, a renewed effort was made. The government wage bill was significantly squeezed via a hiring freeze and below-inflation wage increases, transfers were cut, and spending on infrastructure investments were further reduced (Alesina and Perotti 1996; Honohan 1992 and 1999). This tightening in spending was complemented by a tax reform in 1988 that widened the tax base but decreased marginal tax rates both on corporate and personal incomes and by a one-off increase in revenues due to a tax amnesty (Giavazzi and Pagano 1990; Alesina and Perotti 1996). These measures succeeded in setting the debt-to-GDP ratio on a firm downward path for the longer term. Within the next five years, the debt-to-GDP ratio decreased by 20 percentage points to 88 percent in 1992. Then, with the drop in interest rates and the high growth of the Celtic Tiger years, it fell precipitously, plunging to 36 percent in 2000 and to 24 percent in 2007, the last year before the banking crisis.

Biting the Bullet: The Societal Bases of Resolute Stabilization

The steadfastness of the stabilization efforts is understandable in light of the large corollary harm that fiscal problems were inflicting on Ireland's open economy and on Irish society. Budgetary imbalances fueled inflation, which had a devastating effect on the competitiveness of Irish firms after 1979 when Ireland fixed its exchange rates to those of its lower-inflation European trading partners in the framework of the European Monetary System. Unemployment climbed from 7.8 percent in 1979 to a high of 16.8 percent by 1985, average growth in the 1980s was a third lower than in the preceding decade. Problems with competitiveness directly affected firms and workers in exporting and import-competing sectors but also had indirect repercussions for the sheltered sectors through the decline of domestic demand. Inflation also hurt sections of society whose livelihood was not directly dependent on the health of the economy. Public sector workers repeatedly ran into the problem of wrestling nominal wage increases from the government only to end up with lower take-home pay due to the joint effect of high inflation and fiscal drag (Baccaro and Lim 2007). People dependent on transfers saw the real value of those transfers melt away. No parts of the Irish economy and society were fully immune to the problems generated by inflation, which explains the resolute commitment to deflationary policies throughout the decade.

What bears more explanation, however, is how uncontentious the actual austerity measures were. They placed the entire burden on households while completely sparing business, and yet there was almost no protest from those who were asked to bear the pain. Neither of the packages attempted to increase the fiscal pressure on business. The tax reform that accompanied the stabilization package of 1987 even cut corporate tax rates from 47 to 43 percent (Alesina and Perotti 1996). Measures affecting the income of households, on the other hand, were bold and comprehensive.

Austerity encompassed VAT and personal tax increases, cuts in food subsidies, large reductions in social transfers, and a rollback of public employment and wages. Apart from the tax reform of 1988, which put a stop to the constant increase of tax pressure on households, all the adjustments of the decade required newer and newer painful sacrifices from large swaths of society. Yet, none triggered major social upheaval and few encountered major political resistance.

The exemption of business from fiscal sacrifices can be explained with the dependence of the Irish economy on foreign firms. From the late 1950s, Ireland had increasingly opened up to foreign direct investment and sought to lure investors with tax advantages, for example the Export Profits Tax Relief of 1956, which exempted export profits from half and then all of corporate taxation, or the setting of a uniform low, 10-percent tax rate on profits earned in manufacturing in 1978 (Barry 1999). By 1973, foreign firms accounted for a third of manufacturing employment and their share continued to grow to 50 percent by the 2000s (Kirby 2010). Increasing corporate taxation would have risked reversing the favorable trend in foreign direct investment inflows, causing employment to drop even further at a time of surging unemployment. Therefore, it was not in labor's interest to push for greater burden sharing by business.

With businesses spared, households had to bear the fiscal pain, and they had little incentive to delay the inevitable by arguing about how that pain should be distributed among them. The majority of Irish society could not realistically hope to avoid making sacrifices and therefore had no stake in resisting any austerity package when another was likely to hit it in similar fashion. Rebalancing the budget required very large adjustments and was thus bound to involve significant cuts to some or all of the largest expenditures items (like transfers and public employment) and/ or large, across-the-board tax increases. Most of these measures would affect much of the population fairly uniformly. Irish society was bound to choose "solidaristic" solutions because it was not possible to design austerity packages that would shield large sections of society and still successfully close the fiscal gap.

The reason for this lies in the relative homogeneity of society and the pattern of existing policies, which did not generate large differences in vested interests. Limited income dispersion was an important aspect of social homogeneity. Although income inequality within the Irish population was large in comparison with the rest of Europe, this was caused mostly by a "long thin tail" of the distribution towards higher incomes, but the overwhelming majority of society was concentrated at the low-end of the income scale (McDonough and Dundon 2010). Because of this, tax increases and cuts in food subsidies had similar effect on the bulk of the population. Small income dispersion and the architecture of the welfare system also led to fairly uniform interests concerning social security across the majority of society. In the Irish Beveridge-style system, fairly meager contribution-based insurance benefits were matched by tax-financed assistance benefits for those who did not qualify for insurance, with the entire system centrally operated by the government (Callan and Nolan 2000; McCashin and O'Shea 2009). This precluded insider-outsider conflicts between those who earned eligibility and those who did not. Furthermore, due to the historical origins of the system, agrarian groups and the urban working class enjoyed many of the same benefits (McCashin and O'Shea 2009). Thus, the large majority of society was affected by cuts in social transfers fairly uniformly.

Public servants were the only larger group that had interests distinct from the rest of society. They did try to claim immunity from cuts to their income: even as late as 1986, a teachers' strike still averted a public sector pay freeze. Eventually, their resistance was relaxed, though, and they agreed to a hiring and wage stop in 1987. While it is questionable how long they would have been able to hold their own in the face of large sacrifices demanded from the large majority of the population, public sector workers also had an important material reason to acquiesce in bearing part of the pain of austerity. By 1987, they had repeatedly experienced that continuing inflation and fiscal drag counteracted the effect of any nominal wage increases they achieved in negotiations with the government and left them with ever-lower purchasing power (Baccaro and Lim 2007). Under these circumstances, they were better off with a deal that froze public sector pay but implied lower inflation and involved a tax reform. Thus, by 1987, there was no significant area of public finances outside of corporate taxation that had not been adjusted for the sake of stopping debt growth.

Parties, Unions, and Austerity

These societal foundations of Ireland's experience with fiscal stabilization were clearly mirrored in the stance of the most important political actors: the two major parties, *Fianna Fail* and *Fine Gael*, and the labor movement, encompassing the Labor Party and the unions. Given the untouchability of business due to the dependence of the country on foreign investors, no political actor could single out a group to pay for stabilization outside of its supporter base. At the same time, the economic emergency generated by the decline in competitiveness made stabilization equally urgent for the supporters of every significant political player. Therefore, all political actors embraced austerity after some posturing and took turns in putting into place the painful measures that affected the majority of society.

The two major parties relied on the support of almost identical cross-class constituencies (Donaghey and Tegue 2007). *Fianna Fail* and *Fine Gael*—who between them shared more than 80 percent of the vote in the 1970s and 1980s—drew support from all corners of society, and their voter bases exhibited negligible regional or socio-economic differences (McAllister and O'Connell 1984; Farrell 1999).[10] The Labor Party remained a very distant third, small and overshadowed by *Fianna Fail* both in getting the working class vote and in nurturing links with trade unions (Sinnott 1984; Mair 1990). Given the lack of differentiation of their voters, the two large parties never focused their strategies on kindling (re)distributive conflicts. Their programs had been virtually indistinguishable on economic and social issues in the decades preceding the 1980s (Sinnott 1976; Laver and Hunt 1992). In the face of mounting fiscal troubles in the 1980s, neither party could credibly promise to large groups of voters to find a solution that would shield them from fiscal pain. This strengthened their hands because delay would only increase the magnitude of the problem and force them to inflict even greater pain on their supporters. Moreover, neither large party needed to fear long-term negative electoral repercussions, as it was clear that no alternative strategy was available to either their main rival or to potential political entrepreneurs seeking to enter the political market.

After a brief period of wrangling, *Fine Gael* launched the first wave of stabilization in coalition with the Labor Party. They had already presented parliament with an austerity budget that contained large tax increases in 1981, but that package famously foundered on the resistance of independent members of parliament to the symbolic issue of taxing children's shoes, bringing the government down (Honohan 1999; Hallerberg 2004). After new elections, *Fianna Fail* took over the government and proposed a budget with significant spending cuts, but it lacked the necessary external support to have it passed. After yet another round of elections in 1982, the new *Fine Gael* and Labor coalition was strong enough to pass a budget with significant tax increases and some spending cuts (Alesina and Perotti 1996; Honohan 1999).

Fianna Fail was to launch the second wave of fiscal tightening in 1987. Although it had campaigned for an end to austerity in the 1987 election, it initiated major cuts to the public wage bill, transfers, and investments as soon as it formed a (minority) government (Giavazzi and Pagano 1990; Alesina and Perotti 1996). This second round of stabilization took place in an atmosphere of remarkable partisan consensus as the main opposition party, *Fine Gael*, decided to externally support it in parliamentary voting.[11]

Political consensus behind fiscal stabilization also manifested itself in the emergence of an important social pact: the Program for National Recovery in 1987. Endorsement by the unions lent further legitimacy to the austerity measures and guaranteed the commitment of public sector workers to wage restraint (Marsh and Mitchell 1999; Culpepper 2008). The consent of the labor movement to an essentially neoliberal stabilization package revealed union leaders' conviction that such sacrifices were inevitable. They had learned from their inability to achieve real welfare improvements for their members throughout the 1980s that insisting on higher nominal wages in a high-inflation environment was a self-defeating strategy. They contented themselves with tax cuts in return for losses in transfers and for wage restraint, accepting that this was the most they could accomplish for workers in the given situation (Dellapiane and Hardiman 2012).[12]

The various political actors calculated well in embracing austerity. Voting data shows that the eagerness of the major parties to inflict fiscal pain did not alienate their supporters. Vote shares stayed mostly stable in the 1980s. There was only one exception: *Fine Gael*'s vote did plunge in 1987, the first election after the first round of fiscal tightening started in 1982. However, this is unlikely to be a punishment for the party's espousal of austerity. Rather, it reflects a disappointment with its failure to definitively address the debt problem because the votes lost by *Fine Gael* went to the newly formed Progressive Democrats who embraced fiscal rectitude more openly than any of the old parties (Mair 1990). Voters condoned austerity. Unions also benefited from cooperating in the second round of tightening as their membership started to increase again after a long period of decline. Irish society did not seem to resent its political class for fiscal pain even though the rise of the Celtic Tiger and the spectacular dividends of fiscal stabilization could not be foreseen at the time.

Enduring Foundations of Effective Stabilization

Two decades after the breakthrough that helped Ireland reassert control over its debt, the country faces immense fiscal problems once again in the wake of a severe economic and financial crisis. From a low of 24 percent in 2007, debt surged to a high of 120 percent in 2012 as a result of a catastrophic bank bailout scheme, the collapse of tax revenues, and surging expenditures. The policy response was remarkably similar to the one given to similar problems in the 1980s, both in its resoluteness and in its composition. As soon as the first imbalances appeared, a first austerity package was put into place in 2008, and it was progressively reinforced with successive measures when the proportions of fiscal problems fully revealed themselves. Stabilization affected large swathes of society without much differentiation, while mostly shielding the corporate sector. Welfare spending and public wage expenditures were substantially cut and income taxes, as well as VAT, increased (Dellapiane and Hardiman 2012). The debt-to-GDP ratio subsided under 100 percent in 2015 and is forecast to decline further in the coming years (Ameco).

Just like in the 1980s, adjustment has gone practically unchallenged across the political spectrum. The austerity program launched in 2008 by the *Fianna Fail* government was continued without hesitation by the coalition of *Fine Gael* and the Socialists after *Fianna Fail* was thrown out of government in the 2011 elections. Although unions failed to play the central coordinating and legitimizing role they performed in 1987—in fact, the *Fianna Fail* government deliberately chose to act unilaterally in 2008 and 2009, ignoring the practices of social partnership it had created in the late 1980s—this seemed to make little political difference or to undermine the political legitimacy of painful cuts and tax increases (Culpepper and Regan 2014).

Although the Celtic Tiger years brought impressive prosperity and economic development to Ireland, the underlying social structure and policy arrangements stayed stable enough since the 1980s to still rule out much wrangling in times of fiscal emergency. Overwhelming dependence on foreign investment still precludes increasing the fiscal pressure on businesses, while the interests of households are not polarized enough to make fighting about the design of stabilization worthwhile. The growth of income inequality of the past decades has been limited and was mostly manifested in the upper incomes pulling further away from the rest with middle and lower incomes growing roughly in sync (Nolan and Maitre 2000). The structure of welfare policies stayed roughly the same as before. Consequently, it would still be hard to come up with stabilization packages that place the burden on some groups while spare others, which allows Ireland to be resolute in its austerity efforts.

Conclusion

The Belgian and Irish cases of sustained and substantial debt accumulation in the 1980s demonstrate how important it is for fiscal stabilization that a large portion of society is sensitive to fiscal problems. In both cases, sensitivity to negative side effects arose from exposure to foreign competition. Both the Belgian and the Irish economy are significantly more open than the Italian. With budgetary imbalances fueling inflation, both countries were under considerable pressure to resolve their fiscal issues, which impinged heavily on their ability to compete internationally. This is reflected in the determination with which both countries embarked on fiscal stabilization in the early 1980s—a decade ahead of Italy's first stabilization efforts—drastically improving their primary balances.

At the same time, the comparison of the Belgian and Irish stories also highlighted the role of fiscal polarization in determining the chances for effective and timely fiscal stabilization. In Belgium, the polarizing architecture of social security pitted labor and capital squarely against each other and precluded adjustments to a significant part of the budget. The two sides would cooperate as much as was necessary to keep international competitiveness insulated from fiscal troubles but would not come to a compromise over the gaping hole in social security, which had played such a central role in triggering and fueling Belgium's fiscal problems in the past decades. This prevented Belgium from fully resolving its problems and left it exposed to developments in the financial markets (primarily, changes in interest rates). In contrast, the lack of polarizing fiscal conflicts within the Irish society allowed Ireland to effectively adjust any part of the budget—except for corporate taxation—and to pull itself up by its bootstraps.

The comparison of the two cases also sheds light on the role of institutional structures of policy making in influencing fiscal stabilization. From an institutional perspective, Ireland was worse placed to take decisive action or to engineer the compromises across society needed to make painful changes in the budget. It was ruled by divided coalition or minority governments, and it was lacking effective corporatist mechanisms to handle class conflict. In Belgium, coalition governments were the norm, but a time-honored system of corporatist consultation provided an important centralized forum for engineering compromise. Yet, it was Ireland that managed to effectively make the adjustments to its policies needed to fully regain control over borrowing, while Belgium was mired in debt until exogenous conditions changed. Some of Ireland's successful adjustment efforts involved corporatist consultation, namely the second round of stabilization in 1987, but at other times, like in 1982, they did not, and the last instance of austerity since 2008 took place via an explicit rejection of the system of social partnership. These patterns suggest that it is of lesser importance how the policy-making process is organized than what conflicts of interest need to be reconciled within it.

Finally, comparison of the Irish and Belgian cases also demonstrates the role of policy legacies and path dependence in shaping the underlying conflicts of interests that drive policy making. While the two countries looked back onto different economic histories and had developed very different economic structures, policies inherited from the past also had crucial importance for polarizing preferences towards fiscal stabilization in Belgium and allowing conflicts of interest to remain limited in Ireland. In Belgium, the architecture of social security strongly reinforced class conflict over a very large share of the budget because it provided generous benefits to labor from contributions that bore on business profits. In Ireland, the costs of welfare provision fell on the same social groups that enjoyed the benefits due to the combined effect of limited income dispersion and the complementation of social insurance with tax financed welfare benefits. This meant that any adjustment to the system was bound to affect the same group, reducing the possibility of conflict over this substantial part of public finances.

This chapter, along with the previous one, reviewed the effects of differences in structural variables—exposure to the negative side effects of debt and fiscal polarization—on countries' ability to stabilize their public finances and regain control over excessive debt accumulation. The next chapter approaches the issue from a different angle, to demonstrate the deleterious consequences for sustained large-scale debt accumulation of high levels of distributive polarization and considerable insulation from the negative economic side effects in dramatically different economic, social, and political contexts in Greece and Japan.

FIVE

Fiscal Discord
in Closed Economies

Greece and Japan

Greece and Japan arguably present the two most prominent object lessons about the dangers of sustained excessive debt accumulation. For decades, the two countries failed to properly deal with their fiscal imbalances, which resulted in deleterious debt levels. Greece is now bankrupt, economically destroyed, and at the mercy of foreign lenders, who dictate its policy choices. Japan—currently burdened with a debt stock reaching 250 percent of the gross domestic product—has been severely constrained for the last two decades in its efforts to reorganize its economy and restart growth by a significant debt stock and major fiscal imbalances inherited from the 1970s and 1980s. (Figure 5.1 shows the evolution of the two countries debt stocks since the 1970s.) The comparison of the Greek and Japanese cases highlights the significance of fiscal polarization and limited pressures from international competition in explaining sustained excessive debt accumulation in two countries characterized by very large differences in economic structure and political institutions.

This chapter highlights that, despite very large economic and political differences, the two countries display remarkable similarities in their fiscal patterns. In both countries, fiscal imbalances were initially triggered by politically motivated expansion of spending. Parties in power targeted previously disadvantaged voter groups with new, tailor-made benefits to ensure electoral dominance without counterbalancing the new spending

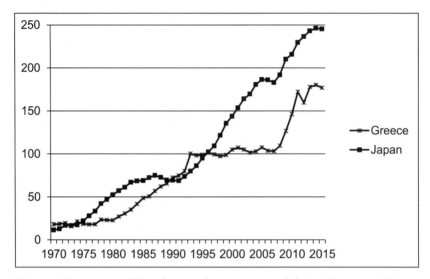

Fig. 5.1. Gross consolidated general government debt in Greece and Japan from 1970 to 2015. Source: Ameco.

with additional taxes or spending cuts elsewhere to avoid alienating the beneficiaries of existing spending and tax arrangements. In Greece, the new left-wing government extended access to public sector jobs, pension entitlements, and state aid to previously "underprivileged" groups in the 1980s, but it failed to curtail access to these benefits for old beneficiaries or to reform taxes and improve tax collection to raise the necessary revenues to pay for the explosion in spending. In Japan, the dominant Liberal Democrats introduced new welfare benefits in the late 1970s to expand their voter base to the urban working class—in response to the shrinking of their rural constituency of farmers and small producers—but they also zealously guarded the tax advantages and the pork-barrel benefits that guaranteed the continued support of their traditional rural supporters. The large structural imbalances created by the new policies were subsequently greatly magnified by economic and demographic shocks in both countries.

In the face of debt growth, successive governments attempted to address the obvious unsustainability of the fiscal trends early on. There were repeated attempts at fiscal reform starting from the mid-1980s in both countries, but politicians retreated and reforms were abandoned in the face of resistance from the groups whose electoral allegiance was crucial to retaining political power. In Greece, successive governments abandoned their efforts to reverse the expansion of the public sector and pensions after it became clear that such attempts meant electoral suicide; and policy makers never even seriously attempted to address the evasion of taxes and social security contributions. In Japan, repeated attempts to introduce and then raise consumption taxes triggered intense resistance and generated significant electoral costs, while attempts to retrench welfare or to rein in the flow of funds that kept the rural economy alive were regularly defeated by resistance from within the long-governing Liberal Democratic Party. Unable to make major adjustments to existing fiscal patterns, political actors tried to proceed in piecemeal fashion and were ready to retreat at the first sign of discontent. This, however, meant that adjustments could not keep pace with the speed of debt accumulation. In the face of ever-growing problems, policy makers resorted to accounting tricks and gimmickry in an effort to conceal at least some of the true proportion of their fiscal issues in both countries.

The electoral price of hurting established vested interest groups proved inhibitive in both countries because of the combined effects of fiscal polarization and relative insulation from the pressures of international competition. The existing fiscal structure, which targeted the benefits of significant spending and tax arrangements closely to specific socioeconomic groups, offered many different avenues for rebalancing the budget and gave strong incentives to different voter groups to punish any political force that proposed to solve the fiscal problem at the price of adjusting policies they had vested interests in. At the same time, the promise of fiscal stability failed to generate countervailing electoral gains since the large majority of both societies were insulated from the negative side effects of growing debt. In Greece, most enterprises were oriented towards the domestic markets, where their competitiveness was maintained by exchange rate flexibility and fiscal benefits, such as state aid, tax exemptions, and the tacit toleration of tax evasion. In Japan, the world famous export sector made up a very small part of the economy and was increasingly moving its production capacities abroad. Furthermore, strict control over inflation and policies to counteract the appreciation of the yen neutralized the possible negative side effects of fiscal problems on international competitiveness (Pempel 2010). Domestic markets, on the other hand, were protected by a complex set of regulatory practices. Under these conditions, the overwhelming majority of society had little immediate stake in fiscal stabilization.

Similar levels of fiscal polarization and relative insulation from the pressures of international competition explain the strong similarities of fiscal patterns in these two otherwise so different countries, which alternative explanations cannot account for. Since Greece and Japan drastically differ in virtually every political institution widely considered central to adjustment capacity and/or to fiscal discipline, one or the other case contradicts the predictions of various theories focused on domestic political institutions. Greece is characterized by "strikingly majoritarian" political institutions, which are usually associated with decisive decision-making and strong adjustment capacities[1] (Lijphart et al. 1988, 21; Spolaore 2004) as well as with strong fiscal discipline (Roubini and Sachs 1989; Grilli et al. 1991). Yet, Greece has been remarkably and persistently unable to adjust economic and fiscal policies in the face of obvious challenges in the past four decades, and it has been considered to be one of the most profligate developed countries. Japan's political system has provided more room to the representation of particularistic interests and has, therefore, been more liable to gridlock and to the subjugation of fiscal balance to particularistic demands for benefits and tax advantages.[2] On the other hand, Japan has had a powerful and autonomous state bureaucracy (Johnson 1982), which makes decisive counteraction against debt growth more likely. Moreover, Japan's strong ministry of finance, famous for its fiscal conservatism, has kept strong, centralized control over spending, enforcing strict limits on the demands of different ministries (Wright 1999; Suzuki 2000; van Hagen 2006). In contrast, the state in Greece has traditionally had limited autonomy from societal forces due to the colonization of the bureaucracy by the parties and the entrenched practice of political appointments in a system of "bureaucratic clientelism" (Mavrogordatos 1997). Prior to the mid-1990s, it also had weak finance ministers, who had trouble enforcing spending ceilings (Hallerberg 2004).

The persistence and scope of the two countries' fiscal problems cannot be fully attributed to economic factors either. In Japan, the collapse of growth in the early 1990s created an immensely difficult context for adjustment, as fiscal tightening threatened to undermine growth and make the debt problem worse. However, there are two reasons to consider debt accumulation a policy failure in its own right, rather than just the corollary of economic problems. On the one hand, the fiscal imbalances that produced such deleterious consequences in combination with weak growth since the mid-1990s had persisted throughout the high-growth years of the late 1970s and 1980s, and only subsided slightly in the exuberant bubble-years of the late 1980s, leaving Japan with a fairly high debt-to-GDP ratio by the time the economy turned for the worse. On the other hand, persistent inability to adjust the entrenched policies that fueled the imbalances of the 1970s and 1980s hamstrung efforts to stimulate the economy in the 1990s and 2000s because existing policies channeled stimulus spending into uses that held little promise of kick-starting the economy (Pempel 2010). From that perspective, fiscal issues contributed to, rather than simply resulted from, Japan's stubborn growth problems in the 1990s and 2000s. In Greece, the debt-to-GDP ratio grew dramatically during the 1980s and approximately stabilized at a very high level from the 1990s onwards despite high nominal growth rates and despite a considerable influx of funds from the European Union, much of which directly boosted government revenues.

Finally, although both Japan and Greece were at times liable to international diplomatic pressures regarding their fiscal policies, these pressures pointed to opposite directions in the two cases and seem to have made little difference for policy outcomes in either case. Due to its position as one of the major economic powerhouses of the global economy, Japan has repeatedly come under diplomatic pressure to stimulate its economy and act as a "locomotive" for global growth. However, while policy makers

TABLE 5.1. Overview of alternative explanations for the similarities of fiscal patterns between Greece and Japan since the 1980s

	Greece	Japan
adjustment	insufficient (piecemeal, no significant breakthroughs in dealing with debt)	insufficient (piecemeal, no significant breakthroughs in dealing with debt)
fiscal polarization	high	high
exposure to intl. competition	limited • moderate openness • domestic market insulated by variety of policies	limited • low openness • domestic market insulated by variety of policies
electoral system	majoritarian	single, non-transferable until 1994 mixed majoritarian-proportional afterwards
party system	two dominant, centralized parties, strong party discipline	predominant pluralism, dominant party highly factionalized
government structure	unitary governments	minority and coalition governments increasingly common from 1980s
corporatism	weak, divided, uncoordinated unions	unions have some influence from 1980s
state strength	weak	strong
fiscal institutions	decentralized until mid-1990s, strong finance minister afterwards	centralized budget control, very strict spending ceilings
economic performance	high nominal growth, EU funds	high growth in 1970s, 1980s major growth issues from 1990s on
diplomatic pressures	pressure to consolidate	pressure for stimulus

showed willingness to succumb to such pressures in the 1970s, they firmly resisted them in the 1980s and instead used accounting tricks to seemingly comply with the wishes of their G7 partners (Wright 1999; Suzuki 2000). Greece, a small, peripheral economy never faced pressures for fiscal expansion. Instead, in the run-up to euro accession and then within EMU, it was to restrain its fiscal deficits in compliance with the Maastricht criteria, but it covertly and overtly violated these constraints. (For an overview of all alternative explanations, see Table 5.1.)

This chapter argues that it is the similarly polarizing nature of the existing fiscal regimes in the two polities and the similarly limited exposure of the two economies that produced such similar fiscal patterns in both countries despite the immense differences in their political systems, economic structures, and international positions. The first half of the chapter explores the Greek case to explain why successive Greek governments were reluctant to use the institutional advantages provided by strong unitary governments and failed to exploit external pressure for fiscal stabilization to enact meaningful reform. It shows that although the two major political parties seemed content to take turns at exploiting state resources to further their electoral goals (Pappas 2013), both initiated significant adjustments to the public wage bill and pensions in the 1980s and 1990s. However, both sides encountered such intense electoral backlash that they abandoned the cause of adjustment. The welfare of populous groups of public employees, farmers, and the owners and employees of SMEs depended more heavily on specific fiscal features—large public employment, various tax favors, opportunities for evasion, subsidies, and specially targeted pension arrangements—than on the macroeconomic fitness of the country. As a consequence, no social coalition emerged that could help a radical adjustment package to succeed—and allow the government that put it into place to survive—in the face of the ire of the negatively affected vested interest groups. The second half of the chapter describes a very similar pattern in Japan. There, attempts by the Ministry of Finance to enact fiscal reform regularly foundered on the resistance of different factions within the long-governing Liberal Democratic Party. Some factions defended pork-barrel spending and tax advantages central to the livelihood of large rural constituencies, others resisted initiatives to retrench welfare or increase tax pressure on the urban population. As none of these societal groups could be discounted from an electoral perspective and neither could be expected to find a positive trade-off between fiscal sacrifices and strengthening public finances, taking on either side had a very steep electoral price that policy makers were unwilling to pay.

Greece's March into Bankruptcy[3]

Greece's fiscal problems started in the early 1980s when the Panhellenic Socialist Movement (PASOK) won its first landslide victory and set out to transform Greek politics and society using the resources of the state. The previous three decades had been characterized by fiscal rigor, which had kept the debt-to-GDP ratio under 20 percent, but policy took a radical turn after PASOK's election to power in 1981. Spending grew one and a half times relative to GDP as public employment was dramatically expanded, welfare entitlements grew, and ailing nationalized companies and banks received generous support (Alogoskoufis 1992). The number of public employees rose by more than a half (OECD 1996). Pension entitlements—which made up the overwhelming majority of total social spending—were made considerably more generous, while eligibility was extended to new social groups, for example, farmers and the self-employed (Close 2002). Public investment was booming, partly thanks to the influx of European funds, while large capital transfers were regularly made to companies in the public sector to make up for their losses and allow them to keep their employees (OECD 1996). The explosion in public spending was compounded by a growing interest burden on an accumulating debt stock. By 1990, interest amounted to almost a tenth of the gross domestic product (Ameco 2008).

In the same period, revenues grew at a much lower rate. Although the newly introduced pension schemes augmented the social security contributions to be collected and consumption taxes grew with the introduction of VAT in 1987—making social security contributions and consumption taxes the overwhelming majority of total revenues at three quarters of the total by the 1990s—revenues could not keep pace with the explosion of expenditure, to a great extent because of large and increasing problems with evasion (OECD 2007). By 1990, the deficit stood at 14 percent of GDP (Ameco 2008; OECD 2001). Debt had grown from 20 to almost 70 percent of GDP, despite high nominal growth (due to high inflation as real growth averaged less than 1 percent over the decade), and it was still on a steeply increasing trajectory.

The alarming trend did not escape the attention of policy makers. After the elections of 1985, the government announced a stabilization plan, which sought to control the rise of the public wage bill through draconian incomes policy and an adjustment to wage indexation, and planned to increase revenues (Alogoskoufis 1992). However, limiting public wage growth failed in the face of a series of public sector strikes, and the political will to push ahead with austerity ran out altogether after PASOK suffered painful losses in the municipal elections of October 1986 (Close 2002; Nicolacopoulos 2005). Although VAT was still successfully introduced in 1987, further adjustment was not pursued and by November 1987, the Minister of National Economy, the architect of the austerity program, was forced to resign.

The 1990s gave a respite from the escalating problems of the 1980s under successive New Democracy and PASOK governments. Yet, Greece arguably squandered an important opportunity in this period to regain control over its alarming debt problem. The headline deficit improved significantly from 14 percent of the GDP in 1990 to (ostensibly) 2.5 percent in 1999 (the revised figures are closer to 6 percent). This led to the approximate stabilization of the debt-to-GDP ratio around 100 percent (or, more accurately, the oscillation of the debt-to-GDP ratio around a slightly increasing trajectory) and earned Greece the right to join the Economic and Monetary Union in 2001. However, much of the improvement was thanks to windfall gains, which provided an important opportunity for reversing, not only roughly stabilizing debt growth. In this period, the influx of funds under the various European structural, cohesion, and agricultural policies tripled, boosting revenues by around 3 percent of the GDP (Saravelos 2007) and stimulating growth to well above the EU average (giving rise to around 3 percent real growth per year on average) in the second half of the decade. At the same time, the interest burden dropped precipitously (from a high of over 12 percent of GDP in 1994 to a little over 7 percent by 2000). Adjustment of the trends that had produced such alarming results in the 1980s played a relatively minor role in the favorable developments of the 1990s.

Spending remained virtually unadjusted. Limits placed on new hiring in the public sector in the early 1990s only managed to slow, but not stop or reverse, the growth of public employment, as regional and local governments were expanded and health and education were explicitly exempted from constraints; whereas other public entities increasingly resorted to hiring "temporary" personnel to circumvent caps (OECD 1996). Similarly, austere incomes policy in the public sector was undermined by special bonuses (OECD 1996). As a result, the public wage bill grew further as a share of GDP. Pension payments also continued to rise despite a pension reform in 1992 that changed the indexation mechanism, tightened eligibility, and somewhat limited the generosity of the system. Capital transfers to loss-making enterprises decreased somewhat on paper, but this was likely due to the adoption of new accounting standards, which took such transaction "below the line" (OECD 1996). Privatization proceeded hesitantly throughout the decade and the government maintained majority shares in companies (OECD 1996 and 2001).

Revenues, on the other hand, did increase significantly, primarily due to bracket creep. Tax brackets were not indexed to inflation from 1992, which doubled direct tax revenues as a percent of GDP in the course of the decade. This boost was reinforced by some successes in the fight against tax evasion; the elimination of certain tax expenditures; and the introduction of a new stock market transaction tax, a withholding tax on government bonds, a new form of property tax, and a progressive income tax on pensions (OECD 2001). Social security contributions grew as a result of the pension reform of 1992, which increased contribution rates for workers in both the private and the public sector, introduced the obligation for civil servants to contribute to their own pension funds, and increased the minimum contribution for the self-employed. The rise of social security contributions was also fueled by the decline in the number of farmers, who make no pension contributions, and their entry into professions that do. At the same time, indirect taxes were lowered to reduce inflation.

By the 2000s, the improvements fizzled out. The primary balance declined precipitously as successive governments used the room to move created by the continued significant drop in the interest burden (3 percent of the GDP between 2000 and 2007 and 8 percentage points from the high of 1994) to compensate society for some of the losses it suffered in the 1990s. Tax brackets were finally corrected to reflect the inflationary effects of the 1990s and rates were cut in 2001 and 2004, causing revenues to fall by more than 5 percentage points (OECD 2001 and 2007). Primary expenditure continued to drift up. In the absence of further corrections, pensions and the public wage bill grew (OECD 2007, Ameco 2008). Capital transfers paid to public companies reached the levels seen in the early 1990s, despite the fact that the accounting changes adopted then still kept most of these transactions below the line. Just as in the case of the improvement of the 1990s, government partisanship seemed to make little difference to the general trends of relapse in the 2000s, as New Democracy and PASOK governments oversaw the fiscal deterioration in turns. The worsening was so pronounced that the primary balance was in the negative by 2004, and the overall deficit hit a low of 7.5 percent. The debt-to-GDP ratio grew above 100 percent. By the time the first effects of the global financial and economic crisis manifested themselves, Greece was in a vulnerable fiscal state, which eventually led to the fiscal disaster well-known to all.

Many characteristics of Greek fiscal policy in the decades between 1980 and 2010 conform to the "fiscal indiscipline" hypothesis. It seems clear that successive governments placed their electoral success ahead of the fiscal stability of the country and pursued policies that would secure votes but eventually led Greece into fiscal disaster. However, repeated attempts, by both PASOK and New Democracy, to initiate major corrections in spending and revenues suggest that governments of both parties were acutely aware of the issue and were willing to take some risks to address it. Some of these attempts (e.g., the introduction of VAT in 1987, the increase in direct tax revenues through bracket creep, or the limited pension reforms of 1992) even yielded considerable results, whereas others were abandoned in the face of electoral backlash. Furthermore, the question remains why fiscal laxity was electorally so consistently successful despite the magnitude of the debt problem, which triggered painful adjustments elsewhere. The next section argues that it was because such a small share of Greek society was exposed to international economic competition and such a large section drew large parts of their income from the government budget. Vested interests in existing policies were strong, while the counterbalancing interests in improving economic fundamentals were weak. At the same time, existing policies were so closely targeted to specific groups that each group could claim that it was possible (and desirable) to stabilize public finances without touching the policies they had vested interests in.

The Dangers of Targeted Populism:
The Societal Bases of Fiscal Laxity in Greece

Political analyses of the past decades of Greek history often focus on the enormous impact of the ascendancy of PASOK to power on the way politics has been conducted since the 1980s. They underline that PASOK instituted a new politics of "bureaucratic clientelism" (Mavrogordatos 1997), "populist democracy" (Pappas 2013), and mass polarization (Kalyvas 1997). What has received less explicit attention, however, is how PASOK's policies in the 1980s transformed the socioeconomic bases of Greek politics using state resources and European funds to nurture large constituencies of state spending, while allowing groups dependent on markets to protect themselves from mounting fiscal pressure. As Mavrogordatos (1997) points out, the practice of building clientelistic relationships through awarding public employment and state aid was a well-entrenched tradition under all of the right-wing and center-right governments in the postwar decades, but PASOK took it to a new level when the party made it the center of its political strategy to extend the privileges enjoyed by the few to the previously "unprivileged" (Kalyvas 1997). This left a profound mark on the structure of fiscal interests by increasing the part of society dependent on income from the state and by generating strong incentives and opportunities for tax evasion.

The proportion of society fully or partially dependent on income from the government surged dramatically. Public employment grew more than one and a half times by the end of the 1980s due to the enlargement of the civil service and the increase in the number of workers in nationalized banks and companies (OECD 1996). Although pay in the public sector was relatively low, such jobs were considered very attractive because of the security of employment and pay (wages were indexed to inflation; promotion and salary increases were independent of performance), the generosity of pension benefits, and the shortness of working hours, which allowed public employees to draw further income from secondary jobs or independent economic activity (Close 2002). The populous group of farmers (still around 25 percent of the population in 1990) added to these dependents of the state as they gained half of their income from national and new European agricultural subsidies (OECD 2001). Many firms were in receipt of state aid: as a percentage of gross value added, public support to manufacturing was the second highest in the European Union (OECD 2001). Finally, the pension system was also extended in the 1980s, making benefits much more generous and granting eligibility to previously uncovered groups, increasing the number of pensioners.

At the same time, the policies of the 1980s also significantly increased the incentives and opportunities for tax and contribution evasion among those who had some flexibility in reporting their earnings. This group includes small- and medium-sized enterprises, their employees, the self-employed, and those *de facto* dependent employees who are officially registered as self-employed to have more room for maneuver in reporting their income.[4] Together, these groups represent the majority of society. The incentives for evasion increased not only due to the growth of fiscal pressure (e.g., due to the introduction of VAT in 1987) but also due to the design of the extended pension system, which created excellent opportunity for sizeable sections of society to win future welfare entitlements without making the corresponding contribution in the present. The specific eligibility rules, replacement rates, and minimum pensions of the pension funds for private sector employees and the self-employed generated strong incentives for these groups to maximize their lifetime income by evading contributions or paying them strategically along their careers and retiring just at the right time (typically: early) to achieve the most favorable life-time benefit-contribution ratio.[5] The significance of the phenomenon of evasion is demonstrated by the fact that the loss of public revenue caused by evasion was estimated to amount to 15 percent of GDP by the 2000s (OECD 2007). While this behavior obviously remained nominally illegal, its potential legal consequences were diminished by periodically granted tax amnesties. Furthermore, many enterprises also had recourse to sec-torally and regionally targeted tax exemptions to legally reduce their tax exposure (OECD 2001).

This policy regime—which mixed populism (the extension of fiscal favors to everyone) with targeting (favoring different groups in differ-ent ways)—delineated five major clusters of fiscal interests. *Public sector employees*—who made up approximately a quarter of the workforce—were attached to their secure jobs and wages as well as to their generous pen-sion arrangements, which allowed them to retire early with decent replace-ment rates (OECD 1996). They bore the brunt of the tax burden not only because they constituted the largest section in society that was unable to evade taxes and social security contributions but also because they could not avail of the exemptions that higher income groups legally had recourse to (OECD 2001). *Farmers* received special help from the state to counterbalance their very low primary income.[6] They received large subsidies from domestic sources as well as from the funds secured by the European Common Agricultural Policy, and they were not even legally required to contribute to their pension fund, which provided rather low pensions. *Enterprises of all sizes* were adamant to hold onto state aid and to preserve the relatively low effective corporate tax rates and a variety of sectorally and regionally based exemptions in an environment where their competitiveness suffered from inflexible regulations and labor market poli-cies. Some major industries, like shipping, were fully tax-exempt (OECD 2001). At the same time, *smaller enterprises* (which make up a large part of the economy) also had an interest in the tacit toleration of evasion. The *employees of smaller enterprises* and the populous stratum of the *self-employed* also had a strong interest in the condonation of evasion as well as in those features of the pension system that allowed them to minimize their contri-butions while still receiving benefits. Finally, those *private sector employees* who worked in jobs that did not allow for evasion (primarily employees of large private companies) were the relatively least favored group. They bore similar tax pressure as public sector employees: although they had higher average incomes, they were protected from the effects of progressivity of taxation by a complicated system of deductions and allowances only available above a certain income. At the same time, they received somewhat less generous pension benefits (OECD 1996 and 2001).

When the unsustainability of the policies of the 1980s was exposed, adjustment was bound to hurt some of these groups. External observers identified a number of ways in which the fiscal problem could be attacked, singling out the largest spending items and the biggest culprits for revenue shortfall: retrenching public employment, pension reform, privatization, broadening the tax base for income taxation, and fighting tax evasion (OECD 1996, 2001, 2007, and 2013). The choice between these measures was bound to be highly contentious, though, because each entailed wildly different incidence of the fiscal pain across powerful groups in society. Cuts in the public wage bill and privatization would have obviously hurt public employees. Scrapping exemptions to widen the tax base and to increase the *de facto* corporate tax rate would have burdened most private enterprises. Broadening the personal tax base through the discontinuation of deductions and allowances would have disadvantaged the employees of large private sector companies. The fight against evasion would have gone against the interests of the large group of people involved in the small-scale economy. Pension reform could potentially have very diverse distributive effects across the different groups, depending on which one of the different pension funds would be most radically reformed.

All of the groups wielded considerable power they could mobilize in defense of their interests. Public sector employees were a numerous voter group and they also demonstrated strong strike potential. From the mid-1980s to the mid-1990s, their strikes led to the highest number of days lost among all OECD countries (Close 2002). Moreover, they also had considerable power to sabotage the policies they disliked from within the state: efforts to limit the public wage bill were repeatedly undermined when wage ceilings and hiring constraints were circumvented by practices such as "temporary" jobs and "special bonuses" (OECD 1996; Mavrogordatos 1997). The self-employed and small business owners represented the single largest electoral group, which made it dangerous to tamper with their pension entitlements or to crack down on tax evasion without easing the *de jure* tax pressure on these parts of society. Farmers constituted a fairly large electoral group, too, and they also regularly resorted to road blockages and other disruptive acts whenever they sought to express their misgivings (Close 2002). Large businesses could mostly count on their political connections, but the big shipping companies could also threaten to move their fleets under different flags when policy conditions were not in their favor (Lavdas 2005). The ability of these powerful groups to stand up for their vested interests meant that decisive fiscal stabilization required overwhelming societal support in order to succeed.

Garnering such support was made difficult by the fact that austerity did not offer immediate benefits to most of society because the overwhelming majority were unconcerned about the potential negative side effects of debt accumulation on the economy. A considerable share of society (public employees, farmers, and companies dependent on state aid) drew part or all of their income from the government. Of those groups that were mostly dependent on the market for their earnings, a large majority were indirectly interested in government largesse because they were oriented towards domestic markets and, thus, had a stake in the maintenance of domestic purchasing power. The populous group of farmers and other self-employed groups in real estate, retail, construction, and small-scale manufacturing, as well as the owners and employees of small- and medium-sized enterprises in the same sectors, were not too concerned about the effects of inflation and overspending on competitiveness. They anyway had little chance of success in export markets due to their perennial productivity problems, while in the domestic markets, their competitiveness and their profit margins were shielded through state aid and large-scale evasion of taxes and social security contributions (EU KLEMS; OECD 1996 and 2001).

The rest of the economy—the owners and employees of large private manufacturing firms, large shipping businesses, and enterprises engaged in tourism—were exposed to the international economy. However, they remained mostly unconcerned about the inflationary effects of budgetary problems because the crawling peg mechanism (which was adopted in the 1970s, made more flexible in 1985, and maintained until 1999) accommodated inflation differentials with main trading partners (Alogoskoufis 1992). Smaller firms and employees had recourse to tax and social contribution evasion, whereas larger firms benefited from export subsidies, often in combination with European structural funds, direct grants, loans, and tax incentives, which contributed to their ability to maintain reasonable competitiveness and profit margins.

In the absence of immediate economic pressures on any of these groups, they had few incentives to voluntarily give in to any adjustment measures that would directly affect their income or to support radical austerity, even if the direct fiscal pain affected other groups. Neither did they have an interest in sacrificing any benefits they received from their political connections in a profoundly clientelistic political system in order to support stabilization-minded political actors. The next section shows that this constellation of societal interests rendered adjustment attempts politically unfeasible.

Parties, Unions, Elections, and the Inability to Adjust

Although it was PASOK whose fiscal policy choices set off the escalation of problems in the 1980s, which eventually culminated in the disaster of the Greek debt crisis, the underlying social interests that were so fundamentally shaped by the policies of the 1980s constrained New Democracy and PASOK equally in their ability to deal with the problems. Both parties attempted to adjust existing policies, and both ran into the same difficulties in dealing with public sector unions, farmers' protests, and, most importantly, voter disapproval.

Due to the genesis of the Greek party system and especially the clientelistic nature of the ties between voters and parties, there is no clear one-to-one correspondence between any of the four large vested interest groups and the two parties. The PASOK-New Democracy opposition has never been based on traditional social cleavages. Given Greece's underdevelopment at the time of the return to democracy in the second half of the 1970s, the industrial base and the industrial working class was too small to structure politics along classical class lines, and there existed no deep religious or regional divisions to shape the party system (Kalyvas 1997). Conflicts about the monarchy and past civil wars still lingered, but the former was put to rest with the referendum of 1974. The latter was used by PASOK in symbolic ways to define itself as an opposition to New Democracy. At the time of its formation in 1974, New Democracy had a vague right-wing or center-right profile defined by its links to business (reflected in its business-friendly macroeconomic policies), its constituency among civil servants, and its support among conservative farmers (Kalyvas 1997; Lyrintzis 2005). These groups had mostly been beneficiaries of the postwar political system under various right-wing governments, as well as the junta that governed the country between 1967 and 1974 (Close 2002; Lavdas 2005). PASOK defined itself as the negation of the postwar years, as the advocate of the losers of that system and as the antithesis of New Democracy (Kalyvas 1997; Lyrintzis 2005). As a result, its policies were directed at distributing the types of benefits—jobs in the civil service and in publicly owned companies, welfare benefits, and state aid—that its supporters had previously had limited access to, via a newly constructed system of "bureaucratic clientelism" (Mavrogordatos 1997).

Consequently, by the time fiscal problems started to manifest themselves in earnest, both parties had important constituencies in all of the major vested interest groups. New Democracy was still the major advocate for business interests and had important support among managerial private sector employees (Lanza and Lavdas 2000; Lavdas 2005); but it also had a crucial base among the old civil servants and public employees, who resented the dilution of their privileges among the masses of new political appointees (Mavrogordatos 1997), and it could also count on the vote of the majority of farmers and the self-employed (Nicolacopoulos 2005). PASOK had a very similar supporter base, although the weights were slightly different. Its strongest base was in the public sector and among lower level private employees, but it also received decent voter backing from farmers and the self-employed (Nicolacopoulos 2005). After the worst years of hostility in the first half of the 1980s, it made peace with the peak business organization (SEV) and engaged in limited concertation with business in the course of the first stabilization package between 1985 and 1987 (Lanza and Lavdas 2000).

This distribution of voter support made it very risky for both parties to move decisively to cut spending on public employees, to reform pension arrangements or to fight tax evasion, because upsetting any of the major groups was likely to cause their vote share to drop enough to make them lose the next election. Furthermore, in the case of policy reforms affecting public sector employees, governments of either color had to count on major confrontations with unions. Even though public sector worker representation was fully colonized by the two parties, who organized their own partisan unions and turned union elections into spheres of partisan competition (Mavrogordatos 1997; Kalyvas 1997), neither party could count on union complacency in the face of policies aimed at reducing public sector incomes. Public sector unions invariably showed remarkable unity and extraordinary militancy when it came to defending the vested interest of public sector workers (Close 2002; Lavdas 2005).

Despite this, public sector employees were the most likely target for adjustment. On the one hand, their wages, pensions, and the capital transfers paid to the loss-making companies that employed them added up to a very large share of the budget. On the other hand, they represented a relatively smaller (albeit still very significant) share of the electoral force than all the other groups that would be hurt by reforms reducing tax evasion, the other major problem undermining fiscal sustainability. However, the electoral repercussions of taking on public employees could only have been ignored if there had been hope that fiscal improvements were going to yield electoral rewards from other groups. Since no groups had an immediate stake in restoring fiscal balance, none could be expected to give up its clientelistic ties to their party and switch electoral camps just to support fiscal stabilization, as both parties had to learn the hard way.

When PASOK attempted to restrain public sector wage expenses in 1985, it got into a major showdown with public sector unions over the issue, which immediately led to its defeat in the municipal elections of October 1986 in its most important strongholds with the largest populations of public sector employees in Athens, Piraeus, and Thessaloniki. Although the government immediately abandoned its resolve to keep the public wage bill down, it went ahead with the introduction of VAT in 1987, which again disproportionately affected those for whom evasion was not an option. PASOK lost the next parliamentary elections in 1989, hemorrhaging votes (almost 7 percentage points compared to the previous elections) to small leftist parties and to New Democracy (Nicolacopoulos 2005).

New Democracy also failed to survive attempting to radically restructure the public sector. It entered government on a program that harked back to its role in the 1970s as a protector of business interests and advocated cuts in public expenditure, privatization, and a reform of the civil service. As a start, it froze public sector pay and attempted to privatize some of the largest public sector firms (e.g., the telecommunications monopoly). It met fierce opposition from public sector unions (Kornelakis 2011). In 1992, the government introduced a pension reform, which afflicted tangible losses on current and retired public sector employees and, to a smaller extent, on private sector employees, despite being a heavily watered-down version of the original proposal. These triggered renewed union protests (Featherstone 2005). After barely a year in power, the party plunged in the polls and lost an important by-election in Athens in 1992. By 1993, it split; the government fell and lost the 1993 elections by a large margin before it could make any headway in achieving any restructuring of the public sector, although the pension reforms stayed in effect and turned out to be the only reasonably meaningful adjustment to the pension system for the next two decades (Nicolacopoulos 2005).

The fiscal corrections that did not immediately cause the electoral demise of the political side that initiated them were the ones that made no full frontal attack on any one vested interest group, but obfuscated, diluted, and slowly introduced changes. Bracket creep between 1992 and 2000—when successive PASOK governments failed to index tax brackets to inflation—resulted in the single biggest fiscal adjustment from the start of fiscal problems until the debt crisis, increasing revenues by 5 percentage points of GDP. Yet, this covert adjustment did not interfere with the electoral success of the party: PASOK was reelected twice (in 1996 and 2000). Similarly, the "gradualist" approach to privatization under the Simitis government in the second half of the 1990s resulted in significant revenues (around 4 percent of the GDP in 1999) but avoided raising the ire of unions because the government only sold minority shares and kept controlling majorities in public companies, thereby retaining responsibility for employment (OECD 2001, Kornelakis 2011). PASOK even managed to introduce two marginal pension reforms (in 1998 and 2002) after retreating on two more meaningful proposals in the face of union opposition in 1997 and 2001 (Featherstone 2005), and pass a minor tax reform in 1997 that selectively weeded out certain tax exemptions and introduced an income tax on government bonds and a real estate tax (which was admittedly difficult to enforce in the absence of a land registry, OECD 2001).

However, such piecemeal, partial, and covert adjustments had very significant limitations. First of all, the corrections they could achieve were too gradual and insufficient in size to deal with the existing imbalances. Second, they did not make a lasting impact on the general fiscal trends since they never even attempted to correct any of the fundamental imbalances of the system. Public sector employment stayed high, the pension system remained excessively fragmented and had the worst problems with underfunding in the OECD, and tax evasion still accounted for a very large share of GDP (OECD 2007). These structural features of public finances constituted fatal flaws in the face of the first effects of population aging, pressure to ensure the purchasing power of public sector pay, and demands to ease the fiscal burden of those who do pay taxes and contributions. In the first half of the 2000s, as the pressure on public finances eased up due to high growth, low interest rates, and the high rate of the flow of funds from the European Union, all of these factors were allowed to exert deleterious influence on public finances. On the eve of the global financial and economic crisis in 2007, at the end of a period of decent growth, the deficit stood at 7 percent of the GDP, higher than in any other developed country. The large deficit, the significant debt stock, and the revelations about accounting manipulations made Greece a prime candidate for market panic and a debt crisis when the crisis hit.

The Formidable Obstacle of Fiscal Polarization: Greek Public Finances after Default

The political events since the start of the Greek debt crisis further confirm just how intractable the political obstacles created by fiscal polarization are.

The foregoing analysis of the fiscal politics of the 1980s, 1990s, and 2000s emphasized the joint role of the polarization of vested fiscal interests and the weakness of economic pressures on large parts of society in preventing the emergence of the necessary social support to strengthen the hands of reformers. The developments of the past seven years, however, show that conflicts of vested interests generate formidable political obstacles to fiscal adjustment even in the face of considerable economic pressures.

Since Greece went officially bankrupt, it has been economically and financially at the mercy of the troika of the European Commission, the European Central Bank, and the International Monetary Fund. The troika provides the necessary funds to avoid complete collapse, but it has also demanded neoliberal reforms to the public sector, to pensions, and to the tax system as a condition for continued funding. For six years since the first bailout, the troika repeatedly issued ultimatums that it will discontinue funding. This would plunge Greece into an even greater economic disaster than it is already in, triggering not only its exit from the common currency but also the crumbling of its banking system, major interruptions in trade, and a collapse of domestic demand. Yet, whichever political actor accepts the troika's demands is ejected from government in the next elections. The old dominant parties have taken turns at and joined forces in implementing the reforms dictated by the troika but faced enormous social unrest with waves of strikes, demonstrations, and deadly riots and were ousted from power. In early 2015, Syriza won the elections on the promise to resist reform ultimatums from the troika.

The enduring resistance to fiscal pain even in the face of direct threats of devastating economic and financial consequences highlights the immense stakes involved in choosing between different adjustment packages in Greece. Fiscal polarization causes vested interests to trump economic exigencies because it concentrates large losses to specific sections of society. For example, public employment has always been a very attractive candidate for adjustment in Greece because the public wage bill and public sector pensions tied down a very considerable share of public spending already in the mid-2000s (more than a third of primary spending, around 13 percent of GDP), which grew to a much larger share in the midst of the economic collapse. However, cuts large enough to make a difference for the budget would fall entirely on a circumscribed part of the population, which has few alternative employment opportunities and would consequently see its income drop drastically if public sector employment was cut and/or public sector pay was slashed. Similarly, tax evasion is an obvious target for reform in Greece. Estimated to amount to around 15 percent of the GDP (OECD 2007), it is an immense drain on revenues. However, it also secures a large part of the income of the sections of society engaged in the small-scale sector. Stakes of these magnitudes are significant enough to matter even in the face of explicit ultimatums and imminent threats of disaster, especially in situations where vested interest groups already suffer from economic hard times.

How Japan became the Most Indebted Country in the World

Intense fiscal polarization has played a similar role in Japan's fiscal troubles despite enormous differences between the two countries in economic structure, political institutions, and even in the main features of the fiscal regimes. Unlike Greece, Japan never formally tied down unusually large amounts of public resources in entitlements or public employment. Both the public wage bill and welfare spending remained modest in international comparison. Tax evasion was not a conspicuous problem either. However, decades of policy practice institutionalized considerable transfers of public funds to geographically and sectorally delineable groups in society and differentiated tax standards along similar lines. The differentiated policies generated very strong conflicts of vested interests between urban and rural areas and high- and low-productivity sectors. They fostered dependency on preferential policies in low-productivity rural areas and fueled resistance to sacrifices in the high-productivity urban groups, especially as economic conditions worsened. Intense societal conflict over fiscal policy gave rise to incessant infighting within the long-governing Liberal Democratic Party (LDP), which housed factions representing opposing societal groups. Factions needed the support of their particular constituencies to maintain their influence within the party, while the party as a whole ultimately needed the votes of both rural and urban populations to stay in power. This power dynamic tied the hands of successive governments for four decades and prevented them from eliciting major fiscal sacrifices from any group for the sake of rebalancing the budget, despite the insistence of the Ministry of Finance on the urgency of fiscal stabilization from the late-1970s.

A Brief Digression on the Difficulties
of Assessing Japan's Public Debt Problems

Before discussing the fiscal trends in Japan in the past four decades and analyzing their political origins, it is necessary to briefly touch on the difficulties involved in assessing Japan's fiscal situation at any point in time. These difficulties arise from two sources. On the one hand, Japan's outstanding debt is partly counterbalanced by an unusually large stock of government assets, diminishing the applicability of gross debt indicators. On the other hand, the practice of government accounting diverges from international standards due to the proliferation of special accounts, which decrease the overall transparency of fiscal transactions (Wright 1999; Suzuki 2000).

Its gross debt-to-GDP ratio of almost 250 percent in 2015 makes Japan by far the most indebted country in the world. However, the gross debt indicator is somewhat misleading because the Japanese government disposes over a much larger asset stock than usual. The net debt-to-GDP ratio is only around 130 percent, which is comparable to Italy's or Portugal's debt ratio in 2015 (IMF WEO Database April 2016). Even in net terms, though, the ratio is obviously still quite high. After all, Italy needed the intervention of the European Central Bank to avert a brewing debt crisis at a significantly lower debt level in 2011, and Greece had similar levels of debt in 2009 before events started to spiral towards default. Nevertheless, markets for Japan's sovereign debt have so far failed to show signs of stress similar to those of Italy or Greece, and the yield on bonds is significantly lower than on many developed country bonds.

Tranquility in the markets for Japanese sovereign debt is usually attributed to the fact that government bonds are predominantly in the hands of domestic investors. While domestic financing currently generates favorable financing conditions, its longer term implications are less benign. Government debt is an attractive investment opportunity for Japanese private banks and government financial institutions, given the abundance of domestic savings, the aversion of these institutions to foreign exchange and credit risk, and the lack of alternative lucrative investment opportunities domestically (Hoshi and Ito 2012; Horioka et al. 2014). However, as the domestic savings stock is expected to decline due to stagnating incomes and population aging, this pool of funds is likely to dry up in the long term. Furthermore, the current equilibrium is highly vulnerable to shocks that change the demand of domestic investors for government debt even in the short term. Even otherwise favorable changes, like a boost in investment opportunities upon an improvement in the Japanese or the global economy, could lead to tighter financing conditions for the government (Hoshi and Ito 2012). Analysts warn that if Japanese banks started to divest of government bonds and the government ran into financing difficulties, the resulting drop in the value of government debt would have devastating consequences for the financial assets of households and banks and, as a result, for the domestic banking system, for the economy, and for society (Ibid.). In this sense, Japan's government debt overhang creates even more daunting risks than the internationally more diversified debt stocks of other highly indebted countries. Although Japan is less exposed to short-term changes in investor sentiments than countries where footloose foreign investors hold the debt, if domestic creditors change their behavior in response to developments already underway, the consequences of a debt crisis will likely be even more devastating than elsewhere, as the losses will have to be practically fully absorbed by the domestic economy.

While it is fairly clear that Japan is by now dangerously indebted even in net terms, the large discrepancy between gross and net debt creates some ambiguity about when the country's fiscal problems turned serious. The gross debt ratio was rapidly rising—from around 10 to more than 70 percent—in the 1970s and 1980s (Ameco), but the net debt ratio never reached 30 percent in this period and only started growing significantly in the mid-1990s after the collapse of economic growth. This suggests—along with relatively low deficit figures for the earlier period—that the fiscal imbalances of the second half of the 1970s and the 1980s were negligible, and Japan's debt problem originates from the economic problems of the last two decades.

However, there are two important reasons not to discount the fiscal problems preceding the economic crisis as minor or inconsequential. First, net debt and deficit figures paint a rosier picture than the reality. They overstate the extent to which the rapid growth of gross debt was counterbalanced by the acquisition of valuable assets due to extensive accounting manipulations increasingly used from the 1980s to disguise pork-barrel spending and subsidies as investment and lending and to move deficits around to various special accounts in the 1980s (Wright 1999; Suzuki 2000). As a consequence, deficits and net debt were likely higher than officially accounted for already in the 1980s. Second, the fiscal problems of the 1980s were seen as serious and pressing at the time. The Ministry of Finance repeatedly warned of a "budgetary crisis," advocated the adoption of principles of "sound management," and put forward one plan for administrative and fiscal reform after another (Wright 1999; van Hagen 2006). The message was not lost on the wider public. Newspapers covered the issue extensively, while public opinion polls showed that "fiscal reconstruction" was considered one of the main policy priorities of the public at the time. As a result, several prime ministers publically pledged to resign if they were unable to eliminate borrowing by a certain deadline (Suzuki 2000). Although the fiscal problems of the 1980s were later dwarfed by the catastrophic debt buildup of the 1990s and 2000s when the economy turned for the worse, rapid debt accumulation in times of high growth was clearly seen as a major problem in the 1980s.

Four Decades of Imbalances: From the 1970s to the 2010s

The first fiscal imbalances appeared in the 1970s as economic growth slowed considerably and welfare policies were expanded. While double-digit growth had created exceptionally favorable fiscal conditions during the 1960s, budgetary constraints became much tighter in the 1970s. Gone were the years when governments could increase spending *and* cut taxes at the same time. At the same time, the governing Liberal Democratic Party came under pressure to increase welfare spending. Pensions and unemployment were upgraded, and free medical care for the elderly and child allowance were introduced. As there was no attempt to cut back traditionally large spending items like public construction projects and subsidies, spending increased considerably. To counterbalance the growing spending pressures, the tax bureau made the first in a long row of attempts to introduce a consumption tax in 1976 but failed in the face of resistance from within the LDP, the opposition parties, and the public (Suzuki 2000; DeWit and Steinmo 2002; Akaishi and Steinmo 2006). A few minor taxes were increased, but they made little difference for the widening fiscal imbalances (Suzuki 2000). As a result, for the first time since the Second World War, the government started to borrow significantly to cover current expenses (Suzuki 2000; Chopel et al. 2005; Estevez-Abe 2008).

Discouraged by its failed attempt to introduce a major new revenue source, the Ministry of Finance embraced "consolidation without tax increases" in the early 1980s and announced that deficits would be eliminated by 1984 through spending control. The new approach received strong support from the business community and the broader public, and a committee made up of central bureaucrats as well as the representatives of business and labor, called *Rincho*, was set up to draft a major fiscal reform (Suzuki 2000). However, the committee's recommendations to cut the largest expenditure items—welfare expenses, farm subsidies, and public works projects—were never actually implemented (Suzuki 2000). Welfare and health care reforms were initiated, but most of these reforms were watered down to an extent that they made little difference to spending or revenues.[7] The Ministry of Finance imposed ever-stronger limits on spending growth, but while these were adhered to in the budgeting process, repeated supplementary budgets, *ad hoc* authorizations, and exemptions undermined their effectiveness in keeping spending under control (van Hagen 2006). Public works spending continued to increase despite repeated budgetary plans to reduce it, while farm subsidies only declined slightly due to a drop in production costs (Suzuki 2000).

Unable to keep its own targets throughout the 1980s, the ministry increasingly resorted to accounting tricks, postponing obligatory payments to special accounts and lower levels of government, cross-subsidizing funds in deficit from funds in surplus, and borrowing heavily from the Fiscal Investment and Loan Program and the Postal Savings System to reduce the discrepancy between plans and outcomes (Wright 1999; Suzuki 2000). Subsidies to local governments for locally provided health care, education, and social services were cut to reduce the deficit of the central government, but since the relevant legislation remained unchanged, local governments had to borrow more to be able to provide the same guaranteed services with lower funding (Suzuki 2000).

Revenue growth helped to partially counterbalance the lack of spending control by the end of the 1980s. Tax revenues grew mostly endogenously as a result of bracket creep of income taxes, especially in the years of exuberant growth in the midst of the real estate and stock market bubble of the late 1980s. Corporate tax rates were also slightly increased—from 40 to 42 percent in 1981 and to 43.3 percent in 1984—and some tax breaks were eliminated (Wright 1999; Suzuki 2000; Estevez-Abe 2008). Although the consumption tax was finally enacted in 1988—after yet another failed attempt in 1986—it made little immediate difference for revenues. It was much lower than originally planned (3 percent instead of 7), it was counterbalanced by income tax cuts meant to soften opposition, and small businesses were allowed to keep the tax (Akaishi and Steinmo 2006). Receipts from the privatization of the telecommunications company, the tobacco monopoly, and the railway system were also used to cover the deficit. The original intention was to use the revenue to reduce outstanding debt, but the incoming funds were eventually used to finance public works and subsidized loans (Wright 1999; Ishi 2000). As a result of privatization and tax buoyancy, the fiscal situation improved considerably and the debt-to-GDP ratio stabilized by the early 1990s, even in the absence of significant spending correction.

However, the fiscal balance proved only momentary. After the asset price bubble burst and growth stalled in the early 1990s, the debt-to-GDP ratio started to grow rapidly. The immediate years after the stock market crash of 1991 brought a series of stimulus packages made up of public works spending, loans, and tax cuts (Suzuki 2000). Simultaneously, social welfare expenditure—hitherto largely stable as a percentage of GDP—started to increase rapidly while income taxes plummeted due to the economic downturn. By the middle of the decade, the debt-to-GDP ratio surpassed 100 percent. Therefore, as growth picked up somewhat by the middle of the decade, consolidation became the priority. The Ministry of Finance argued strongly for the need of tax reform—the introduction of a new, 7-percent consumption tax to replace the one enacted in 1988—and general "fiscal restructuring" of spending in order to bring the deficit below 3 percent and eliminate borrowing by 2005 (Suzuki 2000; van Hagen 2006). The proposal for the new consumption tax was dropped in the face of strong intragovernmental opposition, but the old consumption tax was raised to 5 percent in 1995. As growth turned sharply down, however, further consolidation was postponed and public works expenditure remained at the level of the stimulus years. It was only at the turn of the decade that fiscal reform was back on the agenda.

In the 2000s, the fiscal effort proved more successful. As a first step, the government committed to keeping spending as a percentage of GDP at a constant level. This required major efforts in terms of cuts in public works spending or in terms of social security and health care reform because of the fast growth of social benefit spending due to rapid population aging (van Hagen 2006; Takahashi and Tokuoka 2011). Although the government missed its targets several times, major improvements were achieved in this period. Public works spending—although still high in international comparison—dropped to historically low levels. The share of in-kind social benefits as a percentage of GDP stabilized due to the increase of health-care co-payments while the steep increase of the not-in-kind benefits slowed due to pension benefit cuts (Estevez-Abe 2008). As a result of these measures and thanks to a drop in interest expenses on outstanding debt, spending actually declined as a share of GDP. On the revenue side, social contributions were raised in 2004, while income taxes also picked up somewhat due to the improvement of the economy. By the middle of the decade, the rate of debt accumulation slowed and the debt-to-GDP ratio temporarily stabilized slightly under 190 percent before the global financial and economic crisis derailed Japan's consolidation efforts once again.

This discussion of four decades of Japan's fiscal history highlights that fiscal adjustment efforts were rather timid until the 2000s, despite the persistent discourse of fiscal emergency among bureaucrats in charge of fiscal policy making since the mid-1970s and despite the commitment of political leaders to consolidation. Although favorable economic conditions allowed the fiscal gap to temporarily close at the end of the 1980s, explicit policy measures aimed at correcting the underlying structural imbalances of public finances achieved little before the 2000s. Initiatives to assert control over spending were unsuccessful. Reforms on entitlement benefits were invariably watered down in the face of opposition. Public works spending also conspicuously escaped major cuts before the 2000s. This expenditure item was much larger in Japan than in any other developed country throughout the past decades, both as a percentage of GDP and, especially, as a share of spending. It remained remarkably immune to savings pressures apart from the early 2000s, whereas in most countries, gross fixed capital formation is the first item that suffers at times of fiscal tightening. At the same time, it has consistently been the primary avenue for fiscal expansion when stimulus was deemed necessary.

On the revenue side, the most conspicuous feature of the past four decades has been the consistency of the efforts of the Ministry of Finance to generate more revenues through the taxation on consumption and the failure of these efforts. Although the consumption tax was eventually introduced in 1989—fifteen years after it was initially proposed—and then slightly increased in 1995, the share of consumption taxes has stayed very low. On the other hand, attempts to explicitly increase revenues from personal income taxation are conspicuous by their absence. Corporate tax rates and social security contributions were slightly increased in the 1980s, but they made relatively little difference. Increases in revenues in the past four decades have mostly been driven by favorable phases in business cycles and bracket creep. No matter how adamant about "fiscal reconstruction," policy makers had been mostly unable to assert control over fiscal developments in the past four decades.

The Catch-22 of Fiscal Adjustment in a Polarized Fiscal Regime and a Closed Economy

The persistent inability of policy makers to change important features of Japan's fiscal regime in the past forty years is rooted in the polarized structure of fiscal interests within Japanese society and in the lack of a compelling force for compromise in Japan's closed economy. Failure to retrench welfare benefits, rein in public works spending, or significantly increase revenues through tax reform are all manifestations of the paralyzing effect of strong conflicts of vested interests in the fiscal regime whose main contours were solidified by the mid-1970s. Under that regime, a large share of the population engaged in small-scale, inefficient agriculture, industry, or service—mostly in rural areas of the country—came to crucially depend on a mix of subsidies, public works, targeted welfare policies, and tax advantages for their livelihood. These fiscal benefits have been largely subsidized by high-productivity businesses and labor in urban areas. High productivity businesses have been burdened with very heavy corporate taxes and relatively onerous social security contributions in international comparison. Labor employed in these businesses has born a fiscal burden comparable to the international average, but it has received disproportionately more limited public welfare protection than labor elsewhere. These fiscal relations created irreconcilable conflicts of interests among the low-productivity rural population, high-productivity urban businesses and their workers when it came to fiscal adjustment. Subsidies and public works spending are sacrosanct to the rural population, along with the welfare policies and tax advantages targeted at them. Productive businesses resist further increases in corporate tax pressure, while urban workers are opposed both to cuts in welfare spending and to increased income or consumption taxes.

These conflicts have been all the more difficult to resolve as none of the three groups has an economic stake in fiscal consolidation to make it worthwhile to sacrifice fiscal interests for the sake of stabilization. Fiscal problems have not spilled over into macroeconomic problems like inflation or high interest rates. Therefore, their elimination yields no immediate economic benefit. On the contrary, given the extraordinary significance of domestic demand in Japan's closed economy, fiscal consolidation is likely to damage the livelihood of large sections of society by contracting domestic demand.

Given the conflict surrounding fiscal issues and the lack of incentives for compromise, politicians have always had strong motivation to uncompromisingly defend the fiscal interests of the social groups they were beholden to, lest they be punished with the withdrawal of electoral or financial support. As the electoral power of rural and urban populations has been fairly balanced in the past forty years, the LDP needed the support of both constituencies to stay in power. The fiscal fault line has run across the party, where different factions made sure that there was no attempt to impose fiscal sacrifices on the group whose support they relied on. Therefore, even before the LDP was forced to govern together with other political forces, the hands of LDP governments were tied by the irresolvable conflict between rural and urban Japan. This resulted in a four-decade-long inability to put into place fiscal reforms to stop debt accumulation.

The Socioeconomic Foundations of Fiscal Polarization
in a Dualistic, Closed Economy

Better understanding the highly polarizing fiscal regime and the balance of power that freezes it into place requires briefly investigating the economic roots and political origins of fiscal policies that constitute the regime. The array of fiscal benefits that sustain much of the rural economy originate from the period of rapid economic development in the 1950s and 1960s. In this period of economic take-off, aggregate national income expanded at an astonishing pace, but the large majority of the population was still engaged in low-productivity, small-scale agricultural, industrial, and service activities of limited profitability. This part of the population constituted an incredibly attractive constituency, given its overwhelming electoral power, partly due to the distortion of an electoral system that favored rural constituencies at the expense of urban ones, but mostly by virtue of its still large numerical majority[8] (Estevez-Abe 2008; Steinmo 2010). Political actors were bound to court this constituency by offering ways to benefit from the economic bonanza. Strongly incentivized by the logic of the multi-member electoral system, individual politicians sought to buy electoral support from different sections of the rural population and businesses with closely targeted policies. Liberal Democrats made it a centerpiece of their political strategy to lavish subsidies, public works, and tax benefits on various low-efficiency producer groups such as farmers, the construction industry, and distribution or financial services. They also secured earmarked public pension schemes for farmers and the self-employed. Although highly targeted, together this patchwork of policies became an important pillar of economic well-being for entire geographic areas dominated by low-efficiency sectors (Pempel 2010). It became a deeply entrenched part of the policy structure, not only because the target population came to depend on it but also because it enabled the low-economy sector to thrive and thereby greatly slowed the decline of the political weight of the low-productivity constituency.

Sustained public transfers to rural areas caused neither fiscal nor political problems in the 1950s and 1960s, given the electoral dominance of the population engaged in the low-productivity sectors and the rapid growth of the economy. The necessary funds could be extracted from the high-productivity sectors, which had limited political clout. Workers in these sectors did not constitute a sufficiently large electoral force yet to influence policy making, and their unions only exerted power at the enterprise level (Pempel 1998). Enterprises had considerable lobbying power but not strong enough to countervail the electoral appeal of the low-productivity sectors (Estevez-Abe 2008). Furthermore, the combined effect of rapid economic growth and the lack of extensive public welfare provisions kept fiscal pressure on high-productivity enterprises moderate. Paradoxically, low fiscal pressure also helped to temporarily preempt labor demands for public welfare because enterprises lobbied for—and received—generous tax allowances for providing fringe benefits to their core workers, which appeased the most powerful section of urban labor (*Ibid.*).

Both the political balance of power and fiscal equilibrium was upset in the early 1970s as a result of population shifts, the changing characteristics of the labor market, and, crucially, the slowing of economic growth. With the expansion of the urban population employed in high-productivity industries, urban labor became a more serious electoral force to be reckoned with (Suzuki 2000). Simultaneously, the tightening of industrial labor markets also gave labor greater market power to demand better fringe benefits from employers. The escalation of fringe benefit costs made large companies more sympathetic to—and ready to lobby for—public welfare and social insurance schemes to supplement some of their private fringe benefits (Estevez-Abe 2008). The combined effect of these changes led to the considerable expansion of public welfare policies. But these large spending commitments were taken on at a time when growth slowed in the wake of the first oil crisis and fiscal constraints became tighter. As the flow of funds to rural areas continued unabated, the budget went into deficit.

The new balance of political power entrenched fiscal imbalances for the next four decades to come, as adjustment either to the spending or the revenue side became politically impossible for the governing Liberal Democrats who relied on the electoral support of both urban and rural populations by the end of the 1970s. Significantly cutting back on public works spending, subsidies, tax exemptions, and welfare benefits threatened electoral backlash from the rural constituencies. Appreciably retrenching recently created welfare programs spelled electoral penalties from urban labor. Explicitly increasing personal income taxes on lower income groups or on consumption threatened with electoral repercussions from both groups. Consumption taxes, in particular, were a sensitive issue in Japan, where market protection and the tacit toleration of collusion already kept prices at very high levels as a way to support domestic producers at the expense of consumers (Katz 2002; DeWit and Steinmo 2002). At the same time, high-productivity, internationally competitive businesses started to more vehemently resist the idea of paying higher taxes as profit margins declined (Akaishi and Steinmo 2006). Although they could transfer tax expenses to consumers through price increases in the protected domestics markets, high fiscal pressure dented their international profits (Estevez-Abe 2008). When their lobbying against increases in corporate taxes and social security contributions proved ineffectual in the 1970s and early 1980s, high-productivity internationally competitive businesses increasingly chose to relocate their production abroad and use transfer-pricing techniques to escape high corporate taxes in Japan (Katz 2002; Pempel 2010).

The political constraints arising from the conflicting interests of the three disparate socioeconomic groups were impossible to soften because no group could benefit enough from fiscal consolidation to counterbalance the loss they would suffer from tax increases and spending cuts, and, therefore, none had an incentive to soften its resistance to fiscal pain. On the contrary, beyond its effect on taxes to be paid and benefits received, fiscal adjustment would also impose short-term economic losses on different socioeconomic groups in the mostly closed Japanese economy through contracting domestic demand. Inflation was initially a serious side effect in the 1970s, which caused considerable concern in the famously savings-oriented Japanese society, but it was quickly brought under control by the early 1980s without major fiscal tightening and remained low from then on until the mid-1990s when it turned into dangerous deflation. Although the dynamic, high-productivity, export-oriented sector suffered from the strengthening of the yen, this development was more the consequence of international developments—first the collapse of the Bretton Woods system at the beginning of the 1970s and then the Plaza Accord of 1985—and had little to do with the fiscal stance (Pempel 2010). The prosperity of the 1970s and 1980s—characterized by relatively fast growth, very low unemployment, and sustained current account surpluses—generated no pressures for fiscal correction, whereas the collapse of growth in the mid-1990s generated pressure for stimulus.

Under these circumstances, it was impossible to count on substantial social support for significant fiscal adjustment. Fiscal imbalances remained a problem for bureaucrats to worry about, despite the alarmist discourse, the great public salience of the issue, and the pledges of prime ministers to restrain borrowing. LDP politicians and their factions could not be counted on to compromise the interests of their constituencies for the sake of fiscal consolidation because they had good reason to believe that the electoral punishment would be significant and immediate. They scuttled repeated attempts to significantly retrench welfare, to reduce public works spending, or to significantly increase the taxation of consumption. As politicians went in the direction of least electoral resistance and raised taxes on corporations, businesses relocated. The next section discusses in more detail how societal resistance to fiscal pain was manifested in the partisan-electoral sphere.

Partisanship and Electoral Pressures in a Polarized Fiscal Regime

Since the postwar political history of Japan is practically the story of the Liberal Democratic Party—with various lesser parties, interest groups, and the elite bureaucracy in the supporting cast—the LDP naturally played the central role in the politics of fiscal policy. It was the LDP that mobilized, united, and exploited the electoral potential of the mostly rural, low-productivity sectors from the end of the allied occupation to the present day. It was partially the LDP that channeled the demands of an increasingly powerful labor electorate into policy making, and it was the LDP that furthered the interests of the dynamic, high-efficiency businesses in return for generous financial support. In other words, the conflicts of the three major socioeconomic groups whose interests governed fiscal policy making in the decades since the Second World War played out for the most part through the intraparty power dynamics and strategic choices of the LDP.

Progressive parties played a secondary, limited role in the politics of policy making from the 1950s up to the global financial and economic crisis. They shaped the strategic decisions of the LDP through articulating labor demands, through putting those demands on the agenda, and by demonstrating their electoral appeal—first in local elections and later also on the national stage—and through expressing labor opposition to certain policy changes. However, progressive parties exercised little independent effect on policy choice until the 1990s. From the 1990s, they had a more significant parliamentary and governmental role to directly influence decisions, but—apart from a very brief period when the LDP was out of government in 1993 and 1994—they were minor partners in decision-making until the sweeping electoral victory of the Democratic Party of Japan in 2009.

Similarly, interest groups exerted influence mostly through their connections to LDP, rather than through independent institutional roles. The strong peak associations in business were invited to consult on policy proposals, for example, in the framework of the administrative reform committee, *Rincho* (Suzuki 2000). However, policy proposals rarely survived the political process in their original form. Therefore, business's effective policy influence depended much more on its capacity to lobby the LDP, and this was often more effectively done by particular industry groups than by the umbrella organizations (Estevez-Abe 2008). Trade unions were also invited to committees like *Rincho* but had a relatively low weight even in those consultative fora (Suzuki 2000). Unions lacked policy influence for most of the postwar era because they were mostly focused on the enterprise level, and they were strongly divided at the national level (Pempel 2010). Only after the formation of a unified organization (*Rengo*) in 1987 did unions start to exert more substantial influence, mainly through progressive parties. Even then, unions represented a relatively small share of workers, mostly the most privileged, core workforce, leaving the representation of a considerable cohort of unorganized wage-earners to smaller political parties.

In a similar vein, Japan's famously influential bureaucratic elite was able to shape policy outcomes only within the constraints of the LDP's electoral considerations. Although the Japanese bureaucratic corps had strong organizational autonomy, a strong sense of coherence, a large array of formal and informal powers, and strong networks with powerful politicians, their discretion in policy making was clearly circumscribed by the political needs of LDP Diet members (Suzuki 2000). Although the Ministry of Finance had exclusive authority in compiling the budget, the LDP was incorporated into the budgetary processes, both formally through the so-called Policy Affairs Research Councils and informally through the intervention of senior party officials and members (Wright 1999). Consequently, the Ministry's policy proposals always incorporated the preferences of the party and its clients either as a result of direct intervention or because "anticipated reactions" were taken into consideration in advance (Ibid.).

The Liberal Democratic Party took center stage in politics and gained control of policy making in the years following the allied occupation by tapping into the enormous electoral potential of the population engaged in the low-productivity sector.[9] The LDP developed a network of clientelistic ties that secured the electoral support of diverse rural interest groups through subsidies, tax exemptions, public works contracts, and, later, welfare benefits. Although divided into factions beholden to different interests, the LDP was sufficiently cohesive to provide consistently powerful representation to the interests of the low-productivity sector. Once securely established in power, the LDP was also the natural partner for large, powerful businesses to liaise with, to rely on for keeping tax pressures generally low, and to extract important tax concessions from (Estevez-Abe 2008). When the electoral balance of power started to shift toward urban labor from the late 1960s and early 1970s, the LDP became amenable to wooing labor. As the party lost control over large cities to progressive candidates and suffered setbacks in the Diet elections, the influence of the factions representing urban labor strengthened, which led to the significant extension of public welfare nationwide[10] (Estevez-Abe 2008). By the mid-1970s, half of the LDP support came from labor (Suzuki 2000). This shift toward urban labor effectively turned the LDP into the political umbrella for a "social grand-coalition" of various segments of both the low- and high-productivity sectors of the dualistic Japanese economy.

Relying equally on the electoral support of the population in the low-productivity sector and labor in the high-productivity sector had a paralyzing effect on the LDP when it came to dealing with fiscal problems. In the 1980s, successive LDP governments experimented with a variety of reforms proposed by bureaucrats alarmed by the accumulation of debt. However, the labor faction—often in alliance with opposition parties—watered down measures intended to retrench benefits to wage earners. Simultaneously, rural factions blocked attempts to cut benefits to or increase contributions from farmers and the self-employed (Estevez-Abe 2008). Cutbacks on public works spending and subsidies were sabotaged by supplementary budgets and *ad hoc* authorizations demanded by rural factions (van Hagen 2006). Increases in corporate taxes and social contributions proved to be the path of least electoral—and therefore intraparty—resistance, but they provoked strong resistance from the party's biggest funders and also had their price in terms of encouraging the relocation of competitive companies, which foreshadowed grave economic and employment problems for the future (Akaishi and Steinmo 2006). Introducing a consumption tax would have been closest to a compromise between the different LDP factions because it would have spread the burden of adjustment across the rural and urban populations, but exactly for that reason, it was the electorally most costly option for the party as a whole. Already proposing it in the mid-1970s cost the LDP dearly in local elections. When the consumption tax was finally introduced in 1989—at a much lower rate than originally envisaged and more than counterbalanced by tax cuts elsewhere to soften the blow—it led to the loss of almost a third of the LDP's seats in the 1989 upper house elections and to the loss of the LDP majority (Akaishi and Steinmo 2006).

The policy-making paralysis only intensified as the LDP lost control of the government in the 1990s. As severe economic problems compounded the fiscal ones, intraparty conflict over scarce resources ended in the secession of a large urban faction of LDP Diet members from the party in 1993, leading to the ejection of the party from power for the first time since 1955 (Suzuki 2000). Although the LDP was back in government by

1994, it had to put up with more progressive, urban-oriented parties—the Social Democratic Party and Sakigake—as coalition partners until 1998. This only aggravated the paralyzing effect of the electoral balance between high- and low-productivity sectors on fiscal policy making. Rural policy preferences were briefly excluded from policy making while the LDP was out of government—in this short period, public works spending was cut back—but as soon as the LDP was back in power, they regained their earlier central importance, evidenced by the launching of major new public projects and the reinforcement of farm subsidies (Estevez-Abe 2008). Welfare retrenchment was off the table due to the strong representation of urban labor interests by LDP factions as well as the progressive parties. In fact, the welfare state was expanded in these years (Estevez-Abe 2008). Slightly increasing the consumption tax—offset by large income tax cuts— was the only compromise solution once again. However, just like before, the loss of revenue from income taxes far outweighed the gain from the limited increase of the indirect tax revenue, and even this limited compromise cost the progressive parties dearly in the next election (Akaishi and Steinmo 2006).

In the late 1990s, politics and policies took a new turn that temporarily seemed to resolve the stalemate between the interests of the rural low-productivity sector, urban labor, and high-productivity corporations. The electoral reforms of 1994 increased the need for parties to appeal to broad nationwide constituencies, rather than to particularistic local communities. The LDP responded to these changes with internal reforms that shifted power from factions to the leader of the party, who was now able to provide a clear and unified policy platform to appeal to a broad cross section of voters. Governmental decision-making was also centralized to enable the prime minister to adhere to a clear policy platform (Estevez-Abe 2008). These reforms shifted the intra-party balance of power toward the urban constituencies, whose support was crucial under the new electoral rules and especially in light of the emergence and consolidation of a serious progressive competitor, the Democratic Party of Japan (DPJ), which appealed mostly to unorganized urban voters. Consecutive prime ministers from Hashimoto to Obuchi and Koizumi undertook reforms that improved fiscal balance at the expense of the low-productivity constituencies of the LDP. They reduced public works spending to historically low levels, cut farm subsidies, and reformed health care, but they steered clear of a renewed attempt to increase consumption taxes and even offered limited new social protection schemes to unorganized urban voters (Estevez-Abe 2008). These reform efforts led to the gradual closing of the deficit and the slowing of debt growth.

However, this shift in LDP strategy around the turn of the millennium did not imply that the societal conflict over fiscal resources was definitively resolved. On the one hand, the shift was predicated on the strategic outlook of the leader in whose hands intra-party and intragovernmental power was centralized. When leaders tied to factions with low-productivity constituencies gained the upper hand, the enthusiasm about fiscal adjustment at the expense of rural constituencies waned (Pempel 2010). On the other hand, the LDP's willingness to compromise rural interests had a steep electoral price, and it created an opening that its rivals were ready to exploit. The DPJ—which had originally threatened to outflank the LDP from the left by campaigning consistently with promises of reforms that appealed to the urban electorate—began to exploit rural discontent with the LDP's reforms and tried to capture the LDP's rural constituencies (Lipscy and Scheiner 2012). In the 2007 elections, the DPJ overtook the upper house, and by 2009, they were in government. Despite winning the elections on a platform of change, the DPJ has essentially continued the LDP's old policies, including the restoration of the fiscal position of the rural constituencies through farming subsidies and budgetary support for rural localities (Lipscy and Scheiner 2012). As the global financial and economic crisis sent debt on a path of explosive growth again, the DPJ tried—just as the LDP did several times before—to avoid choosing between its different constituencies by raising the consumption tax as a way of dealing with the country's enormous fiscal imbalances. At the next elections, it was ejected from government. Once back in power, the LDP went back to its old ways of redoubling public works spending in the name of fiscal stimulus (The Economist, Jan 12, 2013).

Political and Economic Change and Enduring Conflicts of Fiscal Polarization

Although electoral reform significantly changed the Japanese party system and the Liberal Democratic Party itself, it did not resolve the underlying societal conflict that has tied the hands of policy makers in dealing with Japan's fiscal imbalances for decades. Albeit they were temporarily suppressed within the LDP, the intense conflicts among the urban and rural populations quickly resurfaced through other channels to prevent meaningful policy adjustment as disgruntled groups found new champions to defend their interests. Just as in the case of Greece, the stakes involved in choosing between specific avenues of fiscal adjustment are too high for different sections of society (and their political representatives) to relax their opposition to unfavorable reforms of spending or taxation, especially since fiscal consolidation does not offer a way out of the severe economic problems of the past more than two decades.

Conclusion

The Greek and Japanese stories demonstrate the paralyzing effect of fiscal polarization on policy reform, especially in conjunction with the insulation of the livelihood of the majority of society from the effects of fiscal imbalances on international competitiveness. Albeit the persistent willingness of policy makers to subordinate the goal of fiscal stabilization to electoral considerations make the two cases seem like textbook examples of "fiscal indiscipline," the profound differences between the two countries—in terms of political and budgetary institutions, ideologies, policy paradigms, the economy, and their position in the economic system—raises the question why it is in these two countries that "fiscal indiscipline" is so unusually persistent and policy makers are so extraordinarily wary of imposing fiscal sacrifices on the electorate. This chapter argued that the electoral price of fiscal pain is prohibitive in both countries because existing fiscal policies generate very strong incentives for large groups in society to resist reforms that negatively affect them, while the economic structure fails to generate incentives for compromise.

Even though existing fiscal policies could hardly be more different in the two countries—in terms of the size of government spending as a share of the economy, the structure of taxation, and the allocation of revenues across spending items—they are very similar in the degree to which they closely target the benefits of public spending and the costs of taxation to specific groups within society. Targeted policies imply that any policy reform is necessarily a targeted assault on the interests of a specific group. Every group has a strong incentive to use its electoral leverage to try to deflect such assaults, especially when stabilization fails to offer hope for compensating improvements in their economic position. Moreover, in the absence of a likely positive impact on the economy, policy makers cannot hope for counterbalancing electoral gains from groups that get to "free ride" on other groups' fiscal sacrifices. Under these conditions, conservative governments in Japan suffered just as serious electoral setbacks after attempts at stabilization as left-wing and right-wing governments did in Greece; Greece's strong, centralized unitary governments were just as timid in attempting reforms as were divided governments in Japan, and Japan's strong bureaucracy and centralized budgetary institutions failed just as manifestly at enforcing fiscal targets in the face of political pressures as the weak Greek bureaucrats did. As a result, Japan borrowed just as relentlessly as Greece, even in the period when its economy was one of the world's strongest and Greece still lagged far behind other developed countries.

The next, concluding chapter revisits all the cases discussed in this book to recapitulate the ways in which fiscal polarization and international exposure influenced the fiscal track records of Belgium, Greece, Ireland, Italy, and Japan. It underlines the variation in the ways in which existing fiscal policies fuel or dampen conflicts between various social groups within different polities and analyzes the ways in which the demands of international economic competition exercise their effects in different political and policy settings. Finally, it ties into broader theoretical debates by investigating the lessons of the case studies about the role of political entrepreneurship as well as institutional and ideational innovations in fostering fiscal adjustment.

SIX

Variations on Three Themes

Social Coalitions, Fiscal Polarization,
and International Exposure

Sustained and substantial public debt accumulation is not simply a governance problem: it is a political-economic phenomenon. Countries may start to borrow for all sorts of economic and political reasons, but failure to restore fiscal balance and stop borrowing once the level of indebtedness reaches proportions that generate substantial economic costs and financial risks is a different matter altogether. Such failure indicates stubborn redistributive conflicts among societal groups within the given polity, which render policy makers helpless even in the face of increasing fiscal vulnerability. Closing a persistent large gap in public finances involves forcing or convincing considerable sections of society to permanently pay more into or take less out of the public purse. Since societal groups have numerous ways of defending themselves against onslaughts on their interests in a democratic polity, major budgetary adjustments require political support or at least tacit acquiescence from a large part of society. Until a specific stabilization package is found that can rely on the support of a strong enough societal coalition, imbalances persist, debt accumulates, and risks mount. Therefore, understanding why a country would drift ever-closer to the edge of the fiscal abyss and when it would eventually turn back requires studying the incentives of different societal groups to ally with other groups in resisting or supporting certain consolidation packages. This, in turn, involves studying the country's existing fiscal policies and economic structure because these factors determine the incentives that different parts of society face.

This book explored the fiscal troubles of five of the most indebted countries of the developed world: Belgium, Greece, Ireland, Italy, and Japan. It found that the polarization-exposure thesis has considerable capacity to explain their divergent fiscal experiences. All of these countries battled with major fiscal imbalances since the 1980s, but only Ireland was able to effectively address its problems relatively early on. Belgium reacted fast but was unable to attack the problem aggressively enough. Italy responded with more than a decade of delay. Greece and Japan never seriously addressed their issues. Analyzing the conflicts and commonalities of societal interests arising from the fiscal *status quo* and the exposure of the country's economy to international competition, and tracing the evolution of social coalitions helped explain the differences in the five countries' fiscal trajectories.

The investigation of these divergent cases highlighted three common themes in the otherwise very different stories of excessive debt accumulation. *First*, they demonstrated the limits of government control over adjustment. A series of failed adjustment attempts in all five countries—a few even in the eventually very successful Ireland—showed that governmental determination in itself is not enough to make reforms succeed and confirmed the significance of societal backing for the ability to inflict fiscal pain. *Second*, the narratives revealed the importance of existing fiscal policies in fueling discord and retarding adjustment or in limiting conflict and facilitating the emergence of a supportive social coalition behind an adjustment package. Where fiscal policies were polarizing—i.e., the costs and benefits of existing policies were closely targeted at specific groups— like in Greece, Italy, or Japan, the high stakes involved in defending particular vested interests induced more intense conflicts about adjustment. Where they encompassed large parts of society, like in Ireland, there was less room for wrangling about how the burden of adjustment should be spread. Where fiscal targeting affected one specific area of public finances, like social security in Belgium, that area was the biggest obstacle to stabilization. *Third*, these stories demonstrated the crucial role of the exposure to international economic competition in inducing large parts of society to form social coalitions in support of adjustment, even if it required considerable fiscal sacrifices from them. Where much of society was insulated from such competition, like in Greece or Japan, the obstacles to fiscal adjustment were insurmountable. Where exposure was very large, like in Belgium and Ireland, reaction to growing fiscal problems was very fast. In the middling case of Italy, the conditions for adjustment emerged gradually as the pressure grew on groups exposed to international competition and triggered a realignment of societal coalitions.

These common themes had different empirical manifestations in the different cases. This chapter provides an overview of their variations across the five countries. The second section gives examples of the diverse ways in which society constrains governments in policy making and demonstrates how supportive societal coalitions emerge to make stabilization possible. The third and fourth sections show how past policy choices interact with socioeconomic structures to give rise to varying degrees of fiscal polarization and exposure to international economic competition in different cases and, thus, how they set the scene for easy or difficult adjustment. These sections also probe into aspects of the effects of policy path dependence and international exposure that received less direct emphasis in the case studies. The section on policy path dependence returns to the claim made in the theory chapter that government size matters little for the difficulty of fiscal reform—only the targeted or encompassing nature of government spending and taxes does—and provides further evidence through an example of swift and relatively uncontentious reform in Denmark, a country of large government. The section on international exposure investigates the impact of international relations by pondering how decisions made outside of the domestic political sphere—primarily the ever-closer European integration and the policy frameworks attached to it—affected the economic and policy context in which the politics of fiscal problems and stabilization played out. It also reflects on the impact of financial internationalization on the constraints under which fiscal policy making operated. The fifth section ties into broader theoretical debates by investigating the lessons of the case studies about the effects of electoral and party systems on policy choice, the benefits of corporatist arrangements, the significance of the strength and organization of the state, and the role of ideational change and political entrepreneurship in making fiscal adjustment possible. The last section concludes with extensions and implications of the findings of this study.

Society versus Government

Although persistent borrowing is often portrayed as the consequence of irresponsible policy choices, the stories told in this book show that sustained excessive debt accumulation has much more to do with the inability to change an existing fiscal course than with a series of reckless decisions.

The severe fiscal troubles of the countries studied here had different roots, but the unsustainability of fiscal trends was recognized fairly early on in all of the cases, and the politics of fiscal policy making revolved around reasserting control over debt growth from that moment on.

In some cases, fiscal imbalances were created by exogenous economic shocks; in others, they were of political origin. In Belgium and Ireland, fiscal problems were triggered by changes in the economic environment. Both countries had pursued policies that kept the debt-to-GDP ratio on a declining path when major economic shocks jolted the budget out of balance in the late 1970s. As growth plunged, unemployment skyrocketed and interest rates surged, previously prudent fiscal policies suddenly yielded significant imbalances, which were compounded by unsuccessful temporary attempts at fiscal stimulus. In Greece, the large budgetary gap was purely political in origin. When PASOK came into power, it used state resources to extend benefits to its supporters without securing the necessary revenues to maintain budgetary balance. In Italy and Japan, politically motivated imbalances were later magnified by adverse economic changes. In Italy, the fiscal rigor of the postwar years was swept away by the social upheaval of the late 1960s and 1970s. Large sections of society violently asserted their claim for fiscal benefits without being able to force other sections to foot the bill of increased spending. The imbalance created by these policy changes became especially consequential when the economy turned for the worse in the 1980s. Similarly, in Japan, the ruling Liberal Democrats introduced welfare policies the 1970s to woo urban labor as their rural supporter base declined without attempting to make their old constituencies pay for the changes. The corresponding stress on the budget grew throughout the 1980s, but it assumed tragic proportions when Japan plunged into a series of recessions from the mid-1990s and faced the first consequences of population aging.

Irrespective of the original reason for excessive borrowing, the unsustainability of existing policies was openly acknowledged and fiscal stabilization became a declared policy goal within a few years of the start of the problem in all of the countries. In Japan, "fiscal reconstruction" and principles of "sound management" ruled the fiscal policy discourse already from the end of the 1970s; various rules were devised to control expenditure growth and a major tax reform was planned. In Belgium, the government announced a "Disaster Plan" to reverse the adverse fiscal and monetary trends as early as 1981, and it put a drastic austerity package in place in 1982, which perpetuated savage cuts for the rest of the decade. It also set out to rebalance the social security system, initiating many reforms.

In Italy, the 1980s were dominated by incessant talk of "risanamento." They saw a series of adjustment plans and reforms to budgetary decision-making to enhance spending control. In the meantime, tax rates were increased and new taxes were introduced while the government tightened the conditions for welfare payments and initiated cuts to health spending. In Greece, the PASOK government sought to restrain the developments it had set off right after it was reelected in 1985 by introducing a draconian incomes policy in the public sector and introducing VAT. New Democracy, on the other side of the political front lines, made renewed efforts in the early 1990s, announcing the retrenchment of the public sector and reforming the pension system. Finally, the 1980s was a decade of austerity in Ireland, too, where two major adjustment packages in 1982 and 1987 introduced dramatic tax increases and spending cuts affecting every item on the budget.

Limits on Governmental Discretion

However, the case studies showed that few of these government initiatives translated into actual adjustments of fiscal policies. The fiscal stories of the five countries draw attention to a wide range of societal constraints on government action and to the various ways in which different social groups could resist adjustments that adversely affected their vested interests in existing policies. Electoral constraints obviously played an important role. Such constraints are usually assumed to work retroactively. This was initially the case in Greece, where both PASOK and New Democracy attempted to drastically adjust fiscal policies (in 1985 and 1991) to then learn that this was very costly in electoral terms. Both parties lost office at the next elections, as they were heavily punished by the social groups that were hurt by their measures. After this experience, both avoided frontal assaults on the vested interests of the largest constituencies. In other cases, electoral influence worked in a more proactive fashion. For example, in Italy, plans to tighten tax collection were withdrawn in 1984 after the small business association, *Confcommercio*, explicitly threatened the government that the vote of small entrepreneurs would be withheld from Christian Democracy if the so-called Visentini law went into effect. In Belgium, Christian Democrats were forced to break up their coalition with the Liberals and abandon plans to retrench the welfare system in the mid-1980s under pressure from the party's labor section. In Japan, the clientelistic ties between individual Liberal Democratic politicians and their voters created the channel for preliminary electoral input.

At the same time, electoral power was only one of the ways in which various social groups could influence and constrain governmental action. Different groups also mobilized their economic power to exert pressure on policy makers. Strikes and strike threats were widely used by labor to resist unfavorable policy adjustment. Strikes prevented cuts in the public wage bill in the 1980s in Greece and Ireland, and they defeated several attempts at welfare reform in the 1980s in Belgium. A decade of strikes had created such a political climate in Italy by the 1980s that successive governments refrained from proposing policy changes to the welfare system altogether. In Italy and Greece, large sections of society also often resorted to civil unrest as a form of protest. Large enterprises had recourse to lobbying, evidenced by the multitude of special tax arrangements targeted to specific sectors, regions, or even firms in Italy, Greece, or Japan. Policy pressure from business was all the more effective when large firms could credibly threaten to exit the national economy. For example, the shipping industry in Greece was fully tax-exempt because it could easily opt to register its vessels under different flags. In Ireland, the high proportion of foreign investors practically excluded the possibility of increasing the fiscal pressure on business.

Some social groups in Italy and Greece also heavily resorted to a less often discussed method of defending their interest from unfavorable policy changes: non-compliance. A minor example of such self-defense is the flouting of hiring and wage freezes in the Greek public sector. The most notable example, of course, is tax evasion. Evasion flexibly responded to changes in tax laws in Italy throughout the past three decades (Chiarini et al. 2013), keeping the *de facto* tax pressure remarkably constant for those who are engaged in the small-scale economy despite large variations in *de jure* tax rates. In Greece, an astonishing 45 percent of the employed labor force falsely registers as self-employed to have the opportunity to self-report their income and, thus, to evade taxes. These practices have had enormous impact on the debt problem in both countries. Obviously, tax evasion is a complicated issue because this form of resistance is sometimes tacitly condoned by policy makers who fail to crack down on evasion. The frequency of tax amnesties, the reluctance to introduce evasion-safe taxes, like the property tax, and the above-cited Visentini affair seem to confirm the widespread opinion that (at least in certain periods) policy makers were complicit in evasion in both countries (Della Sala 1997; Pappas 2013). Nevertheless, noncompliance is a form of societal resistance to policy change that puts policy makers on the defensive and necessitates powerful countervailing action if the redistributive intent of the *de jure* policy change is to be fulfilled.

In fact, none of the forms of societal resistance to policy change discussed here necessarily pose insurmountable obstacles to adjustment.
While all of them have been effectively used in some instances to thwart
policy change, in other instances, they failed to constrain the ability of
governments to adjust policies. The electoral power of the dependents of
the state in the south of Italy, which secured a steady flow of funds to the
South in the 1980s, could not stop governments in the 1990s from cutting
off (in fact, de-institutionalizing) the flow of money. Powerful strikes that
were so effective in blocking welfare reform most of the time in Belgium
proved less powerful at other times and failed to prevent some benefit cuts.
The public employees who successfully resisted pay cuts in the first half
of the 1980s in Ireland decided not to strike but accept lower wages in the
second half of the same decade. Large businesses that insisted on targeted
exemptions in the 1980s in Italy voluntarily acquiesced in increases in the
corporate tax rates in the 1990s. Tax evasion was temporarily pushed back
in Italy in the 1990s when governments took a firm stance and tightened
reporting and introduced new, evasion-safe taxes.

Stating that it requires "governmental resolve" to overcome such forms
of societal resistance or to convince different groups to refrain from putting
up resistance would be tautological: the government has its way when it is
strong enough to have its way. The case studies showed that the extent to
which different social groups were able and willing to use these sources of
power depended on the constellation of societal coalitions, which strengthened or weakened the hands of governments in enforcing policy change.
Strong coalitions formed around the defense of vested fiscal interests made
such forms of resistance effective, whereas coalitions that coalesced around
the need for adjustment discouraged and thwarted them. Coalitions of the
latter kind were much faster to emerge in countries where fiscal polarization was moderate and exposure to international economic competition
ensured that fiscal imbalances generated tangible economic losses for large
sections of society.

Evolving Coalitions

Social coalitions reigning at the time when debt accumulation was identified as a serious problem facilitated resistance to adjustment to the main
contours of fiscal policy. Since fiscal policies that vested interest groups
formed around arose from prior redistributive struggles, they reflected the
balance of power between coalitions of social groups that produced the
extant redistributive arrangements. As long as the constellation of coali-

tions stayed the same, all groups were able to resist onslaughts on their vested interests if they chose to. Therefore, adjustments could only succeed if society universally acquiesced in them or if coalitions realigned in a way that made it possible to overcome the resistance of recalcitrant groups. The politics of public finances in Italy and Belgium exemplify the complex dynamics of conflict, compromise, and changing social coalitions that drive the politics of fiscal gridlock and reform. In Ireland, Greece, and Japan, large realignments of social coalitions did not take place. In Ireland, this was because conflicts about the composition of adjustment were negligible and reforms were put into place without major societal resistance when fiscal problems started to impinge on the economy, obviating the need for political reconfiguration. In contrast, social coalitions failed to realign in Greece and Japan because intense conflicts of vested fiscal interests overpowered economic incentives for compromise.

In Italy, the fiscal problems of the early 1980s were rooted in policies that arose from the "hot autumn" of the late 1960s and early 1970s when labor extorted significant welfare improvements and put business on the defensive about increasing corporate tax pressure. This started a trench warfare of organized labor against a coalition of large and small businesses with the proletariat of the South. Labor's strike potential allowed unions to resist the rollback of welfare. Christian Democracy—entrenched in power by corporate support and the electoral backing of small entrepreneurs and the South—protected businesses from fiscal pressure and channeled funds to the South. Under this balance of power, all of the major fiscal items were untouchable. Adjustment only became possible when some business groups broke away from the coalition that had guaranteed the protection of their vested fiscal interests to form a new alliance with organized labor to restore economic competitiveness. The realignment of coalitions had striking political manifestations in both the electoral-governmental and the corporatist sphere. It destroyed Christian Democracy and the rest of the *pentapartito*, parts of which allied with the erstwhile Communists who reinvented themselves as a moderate center-left party. Unions dramatically reversed their strategy on the most contentious issues of the 1980s and entered into historic compromises with employers. The resulting fiscal adjustment reflected compromises among the groups constituting the competitiveness coalition but also imposed very heavy losses on groups left out of it. The competitiveness coalition later crumbled, and the old coalition among the South and business groups was resurrected, resulting in the end of corporatist consultation, the ascendancy of the center-right electoral alliance over the center-left, and the return to borrowing.

In Belgium, fiscal problems emanated from the social security sector, which became severely underfunded in the wake of the adverse economic shocks of the 1970s and early 1980s. The polarizing fiscal architecture of the system—which provided generous benefits to workers financed from labor cost increasing contributions—embodied a postwar settlement between capital and labor that exchanged wage restraint for entitlements. This exchange had allowed capital and labor to maintain a societal "grand coalition"—manifested both in the dominance of the cross-class Christian Democratic parties and the institutionalized cooperation between business associations and unions—but it generated debilitating conflict when it came to rebalancing social security. Adjustment became feasible only when the social "grand coalition" temporarily gave way to a more limited alliance focused on restoring international competitiveness. Labor groups most acutely exposed to trade (mostly in Flanders) broke ranks with labor groups insulated from the side effects of fiscal problems on competitiveness (mostly in Wallonia) and compromised with business. This realignment manifested itself in changing government composition—as Christian Democrats dropped Socialists for the Liberals as coalition partners—and in the acquiescence of the largest union in benefit cuts in 1982, which rendered strikes by other unions ineffectual. However, this realignment was reversed as soon as the first wave of austerity eliminated the worst side effects of fiscal problems on competitiveness. Christian Democrats reverted to coalition with the Socialists, and unions struck together whenever welfare retrenchment was proposed. The social "grand coalition" was restored on the understanding that welfare reform—either by entitlement cuts or by significant increases in funding—was off the table. Despite draconian austerity in the less clearly redistributive aspects of the budget, the social security deficit continued to fuel debt accumulation. Albeit a steep drop in interest rates from the early 1990s saved Belgium from drifting closer to fiscal disaster, fundamental redistributive conflicts remain unresolved.

In Ireland, the fiscal structure in place at the start of debt accumulation distributed the benefits and costs of government spending fairly uniformly across society as a result of economic underdevelopment and the policies put into place to escape it. Light tax pressure on corporations revealed the dependence of the Irish economy on foreign direct investment and international competitiveness. The bulk of revenues came from consumption and personal taxes, which burdened much of the population fairly evenly due to the strong clustering of incomes at the lower end of the income scale. Reflecting the general precariousness of employment across society, welfare benefits were designed to be available independently of work history. Among these encompassing policies, public employment was the only significant budgetary item that provided specific benefits to a well-delineable group. Otherwise, the uniform incidence of fiscal burdens and benefits and the "untouchability" of business left little room for disagreement about how austerity was to be implemented, especially since persistently high inflation and surging unemployment made macroeconomic stabilization very urgent for large parts of society. Consequently, parties alternating in power—Fianna Fail and Fine Gael in coalition with Labor—did not shy away from large adjustments to VAT, income taxes, and welfare, and they faced limited pushback either from the parliamentary opposition or from unions. Only public sector unions put up resistance in the face of attempts to cut the public wage bill in the first half of the decade, but eventually, they caved in, too, as the real value of public sector pay was consistently eroded by high inflation. By the second half of the decade, fiscal reform received nationwide support.

The Greek case provides interesting contrast to the Irish one because Greece was similarly underdeveloped in European comparison as Ireland, but policies adopted in the wake of the return to democracy—the expansion of public employment, pension benefits earmarked for different social groups, increased state aid to farms and companies, and the toleration of growing tax evasion—strongly polarized societal interests in Greece. Public employees, farmers, large businesses, small enterprises, and the self-employed could each hamstring reforms to parts of the budget they had vested interests in, mainly because any of these groups were able to decisively influence the electoral success of the two large parties—making both New Democracy and PASOK wary of hurting their vested interests—but also because they never shied away from strikes and other forms of civil unrest when they needed to defend their preferred policies. In effect, the political system in place amounted to a social coalition built on the universal plundering of state resources. The stalemate was impossible to break because general macroeconomic stability had much more limited importance to the large majority of people and businesses than the resources they drew or withheld from the state, and, therefore, none of the vested interest groups had an incentive to join another coalition based on fiscal sacrifices and the goal of fiscal stabilization. Policy reform persistently proved to be a losing political strategy, from which both major parties stayed clear of after the mid-1990s. The main contours of fiscal policy remained unadjusted until Greece went bankrupt in the 2010s.

In Japan, postwar fiscal policies entrenched conflicts between dynamic, economically competitive large urban centers and the small-scale, inefficient rural economy. For most of the 1950s and 1960s, geographically imbalanced taxes and government spending were used to channel income from urban to rural areas, but when the urban population asserted claims for more significant government spending on welfare in the 1970s, public finances became structurally imbalanced. However, with the rural population overwhelmingly dependent on state support and urban areas already apprehensive of unequal burden-sharing even before economic hardship befell Japan from the mid-1990s, large fiscal concessions could not be expected from either side, especially since neither side could hope that fiscal sacrifices would alleviate their economic difficulties. On the contrary: since the Japanese economy is overwhelmingly dependent on domestic demand, austerity hurts most social groups irrespective of the actual incidence of fiscal pain. Even the export sector had little to gain from stabilization, as fiscal problems never caused inflation over the international average to undermine competitiveness. Under these conditions, the Liberal Democrats—who, until recent times, continuously held government relying on both rural and urban electoral support—suffered heavy losses of votes every time they tried to make large fiscal adjustments. But the intractability of the societal stalemate is brought into especially sharp relief by the inability of other political actors to redraw the political front lines since the introduction of important electoral reform in the early 1990s. Although the grip of the Liberal Democrats on power gradually loosened, the competitor that eventually ousted them from government adopted their long-term political platform of protecting vested interests both in the countryside and in the cities. At a debt level of two-and-a-half times the GDP, political conditions are still not ripe for radical fiscal reform in Japan.

The five country cases highlight the crucial significance of coalitional alignments for policy stalemate and breakthrough. In each case, social support for governments' attempts to adjust unsustainable fiscal policies emerged only when shared aversion to the growing side effects of fiscal problems outweighed conflicts of vested fiscal interests within large enough parts of society. At the same time, the case studies also showed how different the five countries were in terms of their conflicts of vested fiscal interests and their economic sensitivity to fiscal problems. The next section turns to exploring the roots of these differences in differing economic structures and past policy choices.

The Role of the Fiscal Status Quo

The case studies strongly bring out the importance of conflicts of interests about spending cuts and tax increases in determining the chances for successful fiscal stabilization. They also highlight that different patterns of fiscal conflict are the result of the interplay of past policy choices with economic structures. While structural features of the economy and society obviously played an important role in setting the stage for the politics of fiscal stabilization, the policy paths countries had taken strongly modulated their effect, neutralizing or reinforcing existing economic cleavages and, at times, creating new conflicts independently of the socioeconomic structure. As a result of differences in policy choice, similar economic structures produced very different configurations of vested fiscal interests in different countries and, consequently, different intensities of conflicts about the way fiscal stabilization was to be done. The *size* of government spending, on the other hand, mattered little for the politics of fiscal adjustment.

Varieties of Fiscal Polarization

Major economic cleavages translated into conflicts of interests regarding fiscal stabilization only to the extent to which they were reflected in extant fiscal policies. For example, class conflict was a major obstacle to fiscal adjustment in Belgium, where the large social security sector was designed to redistribute income from capital to labor, but it was subdued in Japan because enterprise-based welfare arrangements put labor and businesses on the same side in the question of welfare spending. In Japan, it was regional disparities that generated intense fiscal conflict due to the institutionalization of the flow of funds from dynamic urban areas to the backward countryside. Regional conflict played a surprisingly insignificant role in the Belgian battles over fiscal stabilization—despite the traditionally large tensions between Flanders and Wallonia and the widening economic gap between the two regions—because there existed no explicitly regional program of redistribution. Even though the welfare system channeled funds across regional boundaries, this failed to impact the coalitional dynamics in the wrangling over social security because workers in both regions had identical vested interests in the perpetuation of the system. Italy was a mixed case. The design of the welfare system stoked class conflict in fiscal matters. At the same time, it also engendered divisions within the ranks of labor due to the highly exclusive eligibility conditions. The interests of large and small businesses also diverged as each followed different strategies to shield itself from high fiscal pressure. This gave rise to more complex coalitional dynamics than the purely class-based antagonism in Belgium, especially since the dynamics were further complicated by redistribution from the North to the South, which introduced a regional dimension into the conflict.

Policies also had the potential to generate conflicts even where economic cleavages were originally mild. Although belated economic development had historically limited the acuteness of class conflict and kept all parts of the country similarly poor in both Ireland and Greece, the structure of conflicts and commonalities of fiscal interests were very different in the two countries by the late-1980s. In Ireland, economic backwardness prompted policies that made the prosperity of society dependent on attracting foreign investors with low corporate tax pressure and otherwise spread fiscal benefits and costs fairly evenly among the large majority of society. This left very little room for conflict when policies needed to be adjusted. In Greece, on the other hand, relative underdevelopment gave rise to policies that linked the welfare of large sections of society to government largesse and targeted specific benefits to different groups. This resulted in a structure of highly polarized vested fiscal interests, which made adjustments to existing policies excessively contentious.

Fiscal Polarization Matters, Government Size Does Not

While the unequal incidence of spending and taxes—and the resulting polarization of vested fiscal interests—had a strong impact on the politics of fiscal stabilization, the size of government spending made little difference. Although it is often assumed that large governments are harder to reform—due to the extensiveness of vested interests generated by the involvement of the government in the economy and the welfare of the citizens (Pierson 2001)—the scope of governments' financial commitments was not associated with more or less success in rebalancing public finances in the sample of cases discussed in this book. Wherever fiscal polarization was intense, stabilization was delayed by political conflict irrespective of government size. Japan, a country whose government spends well below the OECD average, faced equally great difficulties in adjusting its fiscal policies as did Greece with its medium-size government. Belgium and Italy, whose governments spend one and a half times as much as Japan, had significant challenges, although they were more successful in adjusting than either Greece or Japan due to pressures from international economic competition. In the one case, Ireland, where fiscal polarization was low, stabilization was swift and effective. However, since Ireland's government spending is moderate in international comparison, a brief discussion of a case where fiscal polarization was low but government spending was high is necessary to test whether large government commitments interfere with the favorable influence of low polarization.

Denmark—famous for its large public sector—was just as successful in adjusting its fiscal policies as Ireland when economic problems created fiscal difficulties in the early 1980s and again in the 1990s. Encompassing policies similarly limited the scope for political conflict. Welfare entitlements—generous transfers and extensive in-kind benefits—were universally available to all citizens (Green-Pedersen and Baggesen Klitgaard 2009). They were financed from general taxes, which distributed fiscal burden evenly across the population since the redistributive effects of strongly progressive income taxes were counterbalanced by above-average reliance on regressive consumption taxes and relative income equality (Benner and Bundgaard Vad 2001). Corporate taxation was lower than the OECD average, while labor cost increasing social contributions and payroll taxes were virtually absent. The benefits of government spending accrued to and their costs were born by the general population without much differentiation. This left little scope for social conflict about the burden of fiscal reform and limited the room for differentiation in partisan platforms. As a result, governments on both sides of the political spectrum implemented fiscal consolidation, spreading fiscal pain relatively evenly across society without eliciting strong societal backlash or electoral penalties. In the early 1980s, the conservative coalition raised income taxes on individuals and businesses, increasing government revenues by 7 percentage points of the GDP between 1982 and 1988, and cut spending by 6 percentage points in the same period by suspending the indexation of benefits and wages and putting a moratorium on local public investment (Alesina and Ardagna 1998). A Social Democratic government followed suit when public finances came under pressure again from the recession of the early 1990s by tightening unemployment benefits across the board and increasing the focus on reactivation. The extensiveness of government commitments did not prevent extraordinarily large improvements in the budget balance and the swift reversal of debt accumulation.

Besides providing further evidence that government size matters little for successful stabilization, the Danish case also serves as an important complement to the Irish one in highlighting that low fiscal polarization plays an important role in ensuring swift fiscal stabilization in its own right, even when economic pressures from declining international competitiveness are less extreme. Denmark's economy is considerably less open than Ireland's (although still more open than Italy's, Greece's, or Japan's), and its economic problems—in terms of inflation, unemployment, and low growth—were less acute than Ireland's, both in the early 1980s and the 1990s. Yet, stabilization was still swift, radical, and politically uncontentious on both occasions. This example usefully complements the Irish case, where the independent effect of low polarization is more difficult to discern in the presence of extreme economic pressures. While the divergence of the Irish and Belgian paths in the second half of the 1980s showed that differences in fiscal polarization impact the effectiveness of consolidation in similarly open economies, the fact that initially both countries swiftly adopted stringent consolidation measures in the face of pressing macroeconomic problems suggested that when the economy is extremely exposed to international economic competition, incentives for compromise on a stabilization package are extraordinarily strong, which created some ambiguity about the significance of low fiscal polarization on its own for Ireland's steadfast consolidation efforts. Denmark's example corroborates that low fiscal polarization does not play second fiddle to international exposure: the absence of intense conflicts of fiscal interests within the polity matters in its own right. The next section investigates more closely the role of international exposure in the politics of debt accumulation.

Multiple Aspects of International Exposure

The case studies underline the central importance of exposure to international economic competition in helping to foster compromises in countries where conflicts of fiscal interests militated against the coalescence of sufficient societal support behind a stabilization package. Where the performance of the economy was strongly dependent on international competitiveness, large sections of society were sensitive to the competitiveness-reducing impact of the side effects of fiscal imbalances, such as inflation, and therefore, they had an important stake in the restoration of fiscal balance for the sake of eliminating these side effects. While this implies that international exposure is a function of economic openness, the case studies also show that the effect of openness is often modulated by economic policy choices. They also indicate that for countries involved in the ever-closer European integration, these policy choices were subject to the evolving terms of integration. In that sense, the international environment has a double effect on the domestic politics of fiscal stabilization: both through international economic competition and through the channel of international politics. This section investigates both aspects. At the same time, it also reflects on a third type of international exposure—exposure to changes in international financial markets—which received less direct emphasis in the individual case studies.

Economic Openness and Policy Choice

The polarization-exposure thesis advanced at the beginning of this book assumed that in more open economies, macroeconomic side effects of fiscal imbalances affect large sections of society acutely. The case studies show the situation to be more complicated: while economic openness makes high inflation economically harmful for large sections of society, it also influences the extent to which fiscal imbalances are allowed to spill over into such common side effects. Where the large majority of society had a stake in competitiveness, this not only facilitated fiscal compromise but also prompted monetary measures to sever the link between remaining fiscal imbalances and inflation, even at the price of aggravating the debt problem. Belgium and Ireland are cases in point. As they battled with runaway deficits, both countries chose drastic disinflation to shield international economic competitiveness and stopped monetizing their deficits, despite the adverse effects on the debt-to-GDP ratio of the resulting economic slowdown, higher real interest rates, and increased borrowing. Rapidly deteriorating international competitiveness induced initial fiscal compromise and large cuts in collective consumption and public investment in Belgium, but the resulting disinflation insulated competitiveness from further fiscal imbalances, which made possible the re-hardening of the front lines between labor and business and led to a never-ending stalemate in the question of social security reform. In Ireland, where redistributive conflicts were less intense, measures to prevent fiscal problems from spilling over into monetary ones were less consequential for further stabilization efforts.

At the same time, in countries where the exposed sector was a small part of the economy, there was greater room for targeted policies to help exposed industries retain their competitiveness. In Japan, the political influence of industrialists in the dynamic export sector had created a regime of monetary, trade, and industrial policies that guaranteed the competitiveness of the export sector. These policies allowed businesses and workers in this sector to be intransigent when fiscal problems called for adjustment, despite their exposure to international competition. In Greece, the combination of a crawling-peg exchange rate system with subsidies, tax exemptions, and opportunities for tax evasion helped the shipping industry, large manufacturing firms, and the tourism sector prosper despite the macroeconomic problems induced by fiscal imbalances.

Italy presents a peculiar case in this context. Groups exposed to international competition represented a smaller proportion of society in Italy than in Ireland or Belgium. Furthermore, as they remained members of opposing social coalitions, exposed groups lacked the necessary political clout to demand drastic disinflation—which would have hurt the sheltered sectors—or even the complete cessation of the monetization of debt throughout the 1980s. At the same time, the latitude for alternative policies to insulate the exposed sector was much more limited than in Greece (or Japan) due to Italy's participation in the ever-closer European integration. The fixed exchange rate regime of the European Exchange Rate Mechanism (ERM) implied that inflation problems directly bore on international competitiveness while targeted subsidies and tax-exemptions had to be phased out in the Single Market. The mounting pressure on groups depending on international competitiveness eventually triggered the realignment of social coalitions, which made possible the profound fiscal reforms of the 1990s.

When Belgium, Greece, Ireland, and Italy joined the Economic and Monetary Union (EMU) and delegated monetary policy to the supranational level at the end of the 1990s, the policy context changed profoundly. The economy was definitively insulated from the macroeconomic side effects of fiscal problems, as the possibility of monetizing debt at will was ended, and thereby, the most direct channel through which fiscal problems spilled over into inflation was eliminated. In Ireland and Belgium, where international competitiveness had consistently played such an important role in the politics of fiscal policy that the stabilization of the 1980s had already put an end to monetization, this change only institutionalized the *status quo*. In Greece, the end of monetization made little difference for the opposite reason: since international competitiveness was never a decisive factor in fiscal matters, the severance of the monetary link between fiscal problems and competitiveness mattered little. In Italy, however, the end of the threat of returning to the monetization of deficits reduced the incentives for maintaining painful fiscal compromises and led to a relapse in fiscal policy.

European Integration

The effects of the ERM, the Single Market, and EMU on the domestic policy context call attention to the role of the ever-tighter European economic integration in shaping the politics of public debt accumulation in European member states. The policy constraints created by Europe represent an intriguing combination of political and economic forces emanating from the international environment. As integration progressed, each new stage involved significant limits on countries' policy autonomy. The new rules and restrictions were adopted by political fiat, but the countries discussed in this book had no significant influence on them. The motivation to participate in the consecutive stages—and to submit to the attendant rules—arose from various political and economic motives in the different countries. For example, joining the ERM was an economic necessity for Belgium and Ireland, as their highly open economies benefited from minimizing exchange rate volatility. On Italy, however, the constraints of fixed exchange rates were politically imposed, as the country had originally been reluctant to join the ERM and only did so due to intergovernmental arm-twisting. Greece was never under similar political pressure, as its economy was much less significant within Europe. In other words, international economic relations allowed different countries different maneuvering space in policy choice.

Among the various policy constraints created by European economic integration, the adoption of fiscal criteria as a condition for EMU membership stands out as an attempt to directly influence fiscal policy from the European level. Ironically, however, Maastricht—and later the Stability and Growth Pact—exercised much less lasting influence on the domestic politics of debt accumulation than the ERM, the Single Market, or the common currency did. Where EMU-membership was an economic imperative for large sections of society—as in Ireland and Belgium—the bulk of fiscal consolidation had already taken place in the 1980s under pressure to restore international competitiveness. Fulfillment of the criteria required no further radical fiscal reform, especially in light of the rapid easing of the interest burden on the budget. This was especially conspicuous in Belgium, where policy makers' invocation of the euro imperative failed to compel business or labor to acquiesce in major sacrifices regarding social security when relatively minor fiscal corrections sufficed to fulfill the criteria for accession. Where major groups in society had limited stake in the euro, Maastricht provided no new incentive to set aside fiscal conflicts for the sake of resolving persistent problems of public finance. This was the case in Italy and Greece, where there were significant concerns about the effects of accession on competitiveness, and the eventual decision to join was mostly motivated by the government's urge to ease the oppressive interest burden on the budget through the reduction of interest rates in the eurozone. In Italy, the radical adjustments that had already taken place prior to the decision to join the EMU allowed the government to meet the criteria in time with some additional measures. In Greece, governments unable to engage in radical reform relied on the practice of obfuscated piecemeal changes that they had pursued since the early 1990s—complemented by creative accounting—to fulfill the fiscal criteria for accession. In all four countries, Maastricht brought temporary, marginal—and sometimes only apparent— adjustments but no profound changes in fiscal policies.

Financial Internationalization

But participation in the latest stage of European integration changed the context in which fiscal policy operated in more than one way. Apart from the institutional constraints agreed in European fora, monetary and financial integration profoundly affected the financial conditions under which governments could borrow. The rapid convergence of bond yields of the prospective euro members to German levels from the mid-1990s—reinforced by the simultaneous decline of German bond yields themselves—generated remarkable windfall savings. The precipitous fall of yields took place in the context of accelerating internationalization of the holdings of government debt, spurred by the prospect of the elimination of exchange rate fluctuations within the eurozone. Between 1995 and 2005, the share of debt held by foreign creditors went from 22 to 50 percent in Belgium, from 16 to 61 percent in Greece, from 27 to 84 percent in Ireland, and from 15 to 39 percent in Italy (Bruegel database of sovereign bond holdings developed in Merler and Pisani-Ferry 2012).

The massive savings on interest costs—amounting to a drop of 8 percentage points of the GDP from the mid-1990s to the mid-2000s in all four European countries presented here—eased the pressure on policy makers immensely. After more than a decade of ever-decreasing budgetary space and simultaneously snowballing debt levels, policy makers found themselves in the enviable opposite position. They were able to pursue agendas previously crowded out by the costs of debt—and gradually erode primary surpluses generated by prior fiscal adjustments—while simultaneously boasting stable or even declining debt levels. In Greece, the debt-to-GDP ratio roughly stabilized around 100 percent, despite a more than 8-percentage-point deterioration in the primary balance between the mid-1990s and the mid-2000s. In Italy, the debt-to-GDP ratio declined by 15 percentage points over the same period, even though the improvements of the primary balance in the early 1990s were undone by the mid-2000s. In Belgium, the debt-to-GDP ratio fell from over 130 percent to under 90 percent, despite a decline in the primary surplus. (In Ireland, the impact of falling interest rates were dwarfed by the effect of fast growth on both the primary surpluses and the debt-to-GDP ratio. Primary surpluses remained high and the debt ratio soon became one of the lowest in Europe.)

Tapping into international pools of savings helped to minimize the costs of the debt overhang of heavily indebted countries and reduce the political salience of the debt problem. At the same time, the internationalization of government debt holdings also acutely exposed these countries to sudden changes of sentiment in global financial markets. The decade-long lull in the escalation of concern over the debt overhang and the sudden change in financial market conditions in the wake of the global financial crisis led to disastrous consequences in Greece, where a sudden panic over fiscal figures led to a surge of bond yields, which rendered the government insolvent. Italy and Belgium avoided the same fate, although rising yields threatened with debt crisis on a few occasions, prompting officials of the European Central Bank to commit to countervailing measures. (In Ireland, the crisis of the 2010s was mostly unrelated to the debt accumulated during the 1980s.)

In sum, the constellations of interests governing the politics of debt accumulation in different countries were not simply a reflection of domestic economic and social structures. Instead, they were also significantly shaped by an intricate combination of historical and current policy choices, international political pressures, the evolution of the European economic and political order, and financial globalization.

Institutions, Ideas, and Debt Accumulation

The narratives in this book revolved around interests: they explained how the vested fiscal interests and the economic interests of different societal groups motivated their resistance to or acquiescence in fiscal pain, and how the evolving attitude of these groups toward stabilization guided the interactions of various political actors in the quest for a resolution of persistent fiscal problems in different countries. At the same time, the analysis paid much less systematic attention to the role of political institutions or ideational factors in shaping the politics of debt accumulation and fiscal stabilization. Characteristics of the national electoral and party systems, corporatist practices, and the state were presented to elucidate the context in which the different constellations of interests exercised their effect, while ideas featured mostly in the discussion of the ways in which political entrepreneurs rationalized the realignment of social coalitions they sought to profit from. This section turns to these factors and briefly discusses them in a cross-case comparison. It argues that while specific institutional and ideational features corresponded to patterns of political behavior commonly predicted by the literature, they exercised little systematic effect on the overall politics of fiscal stabilization.

Institutions

While the case studies confirm the observation that different *electoral systems* and the attendant different *governmental structures* are associated with different parliamentary and intragovernmental decision-making dynamics, they also highlight that these dynamics had limited independent impact on fiscal decisions in the broader scheme of things. For example, Greece, with its majoritarian electoral system, produced strong unitary governments that could pass decisive austerity measures without drawn-out fights with parliamentary opposition, as evidenced by the 1985 decision on draconian incomes policy, the introduction of VAT in 1987, or the pension reform of 1992. However, upon experiencing the electoral backlash from voter groups not ready to compromise their vested fiscal interests, neither major party was ready to use the majoritarian advantage to introduce further radical reform. In contrast, in Ireland, it took several attempts amid parliamentary squabbles to introduce the first stabilization package because the proportional electoral system made governments overly dependent on close coalitional cohesion and/or outside support. Austerity was nevertheless enacted because packages were repeatedly introduced by both major parties until one successfully passed. Similarly, governments in Belgium had to navigate an especially fragmented parliamentary environment due to the combination of proportional electoral system and a complicated system of checks and balances between linguistic communities. Nevertheless, the "Special Powers Act" of 1982 successfully passed when societal backing for austerity was strong. Later, however, the same obstacles became insurmountable for further reform when social support waned.

Variations in *party systems*, *structures*, and *strategies* show similarly little systematic correlation with the success of fiscal reform. In accordance with theoretical expectations (Haggard and McCubbins 2001), the broad-based catch-all parties alternating in power in Greece and Ireland both wished to maintain compromise in the fiscal domain to limit conflicts of interests within their variegated constituencies, but the compromise they settled on in Greece was to not change the *status quo*, whereas the compromise in Ireland entailed spreading the pain of fiscal reforms evenly across society. The cross-class, centrist Christian Democrats in Belgium sought to broker a compromise between classes based on mutual sacrifices in the early 1980s; the cross-class, centrist Liberal Democrats in Japan settled on a compromise of no sacrifices. In Greece, Ireland, Italy, and Japan, the dominant parties relied strongly on clientelistic ties to mobilize voters in less developed areas, but in Ireland these ties never prevented policy makers from imposing losses on the clientele of their party members, whereas in the other three countries they did. In conjunction with characteristics of the electoral system that forced members of the same party to compete against one another (the multi-member setup in Japan and the practice of preference votes in Italy), these clientele networks created strong factionalism within the dominant parties of the 1980s in Japan and Italy, which helps to explain the intraparty stalemates on fiscal issues in the two countries. However, in Greece the electoral system did not foster intraparty factionalism and conflict, and, yet, governing parties could not bring themselves to impose losses on any of their clienteles.

The political dynamics outside of the governmental-parliamentary-partisan sphere point to similar variance in the role of frameworks of *corporatist intermediation* for the success of policy reform. Corporatist consultation was instrumental to compromise between major socioeconomic groups in several instances of adjustment in Belgium, Ireland, and Italy, but they were neither necessary nor sufficient conditions for reform. In Belgium, apart from the reform of 1982, discord, rather than compromise, characterized class relations in the field of social security, despite established systems of corporatist consultation. In Ireland (in 1987) and in Italy (throughout the 1990s), the resolution of some of the most stubborn conflicts of interest happened in the framework of social pacts. At other times, however, social pacts were absent or explicitly avoided in the reform process, as in 1982 in Ireland and in the wake of the global financial and economic crisis in both countries. In Japan, the formal inclusion of unions and business associations in reform commissions like *Rincho* did little to elicit fiscal compromises from either side, although participation in such commissions was admittedly no real substitute to established systems of interest intermediation. In the case of Greece, it is difficult to say if fiscal reform would have been easier had corporatist consultation tamed the militancy of unions (especially public sector ones), given how consistently workers also expressed their opposition to welfare retrenchment and incomes policies through the electoral channel.

Variations in bureaucratic structures across the different cases call attention to the usefulness of Skocpol's distinction (1985, 9) between state autonomy and state capacity in assessing the role of *institutions of the state* in the politics of fiscal stabilization. While powerful bureaucracies had more autonomy "to formulate and pursue goals that [were] not simply reflective of the demands or interests of social groups" than bureaucracies captured by political parties, the capacity of even the most powerful bureaucratic actors "to implement official goals especially over the actual or potential opposition of powerful social groups" was contingent on the societal backing that the official policy goals enjoyed. Japan's Ministry of Finance—famous for being a major bastion of bureaucratic power—played an important role in initiating "fiscal reconstruction" throughout the 1970s and 1980s by drafting austere budgets, imposing spending limits on special account spending, and putting forward one proposal after another for introducing VAT, but its ability to control outcomes in the face of politicians' fear of electoral backlash was just as limited as the policy influence of ministries in Greece, where bureaucracy was fully colonized by the two major parties. Similarly, technocratic expertise and political independence gave the series of unelected cabinets that governed Italy in the early 1990s remarkable autonomy in formulating policy goals and proposals for radical reform. However, their capacity to put those reforms into place was contingent on the support of the social coalition that had emerged in the early 1990s around the objective of restoring international economic competitiveness. As the Amato government was to learn early on from the resounding failure of its first pension reform attempt, even technocratic governments' power was closely circumscribed by the preferences of the dominant social coalition.

Ideas

The case studies document that major shifts in *policy paradigms* and changes in the *discourse* about fiscal problems in the 1980s profoundly influenced the way policy makers and the public approached growing fiscal imbalances. However, there is no evidence that these ideational shifts helped create the political preconditions for successful stabilization. The conversion from Keynesian ideas of demand management to a focus on monetary stability and austerity is most relevant in cases where—like in Belgium or Ireland—fiscal problems were largely of economic origin and policy makers visibly shifted from attempting to correct problems of growth, employment, and public finances through stimulus in the late 1970s to fiscal tightening and disinflation by the 1980s. But the conversion of policy elites to stability-oriented paradigms was also reflected in the communications of central bank technocrats in Italy and in the resistance of policy makers to domestic and international pressures for fiscal stimulus in Japan throughout the 1980s. The new emphasis on fiscal stability in the 1980s was also strongly demonstrated by the alarmist policy discourse, which ranged from calls for "*risanamento*" in Italy to putting forward a "Disaster Plan" in Belgium to prime ministers staking their tenure in office on the meeting of fiscal targets in Japan. The impact of this discourse on public opinion has been documented in Japan, where polls showed "fiscal reconstruction" to be one of the main policy priorities of the public in the 1980s. However, the general emphasis on fiscal stability in the political discourse in all of these cases stands in marked contrast with the variation in the success of different countries to address their fiscal problems, which depended on the backing of a strong enough societal coalition for an actual stabilization package, not just generalized agreement on the severity of the problem.

From an ideational point of view, the question, of course, is to what extent supportive social coalitions "emerged" or "were cobbled together" by political entrepreneurs using *ideological innovation and new framings* of the problem to appeal to (certain sections of) society. The case studies provide no clear evidence that, in the case of successful stabilizations, political interpretations of the situation played a role in generating supportive coalitions independently of the structure of societal interests. While in Ireland, a "Program for National Recovery" rallied generalized social support for renewed austerity in 1987; the talk of a national "Disaster" in 1981 in Belgium obviously failed to convince diverse social groups that fiscal pain was in everyone's interest. Even though austerity received the necessary social support to succeed, it was not an expression of national unity but of particular Flemish interests. Not only did Walloon labor refuse to fall in line, but even Christian Democratic unions, which decided to make fiscal concessions on behalf of labor in 1982, preferred to signal their amenability surreptitiously, suggesting that they, too, saw this as betraying Walloon labor, rather than averting a nationwide disaster; but they were not ready to openly embrace the latter interpretation of the situation.[1] In Italy, the emergence of the reform coalition of the early 1990s preceded the elaboration of policy platforms of the emergent parties of the Second Republic as the first momentous wave of reforms of the early 1990s took place in a political vacuum under the guardianship of technocrats.[2] By the time the new parties of the Second Republic started to articulate their policy positions, the new societal frontlines had already been drawn between the supporters and opponents of the reforms of the early 1990s. Parties adjusted their platforms and their alliances to this *fait accompli* and did not seek to offer alternative interpretations of conflicts and commonalities of interests.

All of the above examples and cross-country comparisons highlight that while institutional frameworks and ideational factors play an important role in facilitating the persistence of conflict or fostering compromise, they exercised their effect on the politics of debt accumulation and fiscal stabilization strictly in conjunction with the varied constellations of fiscal and economic interests in different countries. The structure of conflicts and commonalities of interests among various socioeconomic groups systematically and decisively impacted the success or failure of attempts to deal with persistent debt accumulation in a variety of institutional and ideational contexts.

Extensions and Implications

This book demonstrated that varying degrees of fiscal polarization and international economic exposure better explain variations in Italy's, Belgium's, Ireland's, Greece's, and Japan's ability to stop debt accumulation than alternative factors do. This final section briefly speculates on how well the polarization-exposure theory might travel beyond these cases and argues that it could well account for other instances of debt accumulation between 1970 and the start of the global financial and economic crisis. (For an overview of all the instances, see Table 1.2 in chapter 1.). By way of conclusion, the section reflects on the practical implications of the theory for policy.

Of the most serious cases of sustained and heavy debt accumulation, only Canada's story was left out of this book. While a detailed discussion of the case is beyond the scope of this section, the many similarities that the Canadian case shows with the Belgian and Italian ones suggest that the polarization-exposure theory explains the Canadian experience well. Between the late 1970s and the early 1990s, Canada increased its debt stock from 43 to 100 percent of the GDP. Just like in Belgium, the origins of the structural fiscal imbalances lay in the dramatic slowing of growth and a sudden increase in the interest rates on the outstanding debt. Just like in Belgium, social spending grew especially dramatically as a share of the GDP due to skyrocketing unemployment, but adjustments to this field of public finances were wrought with class as well as regional conflict. Retrenchment would negatively affect labor in general, but it would hit the Atlantic Provinces especially hard, where unemployment and poverty rates were persistently one-and-a-half times or twice as large as the national average and significant sections of the population lived on transfers financed by taxes and contributions collected in richer regions. Increases in contribution to the unemployment and pension insurance would have further increased fiscal pressure on businesses, which were already at a disadvantage relative to their competitors in the United States due to heavier corporate taxation. At the same time, increasing general taxation to cover the shortfall of social programs threatened to accentuate conflict over regional redistribution. In this polarized situation, compromise required compelling reasons.

Unlike in Belgium, however, the pressure from international economic exposure was only moderate on large sections of society in Canada because the share of exports and imports in the GDP was barely more than in Italy at the time. In the absence of immediate emergency, the protection of vested fiscal interests loomed large in politics. Liberals shied away from fiscal tightening in the first half of the 1980s. When Conservatives took power in 1984, they put forward a stabilization plan that cut collective consumption and investment expenses, made marginal changes to taxation, and refrained from reforms to social policies. The deficit was reduced by 4 percentage points of the GDP by 1988, but this was partly thanks to decent economic performance, and when the economy went into recession again at the end of the decade, borrowing hit new records.

Just like in Italy, the pressure for profound political and policy change built up gradually in sectors and regions most exposed to competition (primarily in manufacturing, concentrated most heavily in the central provinces, but also to some extent in commodity sectors in the west). Although Canada had a floating exchange rate regime and inflation was controlled, exposed sectors suffered increasing disadvantage in trade as the Canadian dollar appreciated due to the influx of foreign capital as investors bought Canadian dollar-denominated debt in increasing quantities. Exchange rate appreciation became especially relevant as trade grew in the wake of the free trade agreement with the United States in the 1988, which was replaced by the North American Free Trade Agreement in 1994. As the trade balance and growth dipped into the negative and unemployment reached levels unseen since the Great Depression in the early 1990s, Liberals campaigned on fiscal consolidation, explicitly promising to reform the unemployment insurance. Not only did Liberals win overwhelmingly, the outgoing Conservatives were obliterated in the elections, as their voters flocked to the Liberals in the central provinces, the new Reform party in the west, and the separatist Bloc Québécois. Having gained a strong mandate for reform and enjoying a comfortable majority in Parliament, the Liberals dramatically retrenched the unemployment insurance system, reduced federal transfers to provinces, and reformed pensions. As a result, the primary balance grew by a whopping 10 percentage points of the GDP by the end of the decade and the debt-to-GDP was firmly set on a declining path.

Although this book has focused on explaining the most serious cases of sustained heavy debt accumulation—in an effort to steer clear of theoretical, practical, and normative controversies about when tolerating fiscal imbalances amounts to a political and policy anomaly (discussed in detail in chapter 1)—there is no theoretical reason why the explanatory power of the polarization-exposure thesis should be restricted to the most difficult cases. The brief discussion of two instances of debt surges in Denmark—between 1976 and 1984 and between 1992 and 1993—in this chapter demonstrated the ability of the theory to explain a scenario where very intense surges of debt accumulation are swiftly checked by decisive stabilization before debt approaches dangerous levels. Furthermore, the similarity of the Danish case to the Finnish and Swedish ones suggests that the theory would probably fit well those cases, too.[3] It would be difficult to comment on cases where debt was growing slowly for decades and stayed in the moderate range before the shocks of the global financial and economic crisis[4] without implying to take sides in the above mentioned controversy about whether, when, and how radically these small but persistent imbalances should have been tackled. It is perhaps worth noting, though, that since minor deficits are unlikely to generate tangible economic losses for any group in society (including losses of competitiveness for the exposed sector), the longevity of these debt trends is not incompatible with the predictions of the model.

Unfortunately, the ability of the polarization-exposure theory to explain variation in countries' ability to deal with their debt problems does not imply that it can generate practical policy solutions. In focusing on the societal bases of the politics of debt accumulation, the theory inevitably forwent generating policy prescriptions for countries that are struggling with heavy debt accumulation but find themselves persistently unable to enact painful policy reforms to restore the balance of public finances. The central importance of societal interests implies that the solution to persistent fiscal imbalances is primarily not in policy makers' hands, and therefore, policy prescriptions are futile. The only short-term policy advice the theory does provide is a cautioning note against too much confidence in institutional panacea and ideational innovations. The theory not only questions the effectiveness of institutional changes within governmental decision-making fora—like technical changes in budgetary procedures or rules constraining policy makers' discretion—but is also skeptical that even radical political reform affecting fundamental institutions of interest aggregation, representation and reconciliation, or the insulation of the state from democratic influences can significantly change a country's ability to regain control over debt growth, unless the political reforms are underlain by reconfigurations in the societal bases of fiscal policy making.

Notes

CHAPTER I

1. Although Japan's net debt-to-GDP ratio is only about half of the gross, it is still dangerously large, on par with that of Greece or Italy.

2. Reinhart and Rogoff (2010) claimed to have found a limit at 90 percent of the GDP, but their results were later discredited by Herndon et al. (2014).

3. Nordhaus (1975), Buchanan and Wagner (1977), Tufte (1978), Alesina and Perotti (1996).

4. Roubini and Sachs (1989), Grilli et al. (1991), Hallerberg and von Hagen (1997), Hallerberg (2004), Hallerberg et al. (2009).

5. E.g., Katzenstein (1985 and 1987), Pierson (2001), Streeck and Thelen (2005), Culpepper (2002 and 2008). For a detailed discussion of this literature, see chapter 2.

6. Economists conceptualize this problem as an example of free riding: fiscal stabilization is a public good whose benefits everyone enjoys (although it is arguably more valuable to those that are more affected by the negative side effects of debt accumulation), but it is rational for different groups to be reluctant to pay for it in the hope that other groups will bear the costs instead of them (Drazen 2004).

7. More precisely, in any moment in time, a group has to weigh the expected value of resisting fiscal pain. This expected value comprises of three parts. One is the gain from successful free riding multiplied by the probability of success. The second is the certain cost of having to endure the negative side effects of debt for longer. The third is the loss from having to eventually give in to bearing a large share of the fiscal pain when the size of the necessary stabilization has grown much larger multiplied by the likelihood that this will happen.

8. In this sense, the book makes a similar point as Hausermann (2010) about the multidimensionality of the politics of policy making, but it also emphasizes that this multidimensionality arises from the simultaneous influence of socioeconomic

structure and existing policies and that the interaction of these multiple dimensions leads to shifts in preferences as time passes.

CHAPTER 2

1. While models exploring the sociopolitical dynamic of economic reforms abound—and call attention to a variety of factors that delay or hasten reforms, from information asymmetry to the imminence of crisis (e.g., Fernandez and Rodrik 1991; Alesina and Drazen 1991; Drazen and Grilli 1993; Laban and Sturzeneg-ger 1994; Cukierman and Tommasi 1998)—Alesina and Drazen's war of attrition model has arguably been the most influential in explaining delay in fiscal stabilization.

2. E.g., Rose (1985), Esping-Andersen (1991), Steinmo (1993), Rosen (1996), Alesina et al. (1999), Rueda (2005), Chopel et al. 2005, Van Kersbergen and Vis (2013).

3. For the classic categorization of welfare systems, see Esping-Andersen (1991).

4. Obviously, at very high levels of debt, continued fiscal problems also increase the risk of financial and economic disaster. This is an issue that affects society fairly uniformly. It is left out of further discussion here because the question at hand relates exactly to why borrowing is allowed to continue so long that even these risks arise. Therefore, such risks are part of the question, rather than the answer.

5. Obviously, Alesina and Drazen's (1991) model itself says nothing about social coalitions since it works with the simplifying assumption of two monolithic groups fighting about the choice between two different distributions of fiscal pain. As soon as the analysis is extended to more groups and a range of different stabilization packages, the issue of coalitions and the composition of packages most suitable to the interest of different coalitions becomes relevant.

6. Party systems and electoral rules shape how societal conflicts play out in electoral politics (Haggard and Kaufmann 1992; Pal and Weaver 2003); corporat-ist arrangements crucially influence how different groups can exercise leverage in policy making outside of the electoral arena (Katzenstein 1985 and 1987); while the autonomy of the state creates room for policy choices that are not simply the result of societal pressures (Skocpol 1985,;Weir and Skocpol 1989).

7. Jacobsen (1995); Yee (1996); Blyth (2002); Mcnamara (1998); Cox (2001).

8. Majoritarian institutions minimize the number of vetoes in the governmental sphere (Haggard et al. 2001), while an autonomous state can bypass bickering vested interest groups to successfully impose fiscal pain on society for the sake of the greater good (Della Sala 1997).

9. In political systems, where parties, unions and employers' organizations encompass large sections of society, conflicts will be settled *within* these interest-representing organizations (Haggard and Kaufmann 1992; Katzenstein 1985; but cf. Baccaro 2003). In some polities, negotiations and compromise are promoted by institutionalized frameworks of consultation in the governmental and corporatist sphere (Lijphart 1999).

10. Party systems evolve (Mair 2006), corporatist actors rise and fall and their interactions change (Baccaro 2003; Culpepper and Regan 2014), electoral rules are amended (Dunleavy and Margetts 1995), states gain and lose autonomy (Della Sala

1997), policy paradigms are adopted and discarded (McNamara 1998), and new ideas emerge to provide focal points for new compromises (Culpepper 2008).

11. The emergence and later demise of the practice of social pacts in many European countries in the 1990s and 2000s exemplifies how institutions geared to foster compromise can be constructed and dismantled, or simply ignored, depending on the evolution of the socio-economic context (Culpepper 2002; Culpepper and Regan 2014).

12. The *public choice school* suggests that the electorate rewards the ability to consume more today at the expense of tomorrow, either because it suffers from "fiscal illusion" and therefore fails to recognize the costs that extra consumption in the present will have in the future (Buchanan and Wagner 1977) or because it wants to transfer the costs of its present overconsumption to later generations (Cukierman and Meltzer 1989). *Political business cycle models* contend that incumbent governments want to reinforce their image as competent managers of the economy and of public finances, so they generate deficit-fuelled economic upswings and provide more public goods from the same amount of tax revenues (Nordhaus 1975; Rogoff and Sibert 1988). Finally, *electoral spending cycle theories* suggest that incumbent political actors want to remind their supporters—and potential supporters—who they should vote for by pleasing them with new targeted spending measures or tax cuts before the elections (Tufte 1978).

13. Alesina et al. (1998) and Brender and Drazen (2008) show that loose fiscal policies tend not to yield the electoral advantage that these theories attribute to them. At the same time, there is evidence that incumbent policy makers still try their luck with such fiscal manipulation sometimes, although not universally (Alt 2007).

14. Weingast, Shepsle, and Johnsen (1981), Grilli et al. (1991), von Hagen (1991), von Hagen and Harden (1996), Hallerberg (2004), Hallerberg, von Hagen, and Strauch (2009).

15. Roubini and Sachs (1989), Grilli et al. (1991), Alesina et al. (1998).

16. While studies on the independent effect of fiscal rules and targets returned mixed results, Mark Hallerberg and his colleagues identify constellations of budgetary institutional arrangements and coordination mechanisms that seem to consistently keep public borrowing in check. In one, policy makers delegate decision-making power to a strong finance minister. In the other, they subject the budget to the terms of a contract previously negotiated between representatives of diverse particularistic interests (Hallerberg 2004; Hallerberg, von Hagen, and Strauch 2009). Hallerberg et al. also convincingly show why one or the other type of coordination works better in different types of governments.

17. Balassone and Giordano (2001), Hallerberg (2004), Hallerberg, Strauch, and von Hagen (2009).

18. Hierarchical decision-making, transparency, centralization, commitment to fiscal targets, and credible penalties for defection from pre-agreed objectives have been consistently associated with lower deficits (Alesina and Perotti 1996; Hallerberg and von Hagen 1997; Hallerberg 2004; Hallerberg, von Hagen, and Strauch 2009).

19. Obviously, the lack of success of the Stability and Growth Pact experiment is no reason to indict the theoretical approach. The European fiscal system can be

(and has been) criticized from the perspective of the "fiscal indiscipline" school itself and failure can be blamed on defects in design: the lack of credible penalties for noncompliance, the insufficient flexibility of its rules, and the unsuitability of the coordination mechanisms it provided. (For a review of the extensive critique of the suitability of the rules and enforcement of the Stability and Growth Pact, see Fischer, Jonung, and Larch 2006.) At the same time, the failure of the Stability and Growth Pact experiment does call attention to the lack of sufficient theorizing about why some countries adopt appropriate budgetary institutions when others do not.

20. Alesina and Perotti (1996) and Hallerberg, von Hagen, and Strauch (2009) point out that this is a major shortcoming.

21. Hallerberg et al. (2009, ch5) suggest that countries in which governments house similar ideological differences across time are likelier to be able to develop the right forms of coordination to deal with those differences. Countries in which intragovernmental ideological distance is consistently small will adopt a delegation approach to budgetary coordination. Countries with consistently large intragovernmental ideological distance will adopt fiscal contracts. Where the distance varies across time, however, it is difficult to consolidate either form of governance. Furthermore, the authors hypothesize that fiscal crises spur the adoption of more effective coordination because experience with such crises makes the electorate more fiscally conservative. They seek to test these propositions quantitatively, but they get ambiguous results. Beyond the obvious problems of operationalizing their explanatory variables—e.g., the difficulties involved in consistently measuring ideological distance across countries and time and in identifying "crises" in both the objective and subjective sense—duly noted by the authors themselves, the regression analysis yields no statistically significant results.

22. Earlier theories in this literature explicitly excluded the possibility that borrowing could be politically costly. Note, for example, the concept of "fiscal illusion" (Buchanan and Wagner 1977). Common resource pool models ignore political costs. Hallerberg's latest work takes a step towards incorporating the political costs of budgetary imbalances into the fiscal indiscipline model by including the fiscal conservativism of the electorate as an incentive for budgetary self-restraint (Hallerberg et al. 2009). However, the concept of fiscal conservativism is arguably too vague to be of real explanatory value.

23. In *Fiscal Governance in Europe*, Hallerberg and his colleagues acknowledge that under certain institutional setups, budgetary decisions might be influenced from outside of the governmental-parliamentary sphere, for example in the field of social partnership, but they leave it to further research to investigate the exact nature of this influence on fiscal problems (2009, 205–8).

24. Seminal pieces in this literature include Katzenstein 1977, 1985, and 1987; Nelson 1990; Haggard and Kaufmann 1992; and Pierson 2001.

25. E.g., Culpepper 2002 and 2008, Hemerijck and Visser 2000, Jones 2008, Katzenstein 1987, Kuipers 2006.

26. E.g., Baccaro and Lim 2007, Baccaro and Simoni 2008, Culpepper 2008

27. Countries that were OECD members for the entire period under consideration.

28. At the same time, the individual country case studies do discuss the trends that can be discerned in 2015.

29. Despite accumulating debt for a long time at low pace (Austria, France, Germany, and Spain), for a moderate time at a moderate pace (the Netherlands, Portugal, and the United States), or at very high rates for short periods (Denmark, Finland, and Sweden), these countries mostly remained under 70 percent of GDP.

30. For concrete analysis of policy structures, see the relevant case studies in chapters 3, 4, 5, and 6.

31. For exact details of the within-country comparisons, see Table 3.1 in chapter 3.

32. For exact details of the most similar case design, see Table 4.1 in chapter 4.

33. For exact details of the most different case design, see Table 5.1 in chapter 5.

34. Qualitative analyses of planned and actual policy measures are favored over quantitative databases, like the one generated by Devries et al. (2011). Devries and his colleagues code formal legislation and budgetary appropriations to capture governmental attempts to deal with a country's fiscal imbalances as a numerical indicator that measures the planned impact of the legislated acts as a percentage of GDP. While it is a useful starting point for gauging policy makers' intentions, this source cannot capture deviations from original government policy that result from political resistance to reform or pick up on changes in policy that arise from the enforcement of previously ill-enforced legislation, like when the government manages to raise revenue by cracking down on tax evasion. Such deviations from official policy and non-legislated changes are often key to understanding fiscal performance.

CHAPTER 3

1. Some of these reforms were aimed at ensuring better planning, others at enforcing discipline on the members of parliament (Ferrera and Gualmini 2004, p64; Padovano and Venturi 2001).

2. Although regular unemployment benefits have historically been trivially small and short in duration in Italy, workers laid off in the restructuring process were entitled to generous income-replacement benefits for up to three years from the so-called the *Cassa Integrazione Guadagni* (CIG) and the *Cassa Integrazione Guadagni Straordinaria* (CIGS) (Bertola and Garibaldi 2003).

3. Early retirement was introduced for redundant workers in 1981, in an effort to dissipate the growing tension over the large number of redundancies (Ferrera and Gualmini 2004).

4. For example, marginal adjustments to pensions included limits on the collection of multiple benefits and defined income ceilings for the entitlement to social pensions (Ferrera and Gualmini 2004, 94).

5. The Amato reform of 1992 significantly tightened eligibility criteria and decreased the benefit levels, but it exempted older cohorts already in retirement or likely to retire within the next decade and was only to come fully in effect by 2032, due to its very long phase-in (Ferrera and Gualimini 2004, 114). The Ciampi reform of 1993 encouraged the development of a second pension pillar and placed penalties on early retirement but left regular pensions fully intact. The Dini reform

of 1995 mandated the phasing in of new, contribution-based formulae for the calculation of pensions and created further disincentives for early retirement. The Prodi reform of 1997 tightened the availability of seniority pensions in the public sector (Ferrera and Gualmini 2004).

6. In 1992 and 1995, corporate tax rates were increased by 1 percentage point and social security contributions by more than 5 percentage points (Bernasconi et al. 2005).

7. The targeted tax exemptions that so severely weakened the revenue-generating capacity of corporate taxes in the 1980s had been phased out in the late 1980s due to the ban on state aid within the Single Market, but many general tax reliefs lingered on into the 1990s. Of these, the tax deductibility of a major local tax (ILOR) from the general corporate tax (IRPEG) was ended in 1993 (Bernasconi et al. 2005).

8. In 1992 and 1993, new taxes on real estate and corporate net worth were introduced. In 1997, a new regional tax (IRAP) on added value replaced many smaller taxes and dues making the fulfillment of tax obligations much more transparent and reducing the opportunities for manipulation of the reported tax base.

9. The move to a defined contribution system begun in 1995 was sped up, the retirement age for women was raised, and the indexation to inflation of higher pensions above was ended (Culpepper 2014).

10. By the early 1990s, old-age pensions accounted for more than an eighth of the GDP and more than a fourth of total expenditure; the deficit of the pension funds accounted for half of the total deficit.

11. Although the electoral law was modified in 2005, this did not have a transformational effect on electoral competition or the party system comparable to the changes of the early 1990s.

12. See, for example, La Palombara 1987 for a vivid description of the failed Visentini attempt to reform tax collection.

13. In an effort to secure lower inflation, the central bank was relieved from the obligation to act as an automatic last resort buyer of government debt in 1981, but the fast growth of debt still prompted policy makers to monetize part of the deficit (Epstein and Schor 1989).

14. Called Italian Social Movement until 1995.

CHAPTER 4

1. Unless otherwise indicated, fiscal data cited in this section are drawn from the database of the National Bank of Belgium (www.nbb.be/belgostat).

2. These financing gap figures are not the official consolidated deficit figures for the different social security funds because the central government covers the financing gap of the social security sector through yearly subsidies. Therefore, the official budget for the social security always balances. Instead, these figures reflect the balance of social security contributions and social benefits paid (source: www.nbb.be/belgostat).

3. Two reforms to the pension system were put into place later—the creation of the Silver Fund in 2001 and the Vandenbroucke law of 2003—but neither affected the balance of outlays and revenues. The Vandenbroucke law set up the legal

framework for a voluntary company-financed second pillar of pension provision, whereas the law on the Silver Fund mandated the setting aside of certain existing funds in anticipation of the effects of population aging (In the end, the Silver Fund was never built up).

4. Parties of different linguistic affiliation competed in largely isolated electoral spheres since the constitutional reform of 1980 designated Flanders and Wallonia as exclusive electoral territories for Flemish and Francophone parties, respectively, leaving the Brussels-capital region as the only shared electoral turf. This caused the "sister parties" on each side of the linguistic divide to drift slightly apart as they adjusted to electoral pressures in their own competitive arenas, but they entered the government together because of the need to ensure the linguistic parity among minsters of the national government that the constitution prescribes (Fitzmaurice 1996).

5. All of these parties changed their names several times during the past decades. Therefore, I am going to refer to them by their ideological label and regional affiliation.

6. The interest organizations representing the *standen*—the Christian workers movement, the union of the middle classes, and the agricultural association—had the right to select candidates on the party's electoral lists. Up to the 1990s, 90 percent of the candidates were nominated by the *standen*. The remaining 10 percent was usually filled by the narrow leadership of the party and former/present ministers (De Winter 1996; Claeys 1996).

7. The word "pact" had only been used once before in 1944 when the foundations of the Belgian welfare state were laid down. By referring back to this earlier, highly important agreement, the government was symbolically emphasizing the gravity of the moment (Kuipers 2005, 96).

8. This is best reflected in the state reforms of the 1970s and 1980s, which divided up the country into three linguistic communities (Flemish, francophone, and German) and three regions (Flanders, Wallonia, and Brussels), creating a curious, two-layer federalized structure (Deschouwer 2009, 48–53).

9. The 1988 Special Law and the 1989 Finance Act devolved many important functions—e.g., economic affairs, transport and communication infrastructure, and education—from the federal level to the regions and communities and allocated 40 percent of VAT and personal income tax receipts to finance them (OECD 2007; Hooghe 1991). The 1999 St. Eloi agreement corrected the allocation rates of VAT and personal income taxes so that Flanders would get more of the income taxes— reflecting its higher tax-generating capacities—in return for higher VAT receipts going to the Walloon side. The 2001 Lambermont agreement, on the other hand, increased the proportion of revenues over which the regions and communities have total autonomy and allowed the regions to set rates and grant exemptions for a range of taxes (IMF 2003).

10. The cleavage that had originally led to the rise of these two parties—different preferences about the degree of political, cultural, and economic independence from the UK—had long faded in relevance by the 1980s (Mair 1992; Laver and Marsh 1992).

11. Fine Gael officially announced—in the so-called Tallaght strategy—that it would support the minority Fianna Fail government in passing any measure that

helps fiscal consolidation (Marsh and Mitchell 1999, Teague and Donaghey 2009).

12. Although some affiliated unions opposed the pact, peak associations strongly pushed for accepting it, and it was eventually adopted (Baccaro 2003).

CHAPTER 5

1. In the four decades preceding the debt crisis, Greece had a majoritarian electoral system (apart from a short interlude of proportionality around the turn of the 1980s and 1990s), which produced two strong, centralized parties held together by strict party discipline. These took turns in forming stable unitary governments, which were unconstrained by corporatist practices, since unions were weak, divided, and uncoordinated outside of the public sector (Kalyvas 1997; Nicolacopoulos 2005).

2. The Japanese electoral regime—the system of single nontransferable votes—in place until 1994 encouraged centrifugal tendencies in interest representation (Cox and McCubbins 2001). The new electoral system mixes elements of majoritaritarianism and proportionality. The party system was long characterized by "predominant-pluralism,'" with the dominance of the Liberal Democratic Party being counterbalanced by several opposition parties. Single-party majority governments increasingly gave way to minority or coalition governments from the late 1980s. Furthermore, the Liberal Democratic Party itself has traditionally been highly factionalized with a large number of distinct and well-organized groups of politicians vying for positions of power (Wright 2002). Trade unions, albeit organised at the enterprise-level, gained increasing influence in policy making from the 1980s (Kume 1998).

3. Any analysis of Greek fiscal policy undertaken after 2010 is hamstrung by the lack of reliable data for the past decades. The well-known scandals involving deliberate falsification and poor accounting discredited Greek statistics to such an extent that none of the usual sources (IMF, OECD, Ameco, etc.) provide data for more than a few years back. The following analysis attempts to circumvent this problem by using older data sources (Ameco data accessed in 2008, printed issues of older OECD reports, and older scholarly journal articles) despite the questionable reliability of the figures. It also incorporates information derived from past OECD country reports about the reforms that were undertaken in the period under consideration and that influenced fiscal outcomes. This provides information about the broad trends in fiscal policy in the period but obviously cannot inspire confidence in the exact figures. Therefore, to the extent possible, the analysis avoids operating with numbers and tries to describe trends.

4. According to the OECD (2001), 45 percent of all employed are officially registered as self-employed.

5. As the OECD's 1996 analysis of the Greek pension system points out, all occupational pensions favor early retirement. At the same time, low contribution requirements (fifteen years) and short reference periods (last five years of employment) generate very strong incentives for private sector employees and their employers to evade contributions altogether for most of their careers, underreport income on which they pay contributions for fifteen years, and only pay contributions based on their *de facto* salaries for the last five years in employment. Similarly,

the self-employed have an incentive to put themselves in the lowest contribution category because decreasing replacement rates do not make paying higher contributions worthwhile.

6. In the early 1980s, farmers still made up 40 percent of the active labor force, but their share declined to under 25 percent by the 1990s.

7. In fact, the most important changes of the health reform of 1982 and the pension of reform of 1985 were purely cosmetic, as they related to the cross-subsidization of various healthcare and pension funds, rather than to creating new revenues or restraining expenditure (Suzuki 2000; Estevez-Abe 2008).

8. Although the share of the rural population shrank rapidly from the Second World War, it was more than 60 percent in 1950, and it still amounted to 35 percent in 1960 (Suzuki 2000). The total share of the population linked to low-productivity sectors is even higher. Steinmo (2010) estimates that the high-efficiency sector still only employs around 20 percent of the workforce. With a public employment rate of around 10 percent, this leaves more than 70 percent of the workforce in the low-productivity sector.

9. Although the Liberal Democratic Party was only formed in 1955—by uniting the former Liberal Party and the Japan Democratic Party—the conservative forces that came to constitute the LDP have been actively organizing rural interest groups and receiving increasing electoral support from them from the end of the allied occupation in 1951.

10. As explained above, this move was also supported by businesses in the high-productivity sector due to the increasing cost pressures of in-house welfare benefits in the wake of the increase in the market power of labor.

CHAPTER 6

1. Later, a similar attempt to elicit fiscal sacrifices in the name of the shared interest in national prosperity in Belgium in the early 1990s fell flat even more obviously. Although Christian Democrats likened their proposal for a Global Pact to the Social Pact of 1944 that had made possible postwar reconstruction and plenty, labor failed to see the parallel and refused to make concessions.

2. Even though the "independence" of these technocrats from "politics as usual" could itself be seen as a political construct to lend credibility to the impartiality and universal desirability of their reforms, the fiasco of their first pension reform proposal demonstrates that the claim of "technocratic rationality" did not secure unconditional support, even from groups that otherwise rallied behind the technocratic government.

3. Sweden saw two bursts of intense debt accumulation between 1977 and 1984 and between 1991 and 1996; Finland had one serious incident between 1991 and 1996.

4. Such cases include slow debt accumulation in Germany since 1975, France since 1981, Austria between 1975 and 2005, Spain between 1977 and 1996, the United States between 1981 and 1993, the Netherlands between 1978 and 1993, and Portugal between 1975 and 1986.

References

Akaishi, T., and S. Steinmo. 2006. "Consumption Taxes and the Welfare State in Sweden and Japan." In *The Ambivalent Consumer*, edited by S. Garon and P. Maclachlan, 213–36. Ithaca: Cornell University Press.

Alesina, A., and S. Ardagna. 1998. "Tales of Fiscal Adjustments." *Economic Policy* 13(27): 489–585

Alesina, A., and S. Ardagna. 2013. "The Design of Fiscal Adjustments." *Tax Policy and the Economy* 27: 19–67.

Alesina, A., S. Danninger, and M. Rostagno. 1999. "Redistribution through Public Employment: The Case of Italy." *IMF Working Papers*, IMF. WP/99/177.

Alesina, A., and A. Drazen. 1991. "Why Are Stabilizations Delayed?" *The American Economic Review* 81(5): 1170–88.

Alesina, A., C. Favero, and F. Giavazzi. 2015. "The Output Effect of Fiscal Consolidation Plans." *Journal of International Economics* 96(S1): S19–S42.

Alesina, A., and R. Perotti. 1996. "Fiscal Discipline and the Budget Process." *The American Economic Review* 86(2): 401–7.

Alesina, A., R. Perotti, and J. Tavares. 1998. "The Political Economy of Fiscal Adjustments." *Brookings Papers on Economic Activity* 1: 1998.

Alogoskoufis, G. 1992. "Inflationary Expectations, Political Parties and the Exchange Rate Regime: Greece 1958–1989." *European Journal of Political Economy* 8(3): 375–99.

Alt, J. E., and S. S. Rose. 2007. "Context-Conditional Political Business Cycles." In *Oxford Handbook of Comparative Politics*. Edited by C. Boix and S. C. Stokes. Oxford: Oxford University Press.

Anderson, Karen M., S. Kuipers, S. Schulze, and W. Van den Nouland. 2007. "Belgium: Linguistic Veto Players and Pension Reform." In *West European Pension Politics*. Edited by E. M. Immergut, K. M. Anderson, and I. Schulze. 297–346. Oxford: Oxford University Press.

Ansell, B. W. 2008. "University Challenges: Explaining Institutional Change in Higher Education." *World Politics* 60(2): 189–230.

Baccaro, L. 2003. "What Is Alive and What Is Dead in the Theory of Corporatism." *British Journal of Industrial Relations* 41(4): 683–706.

Baccaro, L., and S.-H. Lim. 2007. "Social Pacts as Coalitions of the Weak and Moderate: Ireland, Italy and South Korea in Comparative Perspective." *European Journal of Industrial Relations* 13(1): 27–46.

Baccaro, L., and M. Simoni. 2008. "Policy Concertation in Europe: Understanding Government Choice." *Comparative Political Studies* 41(10): 1323–48.

Balassone, F., and R. Giordano. 2001. "Budget Deficits and Coalition Governments." *Public Choice* 106(3–4): 327–49.

Barro, R. 1979. "On the Determination of Public Debt." *Journal of Political Economy* 87(5): 940–71.

Barro, R. J., and X. Sala-i-Martin. 1990. "World Real Interest Rates." *NBER Working Papers* No. 331.

Barry, F. 1999. *Understanding Ireland's Economic Growth*. Basingstoke: Macmillan.

Béland, D., and A. Lecours. 2005. "Nationalism, Public Policy, and Institutional Development: Social Security in Belgium." *Journal of Public Policy* 25(2): 265–85.

Béland, D., and A. Lecours. 2008. *Nationalism and Social Policy: The Politics of Territorial Solidarity*. Oxford: Oxford University Press.

Benner, M., and T. Bundgaard Vad. 2000. "Sweden and Denmark: Defending the Welfare State." In *Welfare and Work in the Open Economy* 2. Edited by F. W. Scharpf and V. A. Schmidt. Oxford: Oxford University Press.

Bernasconi, M., A. Marenzi, and L. Magani. 2005. "Corporate Financing Decisions and Non-Debt Tax Shields: Evidence from Italian Experiences in the 1990s." *International Tax and Public Finance* 12(6): 741–73.

Bertola, G., and C. Garibaldi. 2003. "The Structure and History of Italian Unemployment." *CESifo Working Paper*.

Blanchard, O. 1990. "Suggestions for a New Set of Fiscal Indicators." *OECD Economics Department Working Papers* No. 79.

Blöndal, G. 1986. *Fiscal Policy in the Smaller Industrial Countries, 1972–82*. Washington, DC: IMF.

Blyth, M. 2002. *Great Transformations: Economic Ideas and Institutional Change in the Twentieth Century*. Cambridge: Cambridge University Press.

Blyth, M. 2013. *Austerity: The History of a Dangerous Idea*. Oxford: Oxford University Press.

Borensztein, E., and U. Panizza. 2010. "Do Sovereign Defaults Hurt Exporters?" *Open Economies Review* 21(3): 393–412.

Brender, A., and A. Drazen. 2008. "How Do Budget Deficits and Economic Growth Affect Reelection Prospects? Evidence from a Large Panel of Countries." *American Economic Review* 98(5): 2203–20.

Buchanan, J. M., and R. E. Wagner. 1977. *Democracy in Deficit: The Political Legacy of Lord Keynes*. New York: Academic Press.

Buiter, W. H. 1985. "A Guide to Public Sector Debt and Deficits." *Economic Policy* 1(1): 13–79.

Bull, M., and J. Baudner. 2004. "Europeanization and Italian Policy for the Mezzogiorno." *Journal of European Public Policy* 11(6): 1058–76.

Callan, T., and B. Nolan. 2000. "Taxation and Social Welfare." In *Bust to Boom?: The*

Irish Experience of Growth and Inequality. Edited by B. Nolan, P. J. O'Connell, and C. T. Whelan. Dublin: Institute of Public Administration.

Cameron, D. R. 1978. "The Expansion of the Public Economy: A Comparative Analysis." *American Political Science Review* 72(4): 1243–61.

Caruso, F., F. Mathot, M. Mignolet, M. E. Mulquin, and L. Vieslet. 2002. "Les transferts entre les regions: Realites contemoraines et recul historique." In *La fin du deficit budgetaire*. Edited by E. Callatay. Brussels: De Boeck Superieur.

Chiarini, B., E. Marzano, and F. Schneider. 2013. "Tax Rates and Tax Evasion: An Empirical Analysis of the Long-Run Aspects in Italy." *European Journal of Law and Economics* 35(2): 273–93.

Chopel, A., N. Kuno, and S. Steinmo. 2005. "Social Security, Taxation, and Redistribution in Japan." *Public Budgeting and Finance* 25(4): 20–43.

Claeys, P.-H. 1996. "Le systeme des piliers." In *Les partis politiques en Belgique*. Edited by P. Delwit and J.-M. De Waele. Bruxelles: Universite de Bruxelles.

Close, D. H. 2002. *Greece since 1945: Politics, Economy, and Society*. London and New York: Routledge.

Cox, G. W., and M. D. McCubbins. 2001. "The Institutional Determinants of Economic Policy Outcomes." In *Presidents, Parliaments and Policy*. Edited by G. W. Cox and S. Haggard, 21–64. Cambridge: Cambridge University Press.

Cox, R. H. 2001. "The Social Construction of an Imperative: Why Welfare Reform Happened in Denmark and the Netherlands but Not in Germany." *World Politics* 53(3): 463–98.

Cukierman, A., and A. H. Meltzer. 1989. "A Political Theory of Government Debt and Deficits in a Neo-Ricardian Framework." *The American Economic Review* 79(4): 713–32.

Cukierman, A., and M. Tommasi. 1998. "When Does It Take a Nixon to Go to China?" *The American Economic Review* 88(1): 180–97.

Culpepper, P. D. 2008. "The Politics of Common Knowledge: Ideas and Institutional Change in Wage Bargaining." *International Organization* 62(4): 1–33.

Culpepper, P. D. 2002. "Powering, Puzzling, and 'Pacting': The Informational Logic of Negotiated Reforms." *Journal of European Public Policy* 9(5): 774–90.

Culpepper, P. D. 2014. "The Political Economy of Unmediated Democracy: Italian Austerity under Mario Monti." *West European Politics* 37(6): 1264–81.

Culpepper, P. D., and A. Regan. 2014. "Why Don't Governments Need Trade Unions Anymore? The Death of Social Pacts in Ireland and Italy." *Socio-Economic Review* 12(4): 723–45.

De Winter, L. 1996. "Le CVP: entre gestion et conviction." In *Les partis politiques en Belgique*. Edited by P. Delwit and J.-M. De Waele. Bruxelles: Universite de Bruxelles.

Dejemeppe, M., and Y. Saks. 2002. "A New Light into Regional Unemployment Disparities in Belgium: Longitudinal Analysis of Grouped Duration Data." *IRES Discussion Papers* No. 2002019. Louvain: Universite catholique de Louvain.

Della Sala, V. 1997. "Hollowing Out and Hardening the State: European Integration and the Italian Economy." *West European Politics* 20(1):14–33.

Dellepiane, S., and N. Hardiman. 2012. "Fiscal Politics in Time: Pathways to Fiscal Consolidation 1980–2012." *UCD Geary Institute Discussion Paper Series* No. 201228. Dublin: UCD Geary Institute.

Delwit, P. 1996. "Le parti socialiste (PS)." In *Les partis politiques en Belgique*. Edited by P. Delwit and J.-M. De Waele. Bruxelles: Universite de Bruxelles.

Deschouwer, K. 2009. *The Politics of Belgium: Governing a Divided Society.* London: Palgrave Macmillan.

DeWit, A., and S. Steinmo. 2002. "Policy vs. Rhetoric: The Political Economy of Taxes and Redistribution in Japan." *Social Science Japan Journal* 5(2): 159–78.

Diamanti, I. 2007. "The Italian Center-Right and Center-Left: Between Parties and 'the Party.'" *West European Politics* 30(4): 733–62.

Domar, E. D. 1944. "The Burden of the Debt and the National Income." *The American Economic Review* 34(4): 798–824.

Donaghey, J., and P. Teague. 2007. "The Mixed Fortunes of Irish Unions: Living with the Paradoxes of Social Partnership." *Journal of Labor Research* 28(1): 19–41.

Drazen, A. 2004. *Political Economy in Macroeconomics.* Princeton: Princeton University Press.

Drazen, A., and V. Grilli. 1993. "The Benefit of Crises for Economic Reforms." *The American Economic Review* 83(3): 598–607.

Dunleavy, P., and H. Margetts. 1995. "Understanding the Dynamics of Electoral Reform." *International Political Science Review* 16(1): 9–29.

EC. 1993. "The Economic and Financial Situation in Belgium." *European Economy.* Brusselles: DG Ecfin.

Eggertsson, G. B., and P. Krugman. 2012. "Debt, Deleveraging, and the Liquidity Trap: A Fisher-Minsky-Koo Approach." *The Quarterly Journal of Economics* 127(3): 1469–513.

Epstein, G., and J. Schor. 1989. "Divorce of the Bank of Italy and the Treasury." In *State, Market, and Social Regulation—New Perspectives on Italy.* Edited by P. Lange and M. Regini, 146–66. Cambridge: Cambridge University Press.

Esping-Andersen, G. 1990. *The Three Worlds of Welfare Capitalism.* Princeton: Princeton University Press.

Estévez-Abe, M. 2008. *Welfare and Capitalism in Postwar Japan.* Cambridge: Cambridge University Press.

Farrell, D. 1999. "Ireland: A Party System Transformed." In *Changing Party Systems in Western Europe.* Edited by D. Broughton and M. Donovan, 30–48. London and New York: Pinter.

Featherstone, K. 2005. "'Soft' Co-ordination Meets 'Hard' Politics: The European Union and Pension Reform in Greece." *Journal of European Public Policy* 12(4): 733–50.

Fernandez, R., and D. Rodrik. 1991. "Resistance to Reform: Status Quo Bias in the Presence of Individual-Specific Uncertainty." *The American Economic Review* 81(5): 1146–55.

Ferrera, M., and G. Elisabetta. 2004. *Rescued by Europe? Social and Labor Market Reforms in Italy from Maastricht to Berlusconi.* Amsterdam: Amsterdam University Press.

Fisher, J., L. Jonung, and M. Larch. 2006. "101 Proposals to Reform the Stability and Growth Pact. Why So Many? A Survey." *European Economy* No. 267.

Fitzmaurice, J. 1996. *The Politics of Belgium.* London: Hurst & Company.

Fratianni, M., and F. Spinelli. 1997. *A Monetary History of Italy.* Cambridge: Cambridge University Press.

Frieden, J. A. 1991a. *Debt, Development, and Democracy: Modern Political Economy and Latin America, 1965–1985.* Princeton: Princeton University Press.

Frieden, J. A. 1991b. "Invested Interests: The Politics of National Economic Policies in a World of Global Finance." *International Organization* 45(4): 425–51.

Fukuyama, F. 2004. *State-Building.* Ithaca: Cornell University Press.

Ghosh, A. R., Ostry, J. D., and R. A. Espinoza. 2015. "When Should Public Debt Be Reduced?" *IMF Staff Discussion Notes* No. 15/10.

Giarda, E., P. Onofri, and P. Bosi. 2003. "Italian Budget Policy: A Long Run Overview." Available at http://dx.doi.org/10.2139/ssrn.267897

Giavazzi, F., and M. Pagano. 1990. "Can Severe Fiscal Contractions Be Expansionary? Tales of Two Small European Countries." *NBER Macroeconomics Annual* No. 5: 75–122.

Giavazzi, F., and L. Spaventa. 1989. "Italy: The Real Effects of Inflation and Disinflation." *Economic Policy* 4(8): 133–71.

Ginsborg, P. 2003. *Italy and Its Discontents: Family, Civil Society, State, 1980–2001.* New York: Palgrave Macmillan.

Goldstein, A. 2003. "Privatization in Italy 1993–2002: Goals, Institutions, Outcomes, and Outstanding Issues." *CESifo Conference "Privatisation Experiences in the EU.*

Gourevitch, P. 1986. *Politics in Hard Times: Comparative Responses to International Economic Crises.* Ithaca: Cornell University Press.

Green-Pedersen, C., and M. Baggesen Klitgaard. 2009. "Between Economic Constraints and Popular Entrenchment." In *The Handbook of European Welfare Systems.* Edited by K. Schubert, S. Hegelich, and U. Bazant. London: Routledge.

Grilli, V., D. Masciandaro, G. Tabellini, E. Malinvaud, and M. Pagano. 1991. "Political and Monetary Institutions and Public Financial Policies in the Industrial Countries." *Economic Policy* 6(13): 341–92.

Guerra, M. C. 1993. "Tax Policies in the 1980s and 1990s: The Case of Italy." In *Taxation in the United States and Europe.* Edited by A. Knoester, 328–54. London: Palgrave Macmillan.

Guerrieri, P., and C. Milana. 1990. *L'Italia e il commercio mondiale, Mutamenti e tendenze nella divisione internazionale del lavoro.* Bologna: Il Mulino.

Hacker, J. 2004. "Privatizing Risk without Privatizing the Welfare State: The Hidden Politics of Social Policy Retrenchment in the United States." *American Political Science Review* 98(2): 243–60.

Hacker, J. S., and P. Pierson. 2014. "After the 'Master Theory': Downs, Schattschneider, and the Rebirth of Policy-Focused Analysis." *Perspectives on Politics* 12(3): 643–62.

Haggard, S., and R. Kaufman (1992). "Institutions and Economic Adjustment." In *The Politics of Economic Adjustment—International Constraints, Distributive Conflicts, and the State.* Edited by S. K. Haggard, and R. Kaufmann, 3–41. Princeton: Princeton University Press.

Haggard, S., R. Kaufman, and M. Shugart. 2001. "Politics, Institutions, and Macroeconomic Adjustment: Hungarian Fiscal Policy Making in Comparative Perspective." In *Reforming the State: Fiscal and Welfare Reform in Post-Socialist Countries*. Edited by J. Kornai, S. Haggard, and R. Kaufmann, 77–110. Cambridge: Cambridge University Press.

Hallerberg, M. 2004. *Domestic Budgets in a United Europe: Fiscal Governance from the End of Bretton Woods to EMU*. Ithaca: Cornell University Press.

Hallerberg, M., R. R. Strauch, and J. Von Hagen. 2009. *Fiscal Governance in Europe*. Cambridge: Cambridge University Press.

Hallerberg, M., and J. Von Hagen. 1997. "Electoral Institutions, Cabinet Negotiations, and Budget negotiations in the European Union." *NBER Working Paper* No. 6341.

Häusermann, S. 2010. *The Politics of Welfare State Reform in Continental Europe: Modernization in Hard Times*. Cambridge: Cambridge University Press.

Hemerijck, A., B. Unger, and J. Visser. 2000. "How Small Countries Negotiate Change: Twenty-Five Years of Policy Adjustment in Austria, Belgium and the Netherlands." In *Welfare and Work in the Open Economy*. Edited by F. W. Scharpf and V. A. Schmidt. Oxford: Oxford University Press.

Herndon, T., M. Ash, and R. Pollin. 2014. "Does High Public Debt Consistently Stifle Economic Growth? A Critique of Reinhart and Rogoff." *Cambridge Journal of Economics* 38(2): 257–79.

Hiscox, M. J. 1999. "The Magic Bullet? The RTAA, Institutional Reform, and Trade Liberalization." *International Organization* 53(4): 669–98.

Hiscox, M. J. 2001. "Inter-Industry Factor Mobility and the Politics of Trade." *International Organization* 55(1): 1–46.

Honohan, P. 1992. "Fiscal Adjustment in Ireland in the 1980s." *The Economic and Social Review* 23(3): 285–314.

Honohan, P. 1999. "Fiscal Adjustment and Disinflation in Ireland: Setting the Macro Basis of Economic Recovery and Expansion." In *Understanding Ireland's Economic Growth*. Edited by F. Barry, 75–98. Basingstoke: Palgrave Macmillan.

Hooghe, L. 1991. *A Leap in the Dark: Nationalist Conflict and Federal Reform in Belgium*. Ithaca: Cornell University Press.

Horioka, C. Y., and T. Nomoto. 2014. "Why Has Japan's Massive Government Debt Not Wreaked Havoc (Yet)?" *The Japanese Political Economy* 40(2): 3–23.

Hoshi, T. and T. Ito. 2012. "Defying Gravity: How Long Will Japanese Government Bond Prices Remain High?" *National Bureau of Economic Research* No. 18287.

IMF. 2003. "Belgium: Selected Issues". *IMF Country Report*.

Ishi, H. 2000. *Making Fiscal Policy in Japan*. Oxford: Oxford University Press.

Iversen, T., and D. Soskice. 2001. "An Asset Theory of Social Policy Preferences." *The American Political Science Review* 95(4): 875–93.

Jacobsen, J. K. 1995. "Much Ado about Ideas: The Cognitive Factor in Economic Policy." *World Politics* 7(2): 283–310.

Johnson, C. 1982. "Political Institutions and Economic Performance: The Government-Business Relationship in Japan, South Korea, and Taiwan." In *The Political Economy of the New Asian Industrialism*. Edited by F. C. Deyo, 136–64. Ithaca: Cornell University Press.

Jones, E. 2008. *Economic Adjustment and Political Transformation in Small States*. Oxford: Oxford University Press.

Kalyvas, S. N. 1997. "Polarization in Greek Politics: PASOK's First Four Years, 1981–1985." *Journal of the Hellenic Diaspora*. 23(1997): 83–104.

Katz, R. 2002. *Japanese Phoenix: The Long Road to Economic Revival.* New York: M. E. Sharpe.

Katzenstein, P. J. 1977. *Between Power and Plenty: Foreign Economic Policies of Advanced Industrial States.* Wisconsin: University of Wisconsin Press.

Katzenstein, P. J. 1985. *Small States in World Markets.* Ithaca: Cornell University Press.

Katzenstein, P. J. 1987. *Corporatism and Change: Austria, Switzerland, and the Politics of Industry.* Ithaca: Cornell University Press.

Kirby, P. 2010. *Celtic Tiger in Collapse.* Basingstoke: Palgrave Macmillan.

Kornelakis, A. 2011. "*Mediating EU Liberalisation and Negotiating Flexibility: A Coalitional Approach on Wage Bargaining Change.*" Unpublished PhD diss. London: European Institute, London School of Economics and Political Science.

Krasner, S. D. 1978. *Defending the National Interest: Raw Materials Investments and U.S. Foreign Policy.* Princeton: Princeton University Press.

Krasner, S. D. 1984. "Approaches to the State: Alternative Conceptions and Historical Dynamics." *Comparative Politics* 16(2): 223–46.

Kuipers, S. 2005. *The Crisis Imperative—Crisis Rhetoric and Welfare State Reform in Belgium and the Netherlands in the Early 1990s.* Amsterdam: Amsterdam University Press.

Kumar, M. S., and J. Woo. 2010. "Public Debt and Growth." *IMF Working Papers*, No. 10/174.

Kume, I. 1998. *Disparaged Success: Labor Politics in Postwar Japan.* Ithaca: Cornell University Press.

Laban, R., and F. Sturzenegger. 1994. "Distributional Conflict, Financial Adaptation and Delayed Stabilizations." *Economics & Politics* 6(3): 257–76.

Lanza, O., and K. Lavdas. 2000. "The Disentanglement of Interest Politics: Business Associability, the Parties and Policy in Italy and Greece." *European Journal of Political Research* 37: 203–35.

LaPalombara, J. 1987. *Democracy, Italian Style.* New Haven: Yale University Press.

Lavdas, K. 2005. "Interest Groups in Disjointed Corporatism: Social Dialogue in Greece and European 'Competitive Corporatism.'" *West European Politics* 28(2): 297–316.

Laver, M., and M. Marsh. 1992. "Parties and Voters." In *Politics of the Republic of Ireland.* Edited by J. Coakley and M. Gallagher. London and New York: Routledge.

Legro, J. W. 2000. "The Transformation of Policy Ideas." *American Journal of Political Science* 44(3): 419–31.

Lijphart, A. 1999. *Patterns of Democracy.* New Haven and London: Yale University Press.

Lijphart, A., T. C. Bruneau, N. Diamandouros, and R. Gunther. 1988. "A Mediterranean Model of Democracy? The Southern European Democracies in Comparative Perspective." *West European Politics* 11(1): 7–25.

Lipscy, P. Y., and E. Scheiner. 2012. "Japan under the DPJ: The Paradox of Political Change without Policy Change." *Journal of East Asian Studies* 12(3): 311–22.

Lustick, I. S. 1996. "History, Historiography, and Political Science: Multiple Historical Records and the Problem of Selection Bias." *American Political Science Review* 90(3): 605–18.

Lyrintzis, C. 2005. "The Changing Party System: Stable Democracy, Contested 'Modernisation.'" *West European Politics* 28(2): 242–59.

Mahoney, J., and K. Thelen. 2009. "A Theory of Gradual Institutional Change." In *Explaining Institutional Change: Ambiguity, Agency, and Power*. Edited by J. Mahoney and K. Thelen, 1–38. Cambridge: Cambridge University Press.

Mair, P. 1990. "Ireland: From Predominance to Moderate Pluralism and Back Again." In *Understanding Party System Change in Western Europe*. Edited by P. Mair and G. Smith, 129–43. Abingdon: Frank Cass & Co.

Mair, P. 2006. "Party System Change." In *Handbook of Party Politics*. Edited by R. S. Katz and W. J. Crotty, 63–75. London: SAGE.

Mares, I. 2003. *The Politics of Social Risk: Business and Welfare State Development*. New York: Cambridge University Press.

Marier, P. 2008. *Pension Politics*. London: Routledge.

Marsh, M., and P. Mitchell. 1999. "Office, Votes and then Policy: Hard Choices for Political Parties in the Republic of Ireland 1981–1992." In *Policy, Office or Votes?* Edited by W. C. Muller and K. Strom, 36–63. Cambridge: Cambridge University Press.

Maurizi G., and D. Monacelli. 2003. "Corporate Tax Reform in Italy in the late 1990s and Beyond." Paper presented at the Conference Public Finance and Financial Markets, 59th International Institute of Public Finance Congress, Prague, August 2003, mimeo.

Mavrogordatos, G. T. 1997. "From Traditional Clientelism to Machine Politics: The Impact of PASOK Populism in Greece." *South European Society and Politics* 2(3): 1–26.

McAllister, I., and D. O'Connell. 1984. "The Political Sociology of Party Support in Ireland: A Reassessment." *Comparative Politics* 16(2).

McCashin, A., and J. O'Shea. 2009. "The Irish Welfare State." In *The Handbook of European Welfare Systems*. Edited by K. Schubert, S. Hegelich, and U. Bazant. London: Routledge.

McDonough, T., and T. Dundon. 2010. "Thatcherism Delayed? The Irish Crisis and the Paradox of Social Partnership." *Industrial Relations Journal* 41(6): 544–62.

McNamara, K. 1998. *The Currency of Ideas*. Ithaca and London: Cornell University Press.

Merler, S., and J. Pisani-Ferry. 2012. "Who's Afraid of Sovereign Bonds", *Bruegel Policy Contribution* 2012/02 (accessible at http://bruegel.org/publications/data sets/sovereign-bond-holdings/)

Mintrom, M., and P. Norman. 2009. "Policy Entrepreneurship and Policy Change." *The Policy Studies Journal* 37(4): 649–67.

Moene, K. O., and M. Wallerstein (2001). "Inequality, Social Insurance, and Redistribution." *American Political Science Review*: 859–74.

Molina, A., and M. Rhodes. 2007. "Industrial Relations and the Welfare State in Italy: Assessing the Potential of Negotiated Change." *West European Politics* 30(4): 803–29.

Morcaldo, G. 1993. *La finanza pubblica in Italia (1960–1992)*. Bologna: Il Mulino.

Nelson, J. M. 1990. *Economic Crisis and Policy Choice: The Politics of Adjustment in Developing Countries*. Princeton: Princeton University Press.

Nicolacopoulos, I. 2005. "Elections and Voters, 1974–2004: Old Cleavages and New Issues." *West European Politics* 28(2): 260–78.

Nolan, B., and B. Maître. 2000. "A Comparative Perspective on Trends in Income Inequality in Ireland." *Economic and Social Review* 31(4): 329–50.

Nordhaus, W. 1975. "The Political Business Cycle." *Review of Economic Studies* 42(2): 169–90.

OECD. 1996. OECD Economic Surveys: Greece.

OECD. 2001. OECD Economic Surveys: Greece.

OECD. 2007. OECD Economic Surveys: Belgium.

OECD. 2007. OECD Economic Surveys: Greece.

OECD. 2013. OECD Economic Surveys: Greece.

Ostry, J. D., A. R. Ghosh, and Kureshi. 2010. "Fiscal Space." *IMF Staff Position Note* SPN/10/11.

Padovano, F., and L. Venturi. 2001. "Wars of Attrition in Italian Government Coalitions and Fiscal Performance: 1948–1994." *Public Choice* 109(1–2): 15–54.

Pal, L. A., and R. K. Weaver. 2003. "The Politics of Pain." In *The Government Taketh Away: The Politics of Pain in the United States and Canada*. Edited by L. A. Pal and R. K. Weaver, 1–41. Washington, DC: Georgetown University Press.

Pappas, T. S. 2013. "Why Greece Failed." *Journal of Democracy* 24(2): 31–45.

Pempel, T. J. 1998. *Regime Shift: Comparative Dynamics of the Japanese Political Economy*. Ithaca: Cornell University Press.

Pempel, T. J. 2010. "Between Pork and Productivity: The Collapse of the Liberal Democratic Party." *Journal of Japanese Studies* 36(2): 227–54.

Pescatori, A., D. Leigh, J. Guajardo, and P. Devries. 2011. "A New Action-Based Dataset of Fiscal Consolidation." *IMF Working Papers* WP/11/128.

Pierson, P. 1996. "The New Politics of the Welfare State." *World Politics* 48(2): 143–79.

Pierson, P. 2000. "Increasing Returns, Path Dependence, and the Study of Politics." *American Political Science Review* 94(2): 251–67.

Pierson, P. 2001. "Coping with Permanent Austerity: Welfare State Restructuring in Affluent Democracies." In *The New Politics of the Welfare State*. Edited by P. Pierson. Oxford: Oxford University Press.

Pierson, P. 2004. *Politics in Time: History, Institutions, and Social Analysis*. Princeton: Princeton University Press.

Pochet, P. 2004. "Belgium: Monetary Integration and Precarious Federalism." In *Euros and Europeans: Monetary Integration and the European Model of Society*. Edited by A. Martin and G. Ross, 201–26. Cambridge: Cambridge University Press.

Pontusson, J. 1995. "From Comparative Public Policy to Political Economy. Putting Political Institutions in Their Place and Taking Interests Seriously." *Comparative Political Studies* 28(1): 117–47.

Quaglia, L. 2004. "Italy's Policy towards European Monetary Integration: Bringing Ideas Back In?" *Journal of European Public Policy* 11(6): 1096:1111.

Radaelli, C. 2000. "Discourse and Institutional Change: The Case of Italy in the Euro-Zone." *Queen's Papers on Europeanisation* No. 5/2000.

Regini, M., and I. Regalia. 1997. "Employers, Unions and the State: The Resurgence of Concertation in Italy?" *West European Politics* 20(1): 210–30.

Reinhart, C. M. 2010. "This Time Is Different Chartbook: Country Histories on Debt, Default, and Financial Crises." *NBER Working Paper* No. 15815.

Reinhart, C. M., and K. S. Rogoff. 2010. "Growth in a Time of Debt." *NBER Working Paper* No. 15639.

Reinhart, C. M., K. S. Rogoff, and M. Savastano. 2003. "Debt Intolerance." *NBER Working Paper* No. 9908.

Rodrik, D. 1996. "Why Do More Open Economies Have Bigger Governments?" *NBER Working Paper* No. 5537.

Rogoff, K., and A. Sibert. 1988. "Elections and Macroeconomic Policy Cycles." *The Review of Economic Studies* 55(1): 1–16.

Rogowski, R. 1990. *Commerce and Coalitions: How Trade Affects Domestic Political Alignments*. Princeton: Princeton University Press.

Rosen, S. 1996. "Public Employment and the Welfare State in Sweden." *Journal of Economic Literature* 34(2): 729–40.

Roubini, N., and J. D. Sachs. 1989. "Political and Economic Determinants of Budget Deficits in the Industrial Democracies." *European Economic Review* 33(5): 903–38.

Rueda, D. 2005. "Insider–Outsider Politics in Industrialized Democracies: The Challenge to Social Democratic Parties." *American Political Science Review* 99(1): 61–74.

Sargent, T. J., and N. Wallace. 1981. "Some Unpleasant Monetarist Arithmetic." *Federal Reserve Bank of Minneapolis Quarterly Review* 1981(5): 1–17.

Sheingate, A. D. 2003. "Political Entrepreneurship, Institutional Change, and American Political Development." *Studies in American Political Development* 17: 185–203.

Sinnott, R. 1984. "Interpretations of the Irish Party System" *European Journal of Political Research* 12(3): 289–307.

Skocpol, T. 1985. "Bringing the State Back In." In *Bringing the State Back In*. Edited by P. B. Evans, D. Rueschemeyer, and T. Skocpol, 3–39. Cambridge: Cambridge University Press.

Spaventa, L. 2013. "The Growth of Public Debt in Italy: Past Experience, Perspectives and Policy Problems." *PSL Quarterly Review* 66(266): 291–324.

Spolaore, E. 2004. "Adjustments in Different Government Systems." *Economics & Politics* 16(2): 117–46.

Steinmo, S. 1993. *Taxation and Democracy: Swedish, British and American Approaches to Financing the Modern State*. New Haven: Yale University Press.

Steinmo, S. 2010. *The Evolution of Modern States*. Cambridge: Cambridge University Press.

Streeck, W. 2014. *Buying Time: The Delayed Crisis of Democratic Capitalism*. London: Verso Books.

Streeck, W., and K. Thelen. 2005. *Beyond Continuity*. Oxford: Oxford University Press.

Suzuki, T. 2000. *Japan's Budget Politics*. Boulder and London: Lynne Riener Publishers.

Takahashi, K., and K. Tokuoka. 2011. "Japan: Fiscal Adjustment Plans and Macroeconomic Shocks." In *Chipping Away at Public Debt: Sources of Failure and Keys to Success in Fiscal Adjustment*. Edited by P. Mauro, 177–213. John Wiley & Sons.

Teague, P., and J. Donaghey. 2009. "Social Partnership and Democratic Legitimacy in Ireland." *New Political Economy* 14(1): 49–69.

Thelen, K. 1999. "Historical Institutionalism in Comparative Politics." *Annual Review of Political Science* 2(1): 369–404.

Thelen, K., and S. Steinmo. 1992. "Historical Institutionalism in Comparative Perspective." In *Structuring Politics*. Edited by S. Steinmo, K. Thelen, and F. Longstreth, 1–27. Cambridge: Cambridge University Press.

Tufte, E. R. 1978. *Political Control of the Economy*. Princeton: Princeton University Press.

van Kersbergen, K., and B. Vis. 2014. *Comparative Welfare State Politics: Development, Opportunities, and Reform*. Cambridge: Cambridge University Press.

von Hagen, J. 1991. "A Note on the Empirical Effectiveness of Formal Fiscal Restraints." *Journal of Public Economics* 44(2): 199–210.

von Hagen, J., and G. B. Wolff. 2006. "What Do Deficits Tell Us about Debt? Empirical Evidence on Creative Accounting with Fiscal Rules in the EU." *Journal of Banking & Finance* 30(2): 3259–79.

von Hagen, J., and I. Harden. 1996. "Budget Processes and Commitment to Fiscal Discipline." *IMF Working Papers* W/96/78.

Walsh, J. I. 1999. "Political Bases of Macroeconomic Adjustment: Evidence from the Italian Experience." *Journal of European Public Policy* 6(1): 66–84.

Weingast, B. R., K. A. Shepsle, and C. Johnsen. 1981. "The Political Economy of Benefits and Costs: A Neoclassical Approach to Distributive Politics." *The Journal of Political Economy* 89(4): 642–64.

Weir, M., and T. Skocpol. 1989. "State Structures and the Possibilities for 'Keynesian' Responses to the Great Depression in Sweden, Britain and the United States." In *Bringing the State Back In*. Edited by P. B. Evans, D. Rueschemeyer and T. Skocpol, 107–164. Cambridge: Cambridge University Press.

Wright, M. 1999. "Coping with Fiscal Stress: Illusion and Reality in Central Government Budgeting in Japan, 1975–1997." In *Fiscal Institutions and Fiscal Performance*. Edited by J. Poterba, 349–377. Chicago and London: University of Chicago Press.

Wright, M. 1999. "Who Governs Japan? Politicians and Bureaucrats in the Policy-Making Processes." *Political Studies* 47(5): 939–54.

Wright, M. 2002. *Japan's Fiscal Crisis: The Ministry of Finance and the Politics of Public Spending, 1975–2000*. Oxford: Oxford University Press.

Yee, A. S. 1996. "The Causal Effect of Ideas on Policies." *International Organization* 50(1): 69–108.

Index

accounting manipulations. *See* fiscal gimmickry
adjustment approach to debt accumulation, 13–15, 16, 21, 25, 31, 52
aging, 51, 103, 130, 133, 137, 153, 185n3
Alesina, A., 20, 35–36, 180n1, 180n5
Amato reform of 1992, 172, 183n5
annual budgetary decisions. *See* yearly budgetary decisions
Ansell, B. W., 44
anti-tax-state-dependency coalition (Italy), 71–72, 80, 81
austeriterians: arguments for elimination of debt, 10–11; debate with Keynesians, 9–12; support for spending-based contractions, 11
Austria, debt accumulation in, 7, 183n29, 187n4

balanced budgets, coordination mechanisms, 49, 181n16
Bank of Italy, 69, 70
Belgium, 85–103; austerity measures of 1982, 54, 85, 87, 90, 94–95, 99, 153; austerity measures of 1993, 92, 100–101; class conflict, 158, 161; currency crises, 90, 95; debt crisis threats, 169; debt-to-GDP ratios, 6, 32, 85, 89, 90, 91–92, 103, 168–69; Disaster Plan, 91, 98, 153, 173; Economic and Monetary Union membership, 166; enduring problems of fiscal polarization, 101–3; euro accession, 92–93, 95–96, 100, 167; financial internationalization effects, 168–69; fiscal polarization in, 22–23, 54, 56, 83, 86, 87, 111, 112, 161–64; fiscal trajectory, 85–88, 89–93; Global Pact on Employment, Competitiveness, and Social Security, 92, 100, 101, 185n7, 187n1; Global Plan, 92; growth of debt despite concerns, 2, 12; ideational factors in adjustment, 173; inclusion in sampling, 23, 53, 54; institutional factors in adjustment, 111, 170–72; international exposure in, 4, 54–55, 83, 86, 87, 88, 111, 158, 164–69; linguistic communities, 97, 102, 185n4, 185n8; origins of fiscal imbalances, 153, 158; party system, 97; pension financing, 38; polarization-exposure theory applicability, 87–88, 150–51; political uncertainty in recent years, 102–3; regional conflicts, 101–3; regional economic disparities, 94, 95, 96, 98, 158, 161, 173; social coalitions, 157, 158; Special Powers Act of 1982, 94, 99, 170; standen, 98, 185n6; state reform, 102; strikes, 155, 156; summary of case study, 22–23, 111–12

Italy (*continued*)
  institutional factors in adjustment,
  170–72; international exposure in, 4,
  55, 164–69; origins of fiscal imbalances, 74, 153, 157; pentapartito, 61,
  71–72, 157; polarization-exposure
  theory applicability, 150–51; political
  conditions in wake of crisis, 81–82;
  relapse in debt accumulation, 166;
  risanamento, 64, 76, 154, 173; social
  coalitions, 22, 71–81, 82, 83, 157;
  summary of case study, 22–23, 60–63,
  82–84

Japan, 132–49; alternative explanations
  of fiscal history, 115–18; attempts
  at stabilization, 114–15, 137–38;
  bureaucratic elite, 144; clientelism in,
  144, 154, 171; debt-to-GDP ratios, 6,
  32, 133, 136–37, 160, 179n1; domestic
  financing of government debt, 133–
  34; electoral reform, 146, 160, 186n2;
  enduring conflicts of polarization,
  147–48; financial bubble years, 116,
  136; fiscal polarization in, 23–24, 54,
  113, 115, 118, 138–39, 140–48, 161–
  64; fiscal reconstruction attempts, 134,
  138, 153, 172, 173; fiscal trajectory,
  113–14, 116–17, 135–38; Greece vs.,
  56; growth of debt despite concerns,
  2, 6, 12, 53–54, 138–39; ideational factors in adjustment, 173; inclusion in
  sampling, 53–54; institutional factors
  in adjustment, 116, 170–72; international exposure in, 55, 113, 115, 148,
  160, 165–66; net vs. gross debt, 132–
  35, 179n1; origins of fiscal imbalances,
  113–14, 153, 160; partisanship and
  electoral pressures, 143–47, 148–49;
  polarization-exposure theory applicability, 150–51; rural-urban economic
  disparities, 132, 139, 140–41, 144–45,
  146–47, 160, 161, 187n8; socioeconomic foundations of polarization,
  140–43; summary of case study, 148–
  49, 160

Katzenstein, Peter, 41
Keynesians: arguments in favor of

temporary deficits, 10; debate with
  austeriterians, 9–12; shift to neoliberal
  policies, 23, 87, 88, 172–73; views on
  debt accumulation, 9

labor. *See* organized labor
Labor Party (Ireland), 107–9, 159
Lambermont agreement of 2001 (Belgium), 185n9
large enterprises: in Greece, 125, 126;
  in Italy, 61–62, 75, 76, 77, 80, 82; in
  Japan, 141; varying responses to policy
  needs, 155, 156
legacy policies. *See* policy legacies
Lega Nord (Italy), 76, 77, 78–79, 80
Liberal Democratic Party (Japan): clientelistic ties, 144, 154, 171; factions
  in, 132, 139, 142, 144, 145, 146, 147,
  186n2; formation of, 187n9; inability
  to implement adjustment, 141, 142–
  43, 145–46, 160; introduction of new
  welfare benefits, 114, 140, 153; pressure to increase welfare spending, 135;
  resistance to reform, 115, 118; schism
  of 1993, 145; strategic choices, 143–47
Liberal Party (Canada), 175–76
liberals (Belgium): attempts at stabilization, 154; changing coalition participation, 158; political role, 96–101;
  regional conflicts, 102
liberal unions (Belgium), 97–101
Lustick, I. S., 58

Maastricht criteria, 70, 95, 118, 167–68
majoritarian electoral systems: ability to
  overcome resistance to reform, 180n8;
  in Greece, 116, 170, 186n1; in Japan,
  186n2
Mani Pulite campaign (Italy), 77
Maribel operation of 1981 (Belgium), 91
Mavrogordatos, G. T., 122
Maystadt tax reform of 1988 (Belgium),
  91
methodological considerations: benefits
  of qualitative approach, 52; cases
  chosen for sampling, 53–57; numerical
  analysis combined with policy choice,
  57–58; time period of study, 52–53;
  use of secondary sources, 58–59